PARTICIPATION, ASSOCIATIONS, DEVELOPMENT, AND CHANGE

PARTICIPATION, ASSOCIATIONS, DEVELOPMENT, AND CHANGE

ALBERT MEISTER

Edited and Translated by

Jack C. Ross

Transaction Books
New Brunswick (U.S.A.) and London (U.K.)

Library of Congress Catalog Number: 80-22453
ISBN: 0-87855-423-8 (cloth)
Printed in the United States of America

Library of Congress Cataloging in Publication Data
Meister, Albert.
Participation, associations, development, and change.
Bibliography: p.
Includes index.
1. Social change—Addresses, essays, lectures. 2. Social participation—Addresses, essays, lectures. 3. Associations, institutions, etc.—Addresses, essays, lectures. I. Ross, Jack C. II. Title.
HN18.M3836 303.4 80-22453
ISBN 0-87855-423-8

CONTENTS

ACKNOWLEDGMENTS

We gratefully acknowledge permission from Editions Ouvrières (Paris) to translate and reprint the following materials appearing in the present volume:

Chapters 1, 2, 3, 8, and 11 from *Vers une sociologie des associations* (1972) by Albert Meister; chapters 4, 5, 6, and 7 from *La Participation dans les associations* (1974) by Albert Meister; and chapters 9 and 10 from *La Participation pour le développement* (1977) by Albert Meister.

INTRODUCTION

Jack C. Ross

This volume is composed of three strands—participation, associations, and developement—woven into a complex fabric. No one of them represents solely cause or effect, independent or dependent variables, and each is represented in its relation to social change in more than one dimension. I have prepared the book from three of Albert Meister's recent works: *Vers une Sociologie des associations* (1972), *La Participation dans les associations* (1974), and *La Participation pour le développement* (1977), suggesting a degree of independence of the topics that is not actually the case. There is a high consistency of subject, theory, method, and underlying values throughout that makes it possible to bring the most relevant parts to the English-reading public without the expense and confusion that would attend separate publication of each.

The unity of the book lies in the author himself. For about two decades he has pursued research on associations and participation with continuity and in a wide variety of contexts. He has conducted research in France, Italy, Yugoslavia, Israel, South Africa, Argentina, and Peru. He has studied in Switzerland, France, and the United States. He has edited an international journal of development. I do not know of anyone better prepared from experience to make syntheses and generalizations, and at the same time to see the practical issues of community life. This comes to the surface in pithy observations, like the comment about changes occurring in a commune when the manager saves enough money to buy a new car, up to the final foreboding, almost apocalyptic vision of the future of democratic participation.

A few words of explanation about the sequence of topics are needed to make clear the part I have played and the logic of the topics I have intended. Chapters 1 and 2 are drawn from the first part of *Vers une Sociologie des associations,* and contain definitions and other introductory material of a sociological nature. The framework here is the relationship of types of social participation to types of societies. For the most part these materials adequately introduce the excerpts from the other, more specialized books as well. Chapter 3, also from *Vers une Sociologie des associations,* combines two historical chapters on France and the United States. I have combined them to enhance the comparative aspects of this topic. The issue here is change more than development, by which oversimplified distinction I indicate merely the difference between the unintentional and intentional. Whereas chapters 1 and 2 focus on participation, chapter 3 introduces historical types of associations. Chapters 4, 5, 6, and 7 constitute a unit of sociological studies of both development and change, concentrating on members, member roles, types of associations, and types of participation in a variety of types of societies. This is the heart of Meister's work, grounded in empirical research of his own in a wide range of societies—at once theoretically located and pragmatic. Chapter 8 is similarly grounded in specific research, but is confined to development associations. Chapter 9 and chapter 10 are selected from his works in Africa and Latin America respectively, and constitute a detailed application of typologies and approaches presented in chapter 8. These chapters may be taken also as a unit of study on the contrasts between the decentralist-voluntarist model of development influenced by the United States and Great Britain, through the United Nations and separately, and the French centralist model that has also influenced the Spanish approach. In chapter 11 we return to the most general level, in which the author applies his ideas to consideration of the future of democratic participation in postindustrial society.

The beginning and ending materials are drawn from the earliest of the three books. Outside of a few instances of confusion due to references to contemporary events, this should introduce no problems for the reader. Rather than attempt to rewrite these materials I have chosen to present them as originally written to preserve the integrity of the author's views. In the same spirit I have allowed some duplication of examples and ideas to remain, rather than break the continuity of the author's presentation. On the whole there are remarkably few of these, testifying to the vast resources on which Meister draws.

As this volume took form there were numerous instances in which the author's perspective was different from mine. Reading Meister's review of French and American associationist and participationist traditions, one might have assumed that such national differences would exist. On the assumption that most of my English-language readers share the same intellectual traditions, I would like to briefly review those differences and what I have learned from the close consideration of them that translation and editing has necessitated.

The first and foremost distinction is the meaning attached to the idea of association. The difference between the French and American traditions of thought here is manifold. The first distinction to catch the eye is the American emphasis on voluntary associations and voluntarism, a difference that Meister recognizes and stresses both in his history of American associationism and in his review of American approaches to development. Although the voluntary element has long been present in France, it is assumed by most French writers to have been subdued, both because of the primacy of central authority and because of the tradition of revolutionary action by the French working classes. Interestingly American academic emphasis on the voluntary association stems from a Frenchman, Alexis de Tocqueville, and modern French literature on voluntary associations was stimulated by an American, Arnold Rose, perhaps the most cited referent in French studies. In America Tocqueville is seen as the intellectual father of pluralism and the nonpareil of voluntarism, mostly because he said things about us that we want to believe. After 150 years, Tocqueville continues to be recognized in France as an important intellectual. His contributions are rooted in a corporative tradition based on organic thinking, a strain stemming from Rousseau and beyond, which enters into modern sociology most emphatically with Durkheim. In this intellectual tradition the corporation (the word itself implies an organism, a body, a unity) is an historical entity through (varying by epoch) which workers and owners were ideally united in economic control. The closest English equivalent is *guild.*

The guild and corporation were major topics of intellectual interest at the end of the nineteenth century. In England important scholarly works by writers like Charles Gross and George Unwin (and the more political guild socialists like G.D.H. Cole) followed active attempts by governments to salvage ancient guild documents, paralleled by scholarly and political interest in socialism. French scholarship built on similar governmental collections (the 1879 editions by Lespinasse, for example) featuring significant scholarly analyses by such writers as Augustine Thierry and later Olivier Martin Saint-Léon and Emile Coornaert. The effort to investigate and preserve the organizational tradition was quite similar in the two countries. America had no such tradition and had to get along with Tocqueville as best it could.

In practice the difference between French and American traditions is that American writers have considered voluntary associations a separate entity that glorifies individual freedom to dissent and autonomous responsible action under constitutional guarantees, while French writers consider voluntarism less significant than the right to corporate or even simple group existence that has been repeatedly abrogated, restricted, withdrawn, or suppressed. Although Meister writes accurately and sympathetically about American voluntary associations, when he writes about associations elsewhere voluntarism becomes merely one variable among many describing modalities of participation.

The second significant distinction that takes some getting used to is the stress Meister places on the political nature of associations. Just as Americans have seen voluntary associations as a sacrosanct institution that undergirds the civic order under constitutional guarantees—independent of political interference while free to affect or even organize political life through voluntary political parties and a mostly voluntary church—the French have seen associations as inherently political and the church as ascriptive. Meister does note the distinction between expressive and instrumental associations, and then intentionally sets the expressive ones aside. This is not without parallel in American writing on voluntary associations (Arnold Rose, for example) generally dominated by a liberal-pluralist ideological thrust, often bordering on the puritanical-prudish fringe that does not dare recognize that the Ku Klux Klan or various private clubs of an orgiastic nature are voluntary associations too. Meister knows his bias, but a bias it remains. To be fair it should be mentioned that when the focus is on participation rather than associations, the expressive orientation gets more attention. For Meister associations are primarily instrumental and inherently political in the broadest sense of concern with power or control through struggle. I recall listening to an academic debate between French sociologist Raymond Aron and America's champion Talcott Parsons in the early sixties. Aron's response to Parsons' paper was that Americans are not political enough in their thinking. I believe Meister would agree.

The third prominent issue flows directly from the second. It concerns the matrix of national and regional values that undergirds sociological analysis when it is addressed to political and economic issues, or when it includes them as part of its intellectual processes. I will only address half of this problem: Meister's assumptions, the ones that catch the eye of one not trained in European educational traditions. Here one could quickly become bogged down in a morass of qualifications. I would risk the observation that Meister is a faithful mirror of the long and agonized French tension between the revolutionary motto of liberty, equality, and fraternity, and the reality of centralized power. The result seems to the Anglo-American mind a paradoxical French national idealism, affirming the highest aspirations about human nature, and a painfully honest sociological realism about social facts and their interpretations. The result is a sort of Gallic verbal gesture, to borrow from George Herbert Mead. I have never met Albert Meister, but a long struggle to be faithful to the intent of his vivid prose makes me feel that I would recognize him on sight by the slant of a shoulder when (in the last chapter) he gives vent to his accumulated feelings after twenty years of intense thinking about the future of democracy.

The foremost value of Meister's efforts lies in his action sociology. Not action sociology in the Parsonian tradition, though Meister does draw on it, but in the sense, not as common now as a decade ago, of sociology as involvement and application. He speaks with authority because he speaks from experience and commitment. With the exception of his historical material and some speculative matter, the content of his writing comes not from books but from field research. His admiration for C. Wright Mills is no accident—his research bespeaks the same quality of involvement. This involvement in many respects is closer to anthropology in its orientation to field work, but still faithful to the sociological commitment to measurement. As Meister himself points out, no matter how much empirical data he has gathered about an organization, his best insights come from leisure conversations with workers.[1]

Meister also provides a new sociological perspective on organizational research. Treatment of small organizations in American sociology is relatively rare, compared to the study of bureaucratic phenomena. I recently scanned the latest twenty-five issues of *Administrative Science Quarterly*, our premier journal of organizational research. There was not a single study of a voluntary organization, and very little concern with small organizations of any sort. In the same period the *Journal of Voluntary Action Research* focused exclusively on voluntary associations, almost all of them small. The first of these is slick, expensive; the second is a photocopy production, irregularly published and with a small circulation. The relative emphasis on the two fields is clear. The research is where the money is. Leaving the topic of specialized journals the distinctions are not so clear, and some journals concerned with development are partly oriented to what Meister finds interesting: organizations, especially small ones. He gives us an integrated study of participative organizations, historically relevant and empirically grounded. I do not know of any similar approach in the English language.

Meister offers us a different way of looking at participation. He has seen participation simultaneously from the societal and organizational perspective. Here there are more American contributions to consider. Meister leans heavily on C. Wright Mills and David Riesman, giving some of his observations a strangely outdated quality, and upon Oscar Handlin, historian. These authors share a concern for the individual and his relation to modern society. Meister takes up these same themes on a world scale, but in each case grounded in field research of his own. Small organizations are only one way that the person connects with others to form a world; the alternatives are numerous and each has its consequences. To handle this vast array of possibilities Meister relies heavily on typification (to which I shall return) and gives us an integrated and parsimonious taxonomy of roles and characters, groups, organizations, societies, and consequences. The result is a sense that he has completed his task, that the territory has been covered. This approach is not without its costs. Although the fields of participation, associations, development, and change have all been covered, it is at the expense of that satisfying theoretical tidyness that intellectuals use as a criterion of evaluation. There is an eclecticism here that may be a consequence of what Meister has tried to accomplish. The evaluation of this aspect can only be pronounced with time. On this note we may now turn to a brief overview of Meister's theory and methods.

While Meister draws on a wide variety of sources for data and illustration, the core of his work is empirical research. Here his logic is specifically functional, both at the level of role relations in local social systems and in his interpretation of social systems and cultures. This theoretical orientation is not specified, therefore it may be useful to illustrate it regarding each level at which it occurs. The militant role is a concrete entity, emerging from the social history of struggle. This role is assumed by groups in conflict, regardless of ideological orientation. Individual militants enact their roles in specific groups, in which the person in time comes into tension with role requirements. The militant has certain personality characteristics that suit him for his tasks, or learns to acquire or simulate them. Militantism serves as a channel for social promotion. The militant is like the entrepreneur as to personal requirements and ambitions, and comes to much the same personal ends. In role the two act alike regarding competition and conflict, and their psychological makeup is similar. Both become group creatures.

This is no simple determinism. There are a number of potential outcomes for the militant person, depending on which systems level is most effective: the requirements of his family may lead him to seek security and bureaucratic sanctuary; he may adhere to old goals and ethics, becoming ideologically pure and ineffective; he may become the washed-out faithful amateur. There are other outcomes, each involving certain system relations (not always identified). The same functional reasoning could be traced to a number of institutional realms. Analysis is similar in all cases: action in the militant role is a consequence of system interrelation that the role implies, yet always with a certain looseness, a degree of personal voluntarism by the role incumbent. The person may undertake initiatives, but the results are more or less inevitable within the range of outcomes provided by the system.

The logic of militant groups is similar to that of the militant role. Every action has certain consequences, determined by system relations. The same sort of analysis is applied to the history of American labor, French socialism, African cooperatives, Israeli kibbutzim, and many others. The limited success of most of these groups arises from the consequences of (internal) group role interaction as much as from the resistance of conflicting groups or the difficulties of material objectives. This internal phenomenon has an inexorable quality. People adhere to groups in part for their own ends; careers run their courses; new members do not accept the groups' original goals. Cultural systems change militant groups with inexorable logic: economic success demands rationality and efficacy; redesign of leadership and resource allocation roles drives out emotional enthusiasm; militance gives way to ceremony, and so on. There are options and variations, but the course of militant systems is everywhere the same in the long run: they run down from friction in the machine as much as from rough blows of the environment.

What then of the next level, relations between types of groups and systems? The actors here are larger sets and systems, such as parties, self-management approaches, communes, cooperatives, enterprises, but the logic is much the same. Each is limited by conflict and its own internal friction. People like me who do a lot of teaching try to explain social phenomena in words, and usually end up drawing something on the blackboard to try to represent it, some oversimplified diagram with arrows and circles that we hope gets the point across. When we get only the diagram back on the final examination we usually regret that we were ever furnished with chalk in the first place. But the temptation is strong. So, if I were to try to represent Meister's idea of group on the board, it might be a big drum that its members intend to roll effortlessly toward an objective, but which when filled with liquid unexpectedly comes to a halt far short of its intended destination. In design the drum looks perfect, but when filled with what it is intended to carry it sloshes to a halt. I will omit other possible demonstrations of functional thinking. Of particular interest for those who might wish to pursue the matter are Meister's treatment of the social class system and the nature of individual participation. In each case the reasoning is similar.

Meister's methods may be divided into three main kinds: historical, with ideal typification where appropriate, empirical measurement and hypothesis testing, and ideal typification of observations and measured entities. In chapter 3 attention is turned to the history of associations. Specific groups are treated and events reported, with not very much attention to typification. Meister disavows any special training or skill here, and relies on a relatively limited number of sources, mostly standard authorities. His functional logic is evident in the historical presentation, which taken as a whole amounts to an evolutionary theory.

Materials drawn from societies in which Meister has done research in person are treated in two ways. There are specific empirical research findings verified and accepted as factual relationships. Second, and the basic structural element, there are sets of ideal types, generated at every relevant system level, verified by research facts, or not contrary to experience. The major kinds are those concerned with standard abstract sociological categories, such as roles, groups, associations, motives, strata, societies, and so on. In addition and less prominently, ideal types appear in historical situations, in the Weberian tradition.

While the logic of functional analysis seems to be the dominant feature of Meister's thinking, lending it an overall consistency and unity, other elements in his work are unusually creative. There is the frequent reference to and sympathy for the works of David Riesman and C. Wright Mills—prominent prophets and analysts of the 1950s and 1960s. It is their stridence and methods that seem to awake a response in Meister. These writers were similarly concerned with the relationship of individuals to society, with the decay of radicalism, with values and action. In chapter 11 we find a similar attraction to Chauvey and Decoufflé, writers of the Millsian mood.

Meister's thinking also bears the mark of the work of earlier writers Michels, whom he cites at length, and Pareto, whose political analyses and functional logic present an attractive model. Cited or not, the influence of Michels is clear throughout in the constant attention to the emergence of oligarchic tendencies in the evolution of specific groups. In earlier chapters Meister's economic analysis is based on Marx, and his interest in workers' organizations shows germane sympathies. There are no prominent Marxist themes in most of the social analysis, although in his autobiographical comment in *Esprit* he mentions that he is poised undecided between Marx and Pareto.[2] Marx furnishes more of the topic and occasionally the rhetoric, and Pareto most of the logic and values.

Another influential source is Kurt Lewin, progenitor of group dynamics. Lewin's work was a meld of Gestalt psychology and topographical methodology; his values were not markedly inconsistent with Mills' and Riesman's. Is this the means to understand Meister's marriage of functionalism, often accused of static tendencies and inability to account for change, and a personal desire for the triumph of the common man in his struggle for economic justice through change? For Lewin, individuals were the products of forces upon them. Groups had certain systematic qualities and basic natures, discoverable by empirical research (the group dynamics model appears repeatedly in these essays), but the type of group atmosphere was a matter of choice. Lewin, and even more so his scions, chose democratic group atmospheres, even though the theory did not require it. That is what Meister does. Perhaps the year he spent with the group dynamics workers in the United States had an impact. He chooses democracy, socialism, liberty, equality, fraternity; then his functional-evolutionary thinking leads him to describe a gloomy descent into mediocrity and alienation. Meister's vision, coupled with unquenchable revolutionary idealism leaves us stumbling unsteadily waiting for an uncertain future. I read the final few pages as an intellectual autobiographical statement as well as an analytical summing-up.

Albert Meister was born in 1927 in Switzerland. He studied there and in the United States. He took degrees in Economics, Sociology, and Psychology, and received his doctorate in sociology from the University of Geneva in 1958. He was for several years editor of the *International Review of Community Development.* Early in his career he was associated with the work of Adriano Olivetti in Northern Italy. This was a comprehensive scheme of planning, employment, and development programs. Following this he studied planning and animation in Israel, from where he went on to study the Yugoslav workers' councils. Then his research turned to development in Argentina. Subsequently he entered into travels and research in several African countries, with attention to macrosocial change. Since the publication of the last of the volumes used here he has also done research in Peru. His research has resulted in thirteen books in twenty years, plus four more in collaboration (one in Italian, two in Spanish).

My part in this effort consisted of editing and translation, in both of which Meister graciously gave me complete freedom. I discussed the organization and content of the book with him, but made the final decisions myself. I alone bear final responsibility for the arrangement of materials and translation. I abandoned chronological order for topical sequence. This has resulted in some repetition of minor points, which is preferable to the spottiness that might result from excessive pruning. The result is the first three and last chapters from 1972, with some dated topical comments, and materials written later in the center sections. More recent materials were the result of later writing—the research was complete when the earlier work was published. I have not added substantive explanatory materials on the societies included here. This may affect the uses to which the book is put. University courses on social change and development might require supplementation on these societies; used as a sociology text on social organization it stands alone.

My decisions on translation resemble those concerning content. I wanted the author to speak for himself as nearly as possible. Literal translations from the French produce awkward English; complete paraphrasing emasculates the rich and subtle substance of a beautiful language. My policy has been to lean toward French phrasing, even at the expense of a smoother English style—hence, more than the usual number of gallicisms. Much of Meister's sociological vocabulary has English cognates or literal translations and offers no problems. For some words no good solution could be found. *Cadre* became "staff" or "executive," depending on the situation, and sometimes "structure." *Quartier* became "neighborhood." Other decisions will be evident from the context. In general I have preferred to try to render unique French phrases in English rather than leave difficult parts untranslated.

I would like to express my thanks to my children David, Carol, Sarah, and Lisa Ross, all of whom took on tasks of looking up references or helping with problematic French phrases. My wife Dorothy Ross was especially helpful with fine points of grammar. David Horton Smith assisted in making publication arrangements. Excerpts from Albert Meister's work have previously appeared in the *Journal of Voluntary Action Research*. In every case I have made fresh translations.

MEMORIAL POSTSCRIPT

It was with great shock and much sadness that I learned from Madame Meister that her husband Albert Meister had died suddenly in January 1982 in Kyoto, Japan. I had never met him, but in our voluminous correspondence regarding articles of his that I translated for the *Journal of Voluntary Action Research* and for this volume I came to regard him as a close friend. Through the precision of his scholarly correspondence there always penetrated a humane warmth that was refreshing and supportive. I can only regret that the association could not have been more direct.

I have chosen to not alter the text of my introductory essay. It stands as written before the author's death.

I wish to thank Madame Jacqueline Meister and Albert Meister's colleague Olivier Corpet for their assistance in publication details that the author would have done himself.

NOTES

1. This insight and biographical information is drawn from Albert Meister, "Un sociologue s'interroge," *Esprit* (July-August, 1972): 1-11, a biographical article, and from personal correspondence.
2. Ibid.

1

PERSPECTIVES AND DEFINITIONS

PERSPECTIVES ON ASSOCIATION RESEARCH

Although associations make up a part of the scenery of our daily lives—and perhaps because of that—they have received attention from only a small number of sociologists. It is sufficient to recall the list of groups of which each of us is a part, throw a glance at those innumerable bulletins that invade our mail, or run over the lists of group members that the federations of associations proudly exhibit, to take account of the amplitude of the phenomenon in question. Association, committee, union, council, circle, commission, work, friendly society, movement, and so on, these familiar denominations lead us to ask ourselves the reasons which lead men to form groups and the needs they hope to satisfy through them. Such a search immediately runs up against a lack of information on the groups themselves: what we have is fragmentary and is found in the majority of cases in yearbooks, registers, propagandist declarations, or in moral reports that tell us neither about the functioning of the associations themselves, the way in which their members are tied to them, nor about the attachments members have to them. Sometimes we are more lucky, and can put our hands on an association monograph or, now more frequently, research bearing on certain aspects (leadership, for example) of the life of these groups. Most often it is necessary to fall back on personal inquiry, to pick items from minutes of meetings, or those bulletins that each association feels obligated to publish.

If researchers have not occupied themselves much with associations up to the present, it is, as Arnold Rose notes, because intellectuals often consider them with a certain scorn, taking them for women's clubs with no other preoccupation than chatter, or for groups of fanatics wanting to reform society with their preaching.[1] There are three currents of research on associations and related phenomena. The first is based on historical research, the scientific counterpart of the romantic rediscovery of the middle ages. This current is European and, characteristic of the past century, dried up with World War I. A second trend, sociological in nature, is North American and based on Tocqueville—who marveled at the facility with which Americans constitute associations of all sorts—and has its point of departure in the study of the significance of associations insofar as they sustain and correct democracy. A third current, a contemporary one, at once sociological and historical, originates in political sociology. Such political preoccupations are of two orders: first, the increasingly technocratic character of society striking a blow at the very basis of parliamentary democracy which Western countries inherited from the liberalism of yesteryear; second, the difficulties of popular participation in democratic socialist countries, where it was believed that social ownership of the means of production—the suppression of the causes of class conflict—would lead by itself to a collective and democratic management of the economy and society.

Relevant to these political, and very often militant, preoccupations, research on participation is currently popular. Participation in the firm, in politics, leisure, in one's religion, in development, and so on: our purpose is not to examine the different aspects of participation in various activities and structures. My interest is limited to the associationist framework of participation, when individuals "pool their knowledge or their activity with a goal other than sharing the benefits." The quote is from the definition of the association made in French law. We will specify later on. As to the spirit in which these associations must be studied one can only subscribe to what Max Weber wrote:

> It is a fundamental task of sociology to study those structures which are conventionally dubbed "social" (*gesellschäftliche*), that is, all that which lies in the gap between the politically organized or recognized powers—state, municipality, and established church on the one side—and the natural community of the family on the other. Thus essentially: a sociology of associations in the widest sense of the word, from the bowling club . . . to the political party and to the religious, or artistic or literary sect. . . . First, it will be profitable to investigate systematically the origin of the associations, and the occupational, geographic, ethnic and social provenience of the members. I consider it possible that in the course of time we can create a sort of cadastre of the more important categories of associations and thereby get on the track of the principles of selection of which the associations themselves are, to be sure, unaware generally and which can be determined only out of quite extensive and inclusive material. Along with that we shall have to analyse the means of the associations' working inwardly upon the members, and outwardly in the sense of propaganda and conflict, and finally, the propagated content itself, all in a fresh sociological casuistic.[2]

At more than a half century distance, such a program of research can still be ours; and it is in this very broad perspective that the present materials have been assembled. The remainder of this first chapter has as a goal a summary definition of some concepts which will later be defined with more precision.

THE CONCEPT OF ASSOCIATION

To begin with, we can retain the definition in French law in matters of association: a group based on voluntary recruitment and pooling by members of their knowledge or activities with some other goal than sharing the benefits. This definition does not completely cover the cooperative whose goal is, among others, mutally shared benefit. All the same we will include cooperative societies among associations, for as will be seen, the notion of benefits is not very important to them. This definition of association supposes a certain organization of conduct in the group and a certain codification of rights and duties of members (statutes, charter, etc.). These characteristics define formal groups and I will consider the association one of them.

I will contrast the association with small informal groups in which roles of participants are not codified. Such groups are networks of friends in which personalities of participants play the main roles in the cohesion of the whole. Other distinctions between types of associations shall be introduced; for the moment I will limit myself to reiteration of the distinction proposed by A. M. Rose[3] between associations whose goals and activities aim to express or satisfy members' interests (for example, a leisure-time club) and associations that propose to effect a change in their surroundings by their influence. Rose calls the first expressive associations and the second social-influence associations. The distinction is not very clear-cut: even expressive associations have a certain social influence (the case of a music group that collaborates in a political gathering) and social-influence groups also express the psychological needs of their members. The components "expression" and "social influence" are found in all groups and the distinction is a matter of degree. Still, the distinction is useful: we will indeed occupy ourselves more with social-influence associations—and among them those concerned with contestation—than expressive associations.

VOLUNTARISM AND SOCIAL PARTICIPATION

For the sake of clarity we propose to distinguish *voluntarism* from *social participation,* reserving the first to calls to devotion and the exaltation of participation aimed at by associations' leaders. For example, for coop doctrinaires and propagandists, voluntarism covers the voluntary, free, nonobligatory character of cooperative participation and devotion, and the spirit of sacrifice of members—especially that of leaders and officers. For the sociologist, the concept of social participation emphasizes the time devoted to a group, loyalty to it, and all the militant activity that takes place in more or less free groups that assumes an obligatory character. For the doctrinaire associationist, especially if he is Western, there could be no voluntarism in groups organized or controlled (cooperatives, for example) by an external power (generally the state). The sociologist distinguishes different types of participation according to whether the groups in which they are practiced are of spontaneous creation, stimulated, or even imposed (cf. infra).

In spite of these different preoccupations, both tend to agree on the terrain of operating definitions of voluntarism or participation. Both are defined by conduct simple to observe and record: number of adherents, number of subscribers, participants at assemblies, etc., all variables in the diverse indices of participation.[4] Participation thus observed and translated into percentages or indices does not tell us much about voluntarism and participation. They are only the observable and measurable aspects of very complex phenomena, just as suicide was a means of apprehension of anomie for Durkheim. Studies of the motivation of participation, of voluntarism, militancy, are still very rare. What are the psychological and social needs participation satisfies? Need for identification with a group in reaction to isolation from mass society? Need for communication? Need of affirmation or domination? Or, beyond these psychosocial needs, purely instrumental participation for the satisfaction of material needs impossible to satisfy other than by collective action? And so on. All these needs and still others have been proposed as hypotheses, especially by authors studying modern urban industrial society, and it is above all in works on social change that they are salient.

TYPES OF SOCIAL PARTICIPATION

The concept of social participation is of greater scope than that of voluntarism, limited to participation in associations of voluntary creation and recruitment. We will call this type *voluntary participation.*[5] We must also distinguish an *instigated* (or provoked) *participation* when the setting in which it takes place has been organized by an authority external to the group, without the initiative of participants themselves, and when the group remains more or less placed under this external control. In this case, the association is created as a means to integrate some individuals into a larger project (a national development plan, for example) or as a means to bring about participation in activities that leaders, from the outside, judge desirable (as in certain social service institutions). While the association with voluntary participation is created by members themselves and often with a goal of social demands or opposition to the social environment, the association of instigated participation is an instrument of conformity to the values of global society, values still foreign to the individuals considered. Regarding recruitment, one can again distinguish a *matter of fact participation,* insofar as all individuals belong as a matter of course, although participation is voluntary or instigated. Such is the case of participation in groups or subgroups (of trades, ages, and so on) in traditional and tribal societies. In this case the group exists before the individual and its goal is to incorporate him and bring him into conformity with the social values of his surroundings. We have schematized these distinctions in Table 1-1. Returning to the example above, what doctrinaires call "voluntarism" concerns only the third type of participation found in freely created groupings, founded without any meddling or external instigation. This model of participation (with as little external interference as possible) is currently offered to countries already on the path to development.[6]

TABLE 1.1
Participation Typology

	Creation initiative	*Mode of creation*	*Social Function*
Matter of fact participation	Preexistent group, created by tradition	Ascription	Social control, repetition of behavior desirable by group and milieu
Instigated participation	New group, external creation	Voluntary, at times strongly instigated	Acquisition of new behavior judged desirable by the outside
Voluntary participation	Creation by the group itself	Voluntary	Demands, creation of new behavior on group initiative

Outside of these three types of participation there is also *spontaneous participation*—voluntary, found in small, nonstructured groups. Such groups exist in both traditional and modern societies, although their functions differ: in traditional societies they permit deviance and oppose excessive social pressure; in modern industrial and urban societies, they permit the creation of interindividual links that the instrumentality of modern social relations destroys.[7] Yet another type of participation derives from the evolution of voluntary participation and transformation of voluntary groups in large bureaucraticized organizations: a purely instrumental and functional participation, without voluntary group cohesion that creates an emotional attachment, as is so often the case in voluntary participation.

NOTES

1. Arnold M. Rose, *Theory and Method in the Social Sciences* (Minneapolis: University of Minnesota Press, 1954), p. 50.
2. Max Weber, "Geschäftsbericht," *Verhandlungen des Ersten Deutschen Soziologentages vom 19-22 Oktober 1910 in Frankfurt a.M.* (Tübingen, 1911), pp. 52-60, translated by Everett C. Hughes, in the *Journal of Voluntary Action Research* 1 (Winter 1972): 20, 23.
3. Rose, *Theory and Method,* p. 52.
4. Indices more or less based on the famous participation index of F. Stuart Chapin, *The Social Participation Scale* (Minneapolis: University of Minnesota Press, 1937).
5. Elsewhere I have called this "free" or "organized" participation.
6. We could also show that the poor results yielded by this model (in terms of economic efficacy) originate from its substitution for the traditional model of "matter of fact participation": the latter does not prepare for or is even opposed to the voluntary sector and is totally conceived in terms of maintenance of social control and therefore entirely in opposition to the voluntary participation model oriented to creation of new kinds of behavior.
7. For further details on these different types of participation see Albert Meister, *Participation, animation, et développement* (Paris: Editions Anthropos, 1969).

2

SOCIAL PARTICIPATION AND SOCIAL CHANGE

To begin with it will be useful to clarify the ideas of participation and its structures by means of the ideal type method. This first step must subsequently be adjusted and weighed through minute field study of participation. We can begin from certain characteristics of traditional and modern societies, little by little determined in field research. These have no other justification here than their utility in clarification of hypotheses to be verified by empirical research. The method, then, is only a means to reach a goal.[1] It is equally with respect to their utility for concrete research that it is necessary to utilize the celebrated dichotomies between urban and rural society, between traditional, isolated, sacred and mass societies, mobile, secularized, *Gemeinschaft, Gesellschaft,* between societies based on mechanical solidarity (homogeneous) and those based on the division of labor (heterogeneous), between local community and mass society, and so on.

Although no concrete society possesses in the pure state all the characteristics called traditional or modern, their distribution on a continuum permits ordering different societies and constructing research plans.[2] We can now try to characterize the types of social participation in traditional and in modern society.

SOCIAL PARTICIPATION IN TRADITIONAL SOCIETY

Corresponding to a rudimentary technology, hand tools (and human and animal energy) the goal of the economy is to ensure the subsistence of a limited number of individual members of the society or subgroup. Exchanges with the exterior are very limited, each social unit (family, clan, village) aiming at self-sufficiency. Because of very simple tools and the absence of exchanges, division of labor is organized solely on the basis of age and sex. The surplus of produced goods is put in reserve to be consumed later in egalitarian fashion, or in certain cases distributed unequally when a feudality or a system of chiefs appropriates part of the value increment of social labor. In this case, social stratification rests on an unequal division of land and/or on privileged periodic land allocation. Because of the low value of exploitation capital (tools) the land is the principal capital and its possession determines social prestige.

Society is rural, and social organization, with predominance of the extended family, follows the organization of agricultural production. The family and kinship ties establish the limits of society and determine loyalties and solidarities. The family, the locality or neighborhood, age groups, occupational identities and low mobility, and the restrained size of social units, are responsible for the primary character of social relationships; secondary groups are nonexistent. Social values reflect the stability of the system of life, the inward-looking nature of society, the homogeneity of occupations of the population. They are values of stability, reinforcing social control, opposing changes and initiatives liable to menace social equilibrium. They are centripetal, and turn the group back on itself. Religion and myths explain the past and give norms of conduct for the present. All these factors converge to give unity to life, where no activity is differentiated from others or threatens them: work, leisure, and belief not only do not compete but are relatively undifferentiated.

What could be the forms of social participation in such a milieu, dominated by primary relations? Several characteristics can be mentioned. Due to the stability of society and the importance of the family cell, the oldest individuals, guardians of tradition, have a preponderant influence. Entry into a primary group is not the result of free choice, but depends on involuntary factors: age, birth, sex. The voluntary group does not exist, only the primary group. The social hierarchy is unique, rigid, and perpetuates itself without modifications. It takes pyramidal form: groups and institutions are articulated vertically; they sanction certain social privileges and define the rank to which they are attached. The hierarchy is renewed by appeal to its own elements and the goal of the whole system is its conservation, its immobility. Leadership in name is leadership in fact, insofar as belonging to a prestigious group or family ensures status and authority independent of personal efforts.

The rarity of information exchanges corresponds to economic autarchy. Local society is in effect a global society, and as it does not contain opposed systems of groups and institutions, information is highly centripetal, normative, reinforcing integration of the individual into society. Corresponding to the low level of division of labor and specialization of activities, information is likewise very unspecialized. Individual aspirations are little diversified; they are accepted by the normative system in force and a certain legitimacy is thus conferred on them. In the same way, individual motivations are not contradictory: individual goals and social values coincide. Society is integrated, does not absorb rapid changes and thus does not need social-influence associations; the family and local community suffice to satisfy individual needs.

Just as he does not choose to enter a group, the individual does not take initiatives nor interpret the social norms of primary groups: each situation is well determined by tradition; in unforeseen cases, tradition still dictates behavior under the influence of older persons. Even in the family, individual roles are not open to interpretation. Each one, in every phase of his existence, knows exactly what he must do and what is expected of him. In this sense, sociability is very formal. It is as crushing as the system of roles is rigid and impervious to fantasy or deviance. Fantasy or deviation are themselves prescribed and even encouraged within strict limits: festivals and times of rejoicing (for example, Carnival) function as periodic explosions, limited in time but uncontrolled within their limits.[3] Formal sociability is a rigid system of roles, duties, and individual rights. In sum, a totalitarian society, in the sense that individual life is defined in advance within rigid schemes.[4] Submerged in primary groups, having little experience of an exterior world that his society scorns, the individual develops strong feelings of belonging to these groups. The corollary is a weak capacity for adaptation to change and, as Riesman shows, a type of personality drawing its norms of conduct uniquely from tradition.[5]

SOCIAL PARTICIPATION IN SOCIETIES ON THE PATH TO MODERNIZATION

Two types of modernization have been tried by societies presently modern and developed: the liberal path chosen by Western societies in the last century and, in this century, the socialist way. Although the two may end up with the same results on the economic level, and in order to attain them must destroy the bases and social bonds of traditional society, they resort to different modes of individual participation and explain them through different ideologies. We shall examine some characteristics of societies on the path to modernization and identify their forms of social participation.

Common Characteristics

Society transforms its relations with nature, transcends them thanks to new sources of energy and the development of transportation, production ceases to be confined to the satisfaction of needs limited by its own milieu but is entirely centered on exchange. The demand for products is no longer a concrete demand of a known purchaser but the demand of an abstract public. Exchanges are multiple and markets overflow the limits of society. At this stage of industrialization the investment rate is high and dominant social values are centered on production rather than satisfaction of consumer needs. Fixed capital increases enormously in relation to other factors of production. Workers' tools cease to be their own personal property, due to their complexity and growing cost. Division of labor increases and forced specialization grows amidst trades and professions.

To the importance of fixed capital engaged in production corresponds rational employment of individuals, considered more as factors in production among competing others to the end of maximum efficacy of the economic enterprise. Specialization of economic life differentiates it from other spheres of social life; it becomes a world apart, obeying its own laws and morality. Division of labor, specialization, and hierarchies, in the professions influence other aspects of life. Society is stratified into higher classes (liberal bourgeoisie or socialist intelligentsia) and lower classes still linked to tradition but adopting motivations of the higher classes and aspiring to higher standards of living and the prestige attached to better remunerated professions. Transformations in the economy suppose and accentuate social and geographic mobility.

Mobility is responsible for the explosion of institutions and primary solidarities, familial and local. The extended family disappears and the local group and neighborhood lose importance. Social status and prestige are no longer linked to family membership or to locality, but are determined by personal qualities and professional success. Parallel to the progressive shrinking of the family and other primary groups, the importance of secondary groups increases: groups for professionals, for leisure, interests, political defense, religious opinion, and so on. Proliferation of these groups reflects the economic specialization and witnesses the rupture between different aspects of existence. These tendencies are favored by ecological concentration of economic activities, growing urbanization, and the need to recreate interindividual links substituting those of the old neighborhoods and the extended family.

Specialization and the search for efficacy have repercussions on government institutions and systems of authority: the old families, strata, or social classes holding political power are gradually substituted by the modern state directly serving class interests (bourgeoisie, or working class in socialist countries), that is, the bearers of industrialization. The designation of members of government and the administration increasingly obeys rational considerations rather than traditional solidarities. Population increase, thanks to decrease in mortality, its progressive concentration in urban zones, and often the increase in scope of national territories lead to rationality and impersonality of administrative services.

Dominant ideologies are centered on progress and their latent social function is encouragement of productive activities and restraint of consumption. They are combative, "imperialist," and claim to bear their conception of progress to all humankind. Since traditional society aims to prevent marginality and ensure conformity of behavior through the teaching of tradition, individuals of the society on the path to modernization confront many situations to which tradition has no response. Whence the accent placed on free choice and on mental flexibility of the individual. This type of society does not always encourage marginality, but permits great freedom of behavior regarding central values: the search for profit, power, and prestige. A new type of personality emerges, dominated by values and social goals internalized from birth. For this type of personality and individual, life must serve to realize these socially legitimized goals; his personal blossoming is thus his social realization, the success of the mission that society gives him.[6] Social ends and personal goals coincide, and being rigid, permit little deviance. On the other hand, the means to realize these goals are left to the free choice of the individual. In the two following sections, I will try to show how and how much, in spite of appearances, this type of personality is found in the two paths that modern societies have taken toward modernization.

Liberal Social Transformations

Liberating itself from traditional constraints (disdain for economic activities, prohibition of loans at interest, and so on), liberal society comes to rationalize the motive of economic activity in the theory of homo economicus. It raises into dogma the principle of free competition and nonintervention of the state in domains where the class directing the process of industrialization encounters social resistance (amelioration of workers' standard of living) or more traditional resistance (peasantry, feudalism). The dominant social values are progress and individual liberty. But individual free will can be exercised only in the measure that personal goals are those of society. Far from being immoral or amoral, society submits to a system of rigid values and a strict moral code. If personal profit constitutes the fundamental goal of human activity, economic success is respectable only insofar as it originates productive activities. Work ennobles because it is the creator of riches, thus of progress. Laziness, speculation, and even the simple abuse of consumption degrade the individual, curb his zeal, and retard his liberation. Work and economic success cannot fail to justify any courageous endeavor in a normal individual (that is, adapted to the struggle for life—those who do not succeed are considered weak and unsound)—economic success is considered a sign of health and divine benediction. Although personal, this success is valuable for the progress of humanity, in the same fashion as on the economic level the general interest is viewed as the sum of particular interests.

Success is only socially (and divinely) sanctioned to the extent that the rules of the game are observed. Bourgeois morality (not only in its Protestant version) is as severe as socialist morality (which we will examine later on), but does not emphasize the same norms. Concern for honesty in business, respect for work and private property, prevent society from becoming a jungle ensuring the triumph of the strongest by whatever means. Society is strongly policed, and in terms of liberal countries as a whole, basic values have been contested by only a relatively small number. As we shall see, unions, cooperatives, and political workers' associations have asserted themselves more against the abuses of the system than against its fundamental values. Freedom of enterprise and private property have been contested, but more in relation to abuses expressing lack of precise norms in certain domains, than in principle. Individual liberty implies that the business leader does not infringe his workers' freedom in overstepping the strictly contractual relations that link him to them. By the wages agreed upon, he is giving them sufficient opportunity to rise socially, if only they will do their share, reduce their birth rate, educate themselves, and work even harder—what he gives over and above that is only charity.[7]

Murmurs of pity aside, liberalism is hard, pitiless, as much for the weak as for the unfortunate strong. Hardness accompanies Puritanism: austerity and severity toward oneself permit the bourgeois to justify his hardness toward others. Perhaps more than in the metropolises it is evident in certain overseas colonies that the liberal state, faithful instrument of industrial expansion, has permitted to be opened to European settlement: here the colonist has been able to gain his own welfare by crushing personal work and respecting all norms of honesty of his society of origin in his relationships with populations much less demanding than Europe's.[8] In spite of the different context, the liberal colonial attitude is not different from the liberal attitude during modernization in France.

What are the characteristics of participation in this type of society? Due to a new social stratification, in which the social class directing the process of industrialization occupies the summit, and due to a political power not yet contested (universal suffrage having permitted a sharing of power with other classes, only intervening during the base period of industrialization), the structure of social participation follows class barriers. There were no associations common to the bourgeoisie and the working class in the past century (excepting certain religious and social work associations). Associations tend to become associations for demands or for the defense of class interests. We will later examine workers' associations in detail. Here we will only consider some traits of participation and show how the liberalism of the epoch marked even those associations that gave themselves to the mission of contesting, upsetting, or limiting it.

The mixing of populations caused by industrialization and especially rural influx to the cities ends in the creation of innumerable associations whose functions are at once re-creation of traditional solidarities of the place of origin (notably among rural immigrants) and demands for decent conditions of life in a world that does not occupy itself with such social considerations. These groups are created voluntarily and participation in them is also voluntary. Each association is concerned with its own independence and freedom in relation to other associations. In the same manner that businesses are anxious not to let themselves be absorbed by others, associations compete in their recruitment, define their positions and doctrines (i.e., the product they put on the market) with care, and denounce imitators of their ideas in the same way that businesses take action against those who imitate their patented products. These tendencies are especially apparent among cooperatives which, subject to socialist demands, are so acculturated that they make their independence from the state a fundamental principle of doctrine, going so far as to deny the status of cooperative to those integrated into a planning system such as that of socialist states.

These influences of milieu and epoch are found among militants and officers of associations. Before a struggle and often later, to achieve recognition for their group and recruit adherents, they take on certain traits of the liberal businessman: they consider their association their own creation, protect it from competing groups, adapt the publicity techniques of the business enterprise to their use, are jealous of their power and resist sharing it, prefer to keep total control over a small autonomous group rather than become head of a section of a larger association (just as the heads of small businesses are apprehensive about mergers with larger firms in order not to become mere branch managers).

This kind of behavior often accompanies declarations about the need for and use of federations of associations of the same type, in view of greater efficacy regarding demands or activities. But this unity is far from realization when discussions are held regarding redivision of power among leaders of a unifying group. The need to maintain ideological purity (the quality of the product sold to adherents) is then invoked to oppose fusion. The smaller the association (marginal), the stronger the concern for independence: production cooperatives or, still today, small groups of anarchists, each centered on production of a little bulletin with a minuscule distribution, are examples of associations where fusions are rare, manifesting over and beyond declarations of unity the anxiety over independence characteristic of the small business (be it of ideological or material production). Another example is furnished by the attempts, today abortive, at union of certain leftist political associations in recent years. Big political associations, unions, and cooperatives (consumer coops especially), today huge mass associations, have known the same difficulties regarding the fusions, federations, and unions which make up their history (cf. infra). But just as there still exist today a large number of small independent businesses, there remain a large number of small associations. As we will see in the following section, big associations, like big businesses, set the pace in times when large-scale capitalism—and big associations—have replaced atomic capitalism and small associations.

Associationism has been marked by its milieu and times; all the same, as in the case of leftist associations, it combats a certain form of social organization. The parallel can be pushed further if associationism is examined as an instrument of social advancement similar to the business enterprise in the past century. In the same way that the small private business permitted worker social mobility into the ranks of small owners, associations permitted social advancement (and often, but indirectly, subsequent professional promotion) of innumerable militants. The thundering economic takeoff during the industrial revolution, like the intense popular participation in associations of the same era, is explained in part by opportunities of social ascent offered by free enterprise and atomic associations. In numerous cases associational involvement constituted a complementary instrument of individual promotion: at the moment when the enterprise did not offer enough opportunities for professional promotion, associations were open to candidates for advancement.

Presently giant political associations, unions, social organizations, and the very large capitalist enterprises set the tone everywhere. Small businesses and associations remain instruments of individual promotion, professional or social, but their importance has diminished considerably. Large associations and enterprises do offer opportunities for promotion, but address themselves to a different type of man than the captain of industry or the militant associationist of the industrial revolution. (We will return to this point in the following section.) When most of their demands are translated into laws and regulations, associations find themselves less able to arouse popular participation. Associations permitted social promotion to those lacking the opportunity to follow formal channels of education. With compulsory education and the multiplication of institutions of instruction, a much smaller number of individuals have had to use militancy to achieve advancement. The size and ponderous administrative apparatus of the most important associations discourages militancy based on loyalty, to profit from recruitment of specialists in techniques of handling people. Increasingly associations need technicians who are already trained, rather than responsible members to whom they give the opportunity of training and promotion. Whence the disaffection on the level of participation. As we will see later, for different reasons socialist associations experience the same problems once the basic stage of industrialization is completed.

Socialist Transformations

In reaction to the abuse of freedom, socialist development places the accent on equality and then on economic planning.[9] The latter must permit all regions and enterprises to develop without inequalities—human resources must be distributed as equally as possible to avoid privileges. In the structure of socialist ideology, a severe moral code is elaborated and guides individual behavior: the moral socialist is enjoined to respect collective property and above all to struggle against privilege. Man must be first a militant socialist, putting collective interest before his own. Apart from some domains difficult to socialize (such as small artisanal shops) or still under the weight of tradition (such as the peasantry), the economy is collectivized. The principal motivation of economic activity and social ascent is no longer personal economic success, but the promotion of all. Motivation is ideological and to the extent that the ascendancy of ideology over individuals is powerful, the functioning of economic institutions will be satisfactory.

Under these conditions there is theoretically no difference between associational participation and participation of individuals in the economic management of their society. The two types of institutions are based on maximal participation, the condition of good functioning. Whence the multiplication of apparatus and institutions of popular participation in work and outside, endeavoring to develop civic and socialist consciousness, struggling against all manifestations of privilege (of inequality), seeking to maximize collective interest. Ideological motivation has never been sufficient to ensure dynamic functioning of the economy. Socialist countries have had to reintroduce more personal motivations, based on social promotion and individual professional advancement to the detriment of collective progress.

Although associations of the liberal world follow the private enterprise model, constituting themselves freely and creating competition, associations in socialist societies—like economic enterprises—obey a central plan: their constitution is promulgated by the central power, their activity is planned to attain domains of life where an ideological tonic seems necessary, their institutions and functioning are standardized, and their branches extend to all society. As in liberal society, the state is the instrument of the group or class claiming that its mission is the progress of society. And, as in the liberal world, the classes or strata of the population judged to be retarded (the peasantry, for example) are sacrificed and see their political power very reduced.

Just as the leader of the liberal association resembles the leader of a private business, the socialist association leader tends to resemble the economic director of the planned society. With the exception of Yugoslavia, where democratic mechanisms of self-management sometimes play a role, the socialist economic director is an appointed functionary, charged with precise technical tasks, having to render account of his administration, disposing of a certain employment security whatever the success of the enterprise he directs, called to conform to directives rather than to take risks and initiatives. The association leader reflects these characteristics: the association or section he directs, being important due to its official character, the leader is much more often permanent than is the liberal leader, insofar as he is also a functionary. Due to compatibility of association programs (among themselves and with those of economic organizations) elements of demand—that is, of opposition—give way to acceptance and propaganda in favor of official positions: the association leader presents himself as cultural director, a practical technician. Due to the common ideology that embraces both economic and after-hours life, and because economic planning is elaborated by the same group which establishes political associations, the socialist association director does not differ in personality from the economic director. Both are, according to Lenin's phrase, couriers of transmission between the central organs of political and economic power and the masses insofar as they are workers and citizens.

The liberal association has been a powerful instrument of social promotion, often followed by professional advance. In socialist society, because of compatibility between associational ideology and economic modes of organization, associationist social promotion accompanies professional promotion and vice versa: the business director is almost always an association leader, and the association leader extends to the factory the leadership capacities acquired on the cultural, social, or political level. On the personality level, the man of the socialist society in process of construction does not differ from the man of the liberal construction phase. Their values may be different, and in the socialist variant belief in collective promotion has replaced the motive of economic success. But in both cases values and social goals are strongly internalized and constraining. Individual goals are mapped out and life must serve to realize them. The choice of means in both cases is left free: to realize the goals they believe to be the purpose of their lives—economic success and personal recognition—the constructors of liberal society, like the builders of socialism do not hesitate over the choice of means. Progress or socialism are motivations so strong that they blind those who have power over others.

Values gradually lose ascendancy and socialist society must resort to other motivations to advance construction of the new society. Transformations occur equally in modes of participation: because of decreasing ascendancy of collective values, associationist participation diminishes and, inequalities having appeared in remuneration, professional life offers more possibilities of ascent and satisfaction of consumer needs than militant life. As in the liberal world, militant activities are devalued. They no longer pay off. Although at first these activities are a springboard for social or professional advancement or confer prestige and similar advantages, from the moment they are devalued individuals prefer to concentrate their efforts on professional promotion. Socialist societies, having made their industrial revolution, find themselves in a situation similar to that of the liberal world.

SOCIAL PARTICIPATION IN INDUSTRIALIZED SOCIETIES

Once basic industrialization is achieved, new trends in participation emerge. We shall examine first changes in societal organization. Technological changes, prolongations of the great transformations of the industrial revolution brought about mass production on the basis of new forms of energy. Such increasing rationalization led to entirely automatic production requiring ever-larger markets. These extensions of early industrialization were before long accentuated again by the utilization of atomic energy for industrial ends. These technical developments led to important modifications in the organization of production and in society in general: concentration of capital, gigantic development of the tertiary sector, more interdependence of international markets. Small enterprises have been gradually swept into mergers, bought up or integrated as suppliers for large industries. Although their number remains significant, many are occupied with subcontracting or making parts, the great industrial complexes setting the tone. These trends are the same, whatever the type of economy, liberal or socialist.

Liberal Societies

Here there is in addition a progressive separation between the functions of the capitalist and the manager of the large enterprise. The head of his own factory or of a family factory has disappeared as an important category. Large enterprises have expanded the pool of shareholders to the general public. It is these shareholders, generally owners of a few shares, who have lost (but have they ever exercised?) their right of management of the big business. Isolated, or not participating in shareholders' meetings, they are transformed into puppets, management being reserved to owners of many shares and to the executives they designate at the head of the business.[10].

Growing interdependence of large enterprises, thanks to the game of participation in capital and administrative councils—and as we will see, the need to guarantee sources of raw materials and markets beyond national frontiers—have led to stronger participation in political power (straining parliamentary governments whose rule does not provide for participation of economic powers as such, whence the lobby system and other intrusions into political mechanisms). Thanks to these political influences and to a diminution of competition among large firms due to such mutual participation, big capitalism realizes, by connivance with the state, a sort of unofficial planning of economic activities. Due also to the weakness of union and political associations, questioning the basis of the regime and anticipating a revolutionary transformation, this "planning" benefits from the concurrence of leftist parties and the union organizations. The orientation thus given to the economy and to domestic and foreign politics achieves planning—less thorough, less egalitarian, less official—similar to socialist planning. In the country where this evolution is most marked, the United States, it is the military—those implacable defenders of Western life and organization—who are at the origin of it: under the pressure of military needs and under the control of the Department of Defense, a sector of state capitalism has developed, controlling increasing numbers of industrial firms whose management subsidizes its most important functions: search for capital to launch production (furnished by the state), research for new products (organized by the state), and research into cost control (the army scarcely occupies itself with this). If it is realized that this Pentagon capitalism produced, in 1968, 44 billion dollars of goods and services—more than the combined figures of General Motors, General Electric, U.S. Steel, and Dupont—one gets an idea of the scope of the problem.[11] Certainly this example is special, but from the fact of its size it constitutes an economic model imitated in other sectors (civil aviation, for example), and it is justified to ask if it does not lead the entire economy, increasingly dominated by gigantic organizations, veritable institutions of economic and political power. We will come back to this question, and notably its implications for participation.

Highly automated production diminishes the number of men directly concerned with tasks of production and increases the number of those occupied with questions of organization and planning. Just as the first industrial revolution saw the importance of the primary sector diminish in the active population, the second industrial revolution (sometimes called the passage from electrical energy to electronic techniques) sees a shrinking of the secondary sector. Increasingly complex mass production transforms the notion of the client: although the industrial revolution had seen the concrete client transformed into an abstract public, pressure for disposal of consumer goods now brings talk of publics or potential markets that do not yet consume at all but which it is necessary to conquer. From this comes the prominent role of more invasive publicity that now precedes manufacture and research that informs the manufacturer about the opportunity to put a given product into the market. The diverse forms of market study constitute a tool of this planning taking shape in postliberal societies and more generally in economies attaining a certain threshold of diversification of consumer goods. Facing the necessity to extend markets, the growing ascendancy of big enterprises and services over government was devised as a political instrument of commercial expansion. The current policy of aid to underdeveloped countries is a characteristic example of research for new commercial outlets (especially for products in the third sector—experts, studies, education, and so on).[12]

The interdependence of large businesses, among themselves and with government, on the one hand, and the growth of political organizations and workers' organizations to which they are linked, and their acceptance as a matter of fact of the principles of postliberal society, on the other hand, end in a kind of conflict-ridden cooperation between the big national sectors. Business has been led to observe that the politics of the high levels of popular life directly favor its own growth and that starting from a certain stage of industrialization, strong work legislation, employment security, and fringe benefits become factors in productivity. Hence the multiplication of agreements limiting the powers of contracting parties such as collective contracts, limitation of profits, limits on the right to strike, price regulation, state participation, subsidies to certain social categories, and so on. Beginning from these accords and purely empirical adjustments, a practice and doctrine of planning oriented to the economy is worked out. The profit motive always dominates the economic scene and gives it its dynamism, but the implicit value at the bottom of this planning is social peace, channeling conflicts through institutions of dialogue and more or less imperative behavioral orientation of economic agents.

Masking this reality, liberal ideologies continue to be manifest on the level of phraseology: big entrepreneurial associations always exalt the myth of free enterprise; workers' associations that of socialism. These values, brandished like banners for the sake of public opinion, have lost much of their force. The employer knows that he acts now in a more or less planned economy (but maintaining much freedom to maneuver in it), just as the worker knows that his organizations no longer fight for a socialist society (from which he has already partially won what was essential to him: employment security). The key words of the doctrines and militant enthusiasms of yesteryear subsist, but in a very modified context. We will see later that it is in this novel situation that we must seek to explain transformations in association participation, particularly in the disengagement within associations born in the liberal epoch.

Socialist Societies

The socialist economy also submits to transformations once basic industrialization is achieved. They have been set off thanks to the enthusiasm and sacrifices of militants, themselves born of revolution or national liberation. With them, the principles of equality and collective promotion are disparaged, differentiations in pay and promotion being applied to stimulate the economy. All the recent transformations of socialist economies are aimed at stimulating a lethargic economy. The socialist economy starts from premises completely opposite to those of the liberal economy: what the postliberal economy is coming to consider its central value, social peace, is the departure value of the socialist economy. Equality, collective promotion, suppression of class conflict—all these are the values of fraternity and social peace and the socialist economy rests on the postulate that devotion, fraternity, and intelligence are sufficient motors for its development. Although the profit motive and individual social ascent of the liberal economy are only doctrinal translations of the law of the strongest from the natural world, the motive of the socialist economy is the transposition of intellectual ideals, of contemplation. This is no place to debate the superiority of one or the other of these motives. We limit ourselves to establishing their complementarity.

These differences establish the lack of natural dynamism of the socialist economy and the measures taken by planned societies to increase it: the power accrued by directors of enterprises, the great span of the salary scale, the introduction of competition mechanisms, making plans flexible, renouncing the principle of equality in the rhythms of development among the regions of a country and among socialist countries—all these adjustments are so many breaches in the ideal, creators of tensions, and finally, of possibilities for profit and individual success. As in the postliberal world, the ideologies of the socialist takeoff remain in their vocabulary; speeches continue to celebrate the classless society, fraternity, and equality of socialist development. And, as in liberal society, the difficulties of popular participation in associations born in the course of the period of takeoff must be explained.

Problems Common to the Two Types of Societies

Having broached these problems, largely common to the two types of societies that occupy us here, we now turn to examination of some tendencies on the psychosociological level. In the two types of societies the conditions of social mobility are similar: professional education permitting acquisition of a status in the hierarchy of employees and workers has replaced militantism (socialism) or the spirit of business (liberal society) as the condition of social mobility. A certain employment security being conferred, individuals turn to the search for prestige (and at a certain level of the hierarchy, power) in their professional order. Above all in the highest echelons, the profession seems indeed like an order: the criteria for education necessary for advancement are well defined and often serve as mechanisms of cooptation that operate to separate the candidates; from this comes a strong pressure for group conformity. And, also, for the individual, the need to immediately grasp whatever is available to him and to present to others the image of conformity to the group.

Although in the previous period social ascent originated from a victory over things and from the will over men in a combat to dominate and organize the energies of nature, now it is a question of coming to terms with others, with those on whom depends a promotion in the organizations that are increasingly bureaucratized. The problem, as Riesman says, is no longer material environment but human environment.

The ideals of the preceding period having lost their ascendancy, and not having been replaced by any new system of values, no central value molds the personality of the individual. His conduct appears to be entirely directed according to the evaluations that he constantly makes of his position by relation to others. This "radar personality," according to the expression of Riesman, rests on a keen sensibility to the desires of others and on a great ability to convey to others the impressions they wish to receive. Although in the liberal period and the socialist takeoff period internalized values provide norms and guide behavior, the personality type of the following period no longer has rigid internalized values, is no longer guided by severe norms, and thus offers great flexibility in conduct. What has been internalized are mechanisms that are extremely sensitive to detection of the intentions of others.

This absence of values accounts for the extreme facility in social contacts, the growing informality of interindividual relations, and also for the cold instrumentalism of contacts (the tendencies are not contradictory). The modern individual feels at ease everywhere. Each one realizes that he is an element in the game played by others and his own game is to utilize the others for his own goals. This interdependence of games presupposes the absence of constraining personal values that might put nonrational obstacles in these relationships.

In reference to tendencies outlined above in relation to traditional society, we underline some new characteristics of the structures of social participation. Contrary to traditional society which saw a single hierarchy of groups, modern society sees several hierarchies of groups facing each other and even, in appearance at least, no more hierarchies at all. When the groups have links with one another, the articulations between them are horizontal and not vertical (no relations of inclusion, superiority, loyalty, and so on). The privilege that entry into groups can sometimes confer is no more the mark of social rank: it is more the quality of a person that permits entry into a group, and individuals can conquer positions independently of their personal social origin.

Individual participation is no longer total but differentiated, and extends over several groups. In consequence, the power that each group exercises or claims to exercise will be weaker. In the same measure, the foundation of this power changes. It becomes contractual and the individual is free to initiate membership or resignation from the group, to deal with it on the basis of equality, or not be part of it. It is segmentary rather than totalitarian.

Division of labor in modern society results in some very special information content, diffused by its innumerable groups and institutions. This information has a centrifugal effect on the individual, each group proposing to integrate it and thus placing itself in competition with the others. The aspirations and motivations that undergird them are clearly contradictory, sometimes within the individual himself. That which is legitimate is no longer defined, as previously, by opposition to that which is not in a unique system of values, but fluctuating, unstable, by relation to one of several value systems which, more or less momentarily, influence the individual.

In these conditions, what will be the forms of social participation? Associations submit to the same processes of growth and giantism as enterprises. The game of fusions and unions ends up on the plane of their ideology at a sort of least common denominator: the particular and particularist values of the component associations tend to disappear to the benefit of words of a very general order, capable of rallying the greatest number of adherents. And, especially, it is the functional aspects that dominate in propaganda: the association must serve to realize a precise goal and in the short term. In workers' associations, it is no longer a question of installing a new order but of struggling for this or that practical amelioration.

Individuals do not belong any more for ideological motives but for instrumental goals. In belonging, they reinforce the association and expect from it in exchange some very precise and limited actions. In cases of competition between two associations, there is a fluctuation of preferences according to which is momentarily judged more efficacious.

The weak hold of ideologies tends to reduce the number of militants and responsible volunteers: the number of permanent functionaries paid by the association increases and communication between directors and members no longer rests on personal contacts. The size of the groups having strongly increased and the cost of functionaries having gone up, the association has recourse to indirect communication (newspapers, communiqués, radio, and so on) to maintain contact with its members and diffuse its information and instructions. The use of functionaries and the increase in size lead to a certain bureaucratization: relations with adherents are administrative in character and accountable.

In its propaganda the association very often continues to employ the phraseology of the preceding epoch, but its activities are limited to precise objectives. The key words and slogans of the preceding epoch hang on only in the sectors and backward social categories, backward, that is, by relation to the dominant currents of technical and economic progress. In these still retarded sectors, under modes of thought and organization of the preceding period, ideological appeals still have some success: as in France where Poujadist-type slogans are addressed to small merchants attached to atomic methods of distribution and who are victims of a commercial combination similar to that of industry; or the success of old union slogans among production sectors where work methods and lifestyles remain traditional. Certain associations still dominated by the old values regroup no more than the aged militants and have no hold on the young who understand neither the problems nor the vocabulary of an epoch gone by.

Among professional associations, only the American, and in Europe the associations of executives, show clearly the tendencies analyzed above. Functionalization and the decreasing hold of ideology are the most thorough there. But in many regards they show the way, and these characteristics can be noted more and more in other associations.

This growing functionalism of associations, and more generally the instrumentalization of contacts and interpersonal relations, lead to new forms of associations. Beyond the tendency of individuals to withdraw into their little groups and families, we note the growing appearance of nonrational associations.[13] Everything goes on as if the individual suffered from the devaluation of his participation and of his professional and social contacts: whence the appearance of new forms of valuation (especially religious) and the growing popularity of diverse forms of occultism. Are these new valuations a form of compensation for the rationality of participation and daily contacts of the individual?

Better known, by contrast, is the tendency to withdraw into small groups that are informal, unstructured, and unorganized centers for establishing individual identity and for personalization of contacts.[14] In addition to the sentiment they dedicate to a great cause that has passed them by (sentiment that they find again now in cults and other nonrational associations), the militants of the preceding period permitted giving free expression to needs for friendship, identification, and personalization. As was seen above, the high degree of personalization of associations in the previous period had been a brake on their instrumentalization.

The rationality of participation and of professional and everyday social contacts are often traumatizing for the individual: he can never personalize a relationship, the anxiety over efficacy and rationality must always take precedence over personal considerations, and very few occasions are offered in which he can identify profoundly with a cause or even with some work.[15]

The coldness of this participation and interpersonal relationships—even if they appear cordial and facile on the surface—frustrate the individual in his need to appear as a whole person. The increasing distance from the urban center, the comfort of the habitation—and the ownership of a family auto that prolongs Sunday afternoon—tend also to reinforce the nuclear family. The anticipation of purchase of costly equipment creates common projects shared by couples and unites the family around construction or embellishment of the home. Thus the family unit constitutes a unit of consumption in the same sense, and makes an appeal to the same sentiments of identity as the family unit of production so characteristic of preceding epochs: the modern family project of purchase of an automobile or outfitting a second residence is comparable in its psychological aspects to the little artisanal family workshop of fifty years ago.

The family and its small groups in which the individual feels accepted, with his qualities and faults, and not as the performer of a function, compete with association participation. If one recalls in addition that participation was often in the past dictated by the concern to reinforce employment security—and that the latter is now being in the process of being acquired—there are still fewer reasons for participation.

These problems are largely common to the two types of society examined above: in the postliberal society, as in the developed socialist society, the same disengagement is found in regard to associations and the same withdrawal into small groups. The highly organized societies born of these two apparently opposed paths of change and development are confronted with the same problems.

NOTES

1. The gaps thus produced lead to lack of precision in the concepts used in these ideal types. And the danger consists in reification of these concepts and their substitution in empirical research.
2. For a very useful summary of the characteristics of traditional and modern society, cf. Gino Germani, "Comparación tipíco-ideal entre la sociedad preindustrial rural y la sociedad industrial urbana," in G. Germani and Jorge Graciarena, *De la sociedad tradicional a la sociedad de masas* (Buenos Aires: Departamento de Sociología, 1961), pp. 349-62.
3. It would be appropriate to test the hypothesis that the more formalism there is in the sociability of a group, the greater the chance that this group will organize or participate in festivals intended to channel the need for deviation.
4. We propose the hypothesis that associations in which individuals participate who regret the types of societies that more or less hem-in the personality (these regrets subsist today under different forms of passivism, more or less sentimental, running from corporatism to certain forms of apology for the rural life and the family) will tend to be of the authoritarian type as to norms of member participation and totalitarian as to their activities and ambitions.
5. Cf. David Riesman, Nathan Glazer, and Reuel Denney, *The Loney Crowd,* abr. ed. (New York: Doubleday Anchor, 1953), pp. 26-28.
6. One can recognize here the type of gyroscope personality described by Riesman, p. 31.
7. We will see farther on that one of the most important currents of modern associationism (set off with the British settlements) has taken its point of departure precisely in a charity movement.
8. The case seemed very clear to me in a colonized country like Kenya, where the British colonists experience no interference with luxurious living in the midst of a miserable African population. The fact of having worked very hard and surmounted repeated obstacles constitutes for them the psychological justification of their economic success. The part they have given to the natives appears sufficient to them, and the latter ought to accept the rationale that they did not know as well how to use their opportunities.
9. I have tried to show elsewhere how the principle of planning is the corollary of the principle of equality. Albert Meister, *Où va l'autogestion yougoslave?* (Paris: Anthropos, 1970).
10. It is appropriate in this regard to distrust the thesis of big American capitalism that a sort of democratization has been achieved due to the wide dispersion of stock shares, or the pretended separation of management and ownership. On

this subject see C. Wright Mills, *The Power Elite* (New York: Oxford University Press, 1959): pp. 121-22.

11. Cf. Seymour Melman, "Pentagon Bourgeoisie," *Transaction* 8 (March-April, 1971): 4-12. See also the debate organized by *Nouvel Observateur*, 1971.
12. Cf. Albert Meister, *L'Afrique peut-elle partir?* (Paris: Editions du Seuil, 1966).
13. By design I do not employ the word *irrational*, for what these new groups intend above all to contest is the type of rationality I have tried to analyze.
14. See also David Riesman, "Flight and Search in the New Suburbs," *International Review of Community Development* 4 (1959): 123-36.
15. It has often been noted that in administrative and bureaucratic situations the individual who identifies more with his work has the least chances of advancement. Too centered on his work, personalizing it too much, he neglects others, forgets the game that he must play, and becomes only an element in the game of the others.

3

A BRIEF HISTORY OF ASSOCIATIONISM IN FRANCE AND THE UNITED STATES

Although our goal is the sociological study of modern associations, it is indispensable to go back to the past to understand present trends. It is particularly interesting to compare associationist developments in two very different societies: France, where associations, and particularly workers' associations, are slowly ridding themselves of their medieval elements, and the United States, where mass immigration and the break with European traditions give different characteristics to associations.[1]

THREE STRANDS OF MODERN FRENCH ASSOCIATIONISM

It is generally agreed that the history of modern French associations begins in 1848. The political and legal changes that took place then, coinciding as they did with the apogee of the industrial revolution, make it possible to begin there without much error. Nevertheless, certain old forms of organization passed through this revolutionary era with little change—mutual associations, for example—and traces of other types influenced the new kinds. The surviving forms may be grouped under three heads: corporations, trade guilds (*compagnonnages*), and mutual associations. The Roman and Germanic associations that left their imprint on each must be ignored here.[2]

The corporative strand may be traced to the eleventh century, though it was not until late in the thirteenth century that the great codification of corporation statutes prepared by Etienne Boileau prepared the way for the great expansion that was to follow. The corporation (which resembles the English guild as to organization and purposes) brought together in one organization three classes of artisans: apprentices, valets (or journeymen), and masters. Authority was in the hands of experienced sworn masters, the *prud'hommes.* Beside these corporations of sworn tradesmen were the regulated trades under direct rule of the municipalities, and the free trades, under police rule. The corporative groups, of most interest in this associationist history, grew in power and exclusiveness over the centuries. In 1776 an edict by Turgot suppressed them. There followed a brief revival that was brought to an end in 1791.

Beside the corporations were religious fraternities (*confréries*), which probably predated them. They were associations, often of workers of the same trade, which met for purposes of religious ceremonies, fellowship, and charity. The trade guilds arose from the increasing closure of the corporations against journeymen. These associations were at times forced into secrecy, and adopted numerous myths of origin, secret rituals, and obligations. In the eighteenth century they organized many strikes. Some associations survived into the nineteenth century.

The mutual associations were organizations for mutual aid, separate from the corporations and trade guilds which provided the same services for themselves. Similar organizations existed in England, where 5,000 were counted in 1801.[3] Beside the organizations for mutual aid grew associations for welfare, each related to governmental or religious efforts in complex ways. The mutual organizations were the only ones to survive relatively intact through the suppressions of 1791. They constituted a way of meeting, at the expense of private charity, the needs not met by public assistance. Because they were considered a means to contain popular aggression, the mutual aid associations benefitted from the tolerance of the liberal state.

MATURATION OF THE NEW FRENCH ASSOCIATIONAL FORMS

In what measure were the ancient forms of association perpetuated in spite of the repressive law of Le Chapelier in 1791, and subsequent interpretations, and to what extent have they aided in the birth of new types of associations? The same three strands will be followed: corporations, trade guilds, and mutual organizations.

Prolongation of the Corporation

As early as 1806 a new form of labor regulation emerged in Lyon. Commissions were formed of manufacturers' delegates and shop heads. Workers were excluded. These new councils of *prud'hommes* were not true corporations, though they attempted regulation of work through similar means.

The End of the Trade Guilds

The trade guilds were accustomed to clandestine operations and thus escaped some of the suppression that was the lot of other associations. Nevertheless, struggles among their three factions had weakened them, and attempts at synthesis or reform had only moderate success. One of these, led by Flora Tristan in 1842-43 proposed a world union of male and female workers. The trade guilds died out because they were bypassed by events. Their form of organization was suited to artisanal production, but this was the industrial age. Even though they decreased steadily in numbers and importance, their influence has been passed on through their rituals and customs to other organizations. Some 2,000 members were said to exist in 1945.

Mutual Aid and Resistance Associations

Although the law of Le Chapelier forbade the mutual associations for the same reason as all the other associations, the public powers were more tolerant toward them. The prolongation of the old religious fraternities, they sometimes presented themselves as religious and charitable groups and the repression was then ill at ease in their regulation. Certain mutual associations recruited their members in diverse professions and thus found themselves less of a target of the law than groups of pretended common interests. That does not suffice to explain the success of mutual associations under the Restoration. It is necessary to mention again that the more unifunctional character of these groups, by comparison with the corporations and trade guilds (and through that, the absence of complicated and rigid rules in their functioning), rendered them more adaptable to transformations and more flexible in camouflaging the societies of resistance created behind their charitable façades.

From the beginning of the nineteenth century professional workers' mutual associations were constituted in all the large cities. The public powers sometimes considered them with distrust and as at Grenoble in 1803,[4] permitted them to give aid in cases of involuntary unemployment but not in cases of voluntary unemployment (strikes). In 1806, the prefecture of police of Paris prohibited the purely professional mutual associations, but from 1808 the authorities closed their eyes and satisfied themselves with the registration of a few members from another profession in the society.

Due to their charitable goals, the politics of repression of the mutual associations was not as harsh as in the case of other associations; all the less so because many mutual associations deliberately withdrew from their mutual aid functions without joining others in their demands. Such factors explain the survival of this or that society. Thus from 1805 to 1847 the Philanthropic Society in Paris played the role of control office of mutual aid societies of the city. At the end of 1823 there were 160 societies in Paris, of which 132 were professional associations with a total of 11,143 members. In 1840 there were 234 societies.

Even when the societies had only mutual aid in mind, solidarity developed among their members and they quickly expanded their aims to include work conditions. The mutual association gradually evolved into a resistance society. Sometimes a mutual society was simply created to hide a resistance association whose goal was resistance to a tax, or to employers' salary schedules. The hatters were the first to adjoin a secret treasury to their aid society. The meetings were apparently clandestine, the society had no official seat, and it did not appear in negotiations.

Each time a strike broke out, the mutual association was accused of having fomented it and was dissolved; it nevertheless reconstituted itself only to be dissolved anew at the next strike, and so it went. Clandestineness was the rule. Eighteen thirty marks a turning point in the strategy of the workers. Until then they had laid claim to the intervention of authorities to regulate work conditions as they had done during the many centuries of corporation rule. By contrast, at this time they ceased to address themselves to the public authorities and bore the burden in their own organization and attempted to negotiate directly with their employers. Several professions imitated the typographers and constituted secret treasuries.

Mutual associations were submitted to article 291 of the Penal Code, which demanded an authorization for all societies of more than twenty members. To evade the law, numerous societies constituted themselves into sections of less than twenty members; this infraction led to the law of April 10, 1834 which declared that article 291 must also be applied to organizations of fewer than twenty members or to their sections. In addition, the law sanctioned punishing not only the heads but also all members by fines and imprisonment. It was not directed solely against professional associations but also against associations for republican propaganda. Hence the multiplication of secret societies after 1834: the Revolutionary Legions, the Families, the Democratic Falanges, the Seasons, the Egalitarian Workers, and so on. Several were influenced by Socialists or Communists and their tone was always aggressive. More and more, political action was considered the prolongation of the Grand Revolution, the completion of the political and social revolution.

Starting in 1840 the "banquet campaigns" extended to all of France with their propaganda for the democratic and social republic. The refusal, on February 21, 1848, of authorization to terminate the banquet campaigns in Paris and the undercover activity that had accompanied them set the spark to the powder. On the 23rd an incident between the troops and the crown provoked the departure of Guizot. The fall of the monarchy was only a question of days.[5]

Doctrinal Contribution

Even if socialist and associationist doctrines do not enter into our thesis, it is all the same necessary to pose the problem of their relations with the creation and development of associations. Have these doctrines favored this development, have they preceded or, to the contrary, have they drawn some of their ideas there, later introduced into their socialist systems? We will propose these questions in relation to Babeuvism, Saint-Simonianism, Fourierism, and Proudhonism.

Babeuvism. In what measure has Babeuf, this red flower of the revolution, influenced the associationist development through his socialism, and more particularly by his demands for economic equality among individuals? After their arrest, the conspirators showed in the course of their testimony the precision of their plan of insurrection and distribution (confiscation of goods of exiles and of enriched functionaries, abolition of inheritances, common exploitation of the soil, centralization, then redistribution of products). The influence of these ideas on some Forty-Eightist Communists, Blanqui, for example, has been demonstrated. In Babeuf is found one of the first formulations of the idea of economic equality beyond political equality. This idea was to remain the central point of the production workers' associations and of socialism in general. We will return to it.

Saint-Simonianism. Saint-Simonianism does not fall back before collectivism: aided by the power of the banks and regenerated by the methods of industry, the state would be the great lender, the distributor of work, and the organizer of production. Pronouncing itself equally for the abolition of the right of inheritance, Saint-Simonianism moved in the direction of socialist ideas. The Saint-Simonians did not visualize a popular current in their recruitment; there was an identity of points of view before similiar situations rather than a convergence of ideas with popular demands. In the search for filiations in their ideas, we must subscribe to the opinion of Bouglé who sees in efforts to bypass capitalism a kinship with Saint-Simonian ideas: state control or nationalization under state control or with state participation would be examples of it, like the awakening to social responsibility on the part of heads of industry before the anarchy of liberalism.

According to Bouglé, another Saint-Simonian influence may be seen on the international plane. For peace to be realized among nations it is necessary, Saint-Simon said, that they habituate themselves to solidary action, that they associate themselves in great international works:

> Perhaps Saint-Simon does not yet have his statue at Geneva, and the national delegates who meet there have not felt the need to render him the

> solemn homage that they have, for example, rendered Rousseau. There are nevertheless some pathways of influence that should not be neglected a priori. None would contest, for example, that the Leagues for Peace that constituted themselves in Europe before 1870, then before 1914, have blazed the trail to the League of Nations. Now, one of the most active of these leagues, the one that met in Geneva from 1867, the League for Peace and Liberty, is entirely the child of the Le Monnier, the very same person who created the journal *United States of Europe,* and Le Monnier was touched in his own time with Saint-Simonian grace. We identify here only those strands which otherwise remain invisible.[6]

Fourierism. Although Saint-Simonianism addresses itself especially to producers, Fourier gives primacy to consumers. He was at once a declared enemy of intermediaries, merchants, and industrial concentration. His favor goes to the farmer, and to cultivate the land well would be the first ambition of his phalansteries. We would say today that Fourier took more interest in microsociological analysis than in reform on the global level. In his grand design he accorded more place to the description of sociability in the basic unit, the phalanstery, than to relations between the latter and the state, which was to coordinate the interphalanstery economy on a federalist basis. In his 1848 book *Socialism before the Old World; or The Living before the Dead,* Considérant hopes that little by little phalansterian socialism will surpass collectivist socialism. Capital, work, and talent are the three necessities for associations of the Fourierist type.

The influence of Fourierism on the development of associations has long been discussed. It is necessary to distinguish several sectors of influence. The best known and most authentic that depends on Fourier's thought is that of the phalansterian and communitarian sector: Guise, Condé-sur-Vesgre, Cîteaux, in France, and the Brook Farm writers in the United States, to cite only the best known. Fourier's influence on consumers' cooperatives seems very direct. They realize an idea of Fourier as to the suppression of the middleman between the consumer and producer. Although the famous cooperative principles are of English inspiration, Charles Gide recalls that the precursor of this type of cooperation was Fourier.

Proudhonism. The inverse of Saint-Simon and Fourier who confer primacy to capacities and remuneration of talent, Proudhon is the father of equality. He is libertarian and hostile toward the state. Mutualism in all branches of production and services (a banking system of exchange of products and services against work) perhaps found its origin in the principles of mutual aid associations. Proudhon extends them to all sectors of economic activity. Little by little, closed systems of mutual exchange must communicate and join in federations with others and gradually conquer all society and replace the state by the federation: "the workshop will replace the government" and consequently economic activity will suppress political activity.

At first opposed to the production association—which was often proclaimed at the time to solve all problems—Proudhon later reintroduced it into his system relative to mutual contracts between groups of workers. It was the same with private property which he reintroduced into his theory, above all for rural situations: it is necessary that peasants be masters of their land but that they associate for the exchange of their products. Thus mutualist and federalist organization will safeguard equality of individuals without harm to their liberty.

Three great influences of Proudhon's thought can be distinguished. First, on anarchism, in the sense that certain anarchist currents of thought concern proposals to organize society through autonomous groups, independent of central power and capable of putting order into the economy without recourse to it. There was also the influence on the French delegations to the first congresses of the International. To the collectivist theses of the delegations, the French opposed Proudhonist theses of reciprocity and equality of exchange. Finally, there was the influence on syndical thought and on the relations between syndical and political action. F. Pelloutier, in particular, was influenced by Proudhon and sought through the Labor Exchange to deliver the workers from the dominance of Marxist and Guesdist thought.

In this brief account, the miserable situation of the working class has perhaps not been emphasized enough as the backdrop and motor of the development of associationism. As Buret has said, wage workers are the "isolates of the nation," they consider employers "as men of a different class, opposed, and even enemies," because they find themselves "put outside of the civic and political community, alone, with their needs and their miseries."[7]

The prohibition of associations and the absence of labor legislation produced not only optimal conditions for rapid industrialization of the country and the enrichment of those who conceived it and directed it, but also vividly illuminated the pure state of exploitation of one class by another. The iniquity of the laws on associations which always, and during this period, let the chambers of commerce subsist (which permitted employers to meet and discuss their common interests[8]), the miserable wages, the work of women and children, the duration and conditions of work, the work permit and police repression—all this must have been on the minds of workers as the Revolution of 1848 began. These facts alone explain the importance and concrete nature of demands such as those of one minister of progress, for "the end of exploitation of man by man," for the organization of labor.

In addition to conditions of life and labor, workers were doubly the isolates of the nation: the old institutions of mutual aid and succor disappeared with the revolution, and those that subsisted were incapable of adaptation to the new conditions (trade guilds) or, if they did adapt (the mutual associations), remained inefficacious when faced with economic needs to satisfy, political inequality to destroy, and social legislation to construct. There was isolation by lack of structures of action as well as isolation by lack of men instructed about and devoted to the workers' cause. In spite of the role they could have played, the intellectuals did not truly penetrate the working class. The latter had its own elite to form. This elite already existed before 1848, aware, and ready to organize and act.

Just the same, during these years, the influence of socialist theorists on the organization of the working class and its slogans does not seem to have been so considerable as historians have long supposed. That is what R. Gossez has been able to show in his thesis on the associations of the Second Republic. Rather than a direct influence by the thinkers, there was a social climate that inspired both the philosophers and the advanced elements of the working class. Both came to the same conclusions in their analyses of economic life, and reacted in a similar manner: they all sought to find in their milieu ways out that they themselves designed, solutions which were "in the air." If at a certain moment the juncture was made between projects derived from daily experience and the systems of philosophers, it is better to speak of the analogy of thought rather than its continuity.

These conditions of life, this isolation in the midst of the nation, explain why the demands of 1848 for economic changes rapidly became social and political. The three domains are only aspects of an indissoluble whole. From these beginnings, syndicalism was affirmed in this triple emphasis, and we will have again occasion to verify, in relation to other associations as with labor unions, that the loss of one of these goals has repercussions on the pursuit of the others and impoverishes them.

1848: ASSOCIATIONIST EXUBERANCE

During the three years prior to 1848, France underwent the effects of rapid industrialization and growing urbanization. The young working class was harmed by the increase of the price of bread as the result of poor harvests in 1845 and 1846. Troubles broke out all through the northwest, but the insurrections of the "prisoners of hunger" were pitilessly suppressed. Unemployment reached the endemic state and within the factories the process of leveling of qualifications was growing obvious. The feeling of isolation, of the absence of all future in their condition, the end of hope to one day acquire an independent economic situation, was increasing among the workers.

All these facts explain why, in addition to the matter of wage rates, the point of departure of all their claims, the working class moved rapidly toward organization of the professions. In addition, the sudden arrival of universal suffrage and the egalitarianism of the first months of the revolution made those autocratic cells, the businesses born of industrialization, appear still more odious. The research of Gossez[9] brings to light the following facts: (1) the point of departure of the workers' claims was the demand for the replacement of individual bargaining between employer and worker, by what we would now call collective contracts; (2) the passage, after the June days, from corporative to cooperative organization, the latter being conceived as a temporary solution to eventually arrive at the former; (3) the separation between these workers' claims and, in the months that followed, those of the corporative organization, and the systems proposed by the ideologists. In this perspective we will successively examine the new institutions brought about by the February revolution, the attempts to pass from the administration of men to the administration of things, and finally, the start of the repression beginning with the June days.

The Days of February and the Institutions of the Revolution

From February 25, a workers' troop, led by workers, claimed the right to work. Louis Blanc, whom the crown proposed to constitute the provisional government, together with Albert, made himself spokesman of this demand. The Republic recognized the right. On February 25, the day fixed for the proclamation by the Republic, a workers' deputation claimed the creation of a Ministry of Progress charged with setting up the organization of work. The government refused this request and directed it toward the Commission of Government for Workers which met at Luxembourg under the presidency of Louis Blanc.

Elections immediately took place for the Commission of Luxembourg. The workers elected three delegates per profession and three employers by industry. This came to 242 worker delegates and 231 employer delegates. From this number a permanent mixed committee of 20 members was elected. The commission began to play the role of a council of *prud'hommes*: it decreed a working a day of ten hours in Paris and eleven in the provinces, and minimum wages.

The decree of February 25-29 proclaimed liberty of association which was to be entered in the Constitution of November 4, 1848. The secret societies immediately transformed themselves into clubs and 145 clubs of all natures erupted. Certain ones were socialist, like that of Barbès—the Club of the Revolution—to which Proudhon and Pierre Leroux belonged, and which summoned the government to nationalize the Bank of France, insurance companies, railroads, mines, and canals. Freedom of the press was proclaimed and 170 newspapers were immediately created. On February 28 the government also proclaimed the national workshops. The articles published during the course of the previous years by Louis Blanc had popularized the idea of organization of work. He advocated the creation of a minister of work, financed by the products of the big businesses (mines, railroads, banks, insurance companies), and redeemed by the state. With these sums the state was to create social workshops, agricultural colonies, and production associations.

Blanc was to spend the rest of his life denying the paternity of these part state, part cooperative projects, only a caricature of his idea. Marie, who was charged with organizing them, viewed them as simple charity shops, such as certain villages had already known. Vast yards for navvying, specially organized for supervision, they served more for daily distribution of an indemnity for unemployment rather than as useful public works. The yield was ridiculous and justified Marie's comment, who spoke of "the organization of alms," scoffing at the myth of the "organization of work." At the end of March, the national workshops grouped 40,000 workers; by May there were 100,000. Neutralization of the workers' forces obtained by this means cost the young Republic too dearly, and attempts to suppress the shops launched the combat of June 23-27.

Meanwhile, elections to the Constitutent Assembly took place on April 23 and the Assembly met on May 4. The economic and financial situation of the country was disastrous. The bourgeoisie retook the initiative, and the weary workers who sensed that victory was escaping them, were finally vanquished by this clever politics, this "dictatorship of eloquence," as Gaston-Martin called it,[10] which apparently always triumphed over good sense.[11] In mid-May, Louis Blanc quit the presidency of the Commission of Luxembourg, which soon disappeared. The June days and the repression that followed them marked the start of a reaction against the popular forces and opened the way to the coup d'état of December 2, 1851, which abolished the constitution and led to the Empire one year later.

This brief review of political events provides a background to experiences that are more profound and relevant to the organization of work on the part of the workers themselves.

From the Administration of Men to the Administration of Things: Corporative Associations

In addition to spontaneous wage demands, the working class contributed to the revolution the old idea of the corporation, an idea that remained very much alive in the shops. In the processions of February the workers paraded behind the banners of their corporations. But the essential difference is that in these corporations the masters were not represented, only the workers. The corporations had already asserted themselves, and attempts at union among them had taken place: in 1839 the Typographical Society created a special chest to come to the aid of other corporations; in 1845 on the initiative of the same society, the Central Committee of Corporations was created (by means of which worker delegates to the meetings at Luxembourg were elected).

In March 1848 the Central Committee of Corporations gave birth to the Central Committee of Workers of the Department of the Seine, which was to publish the *Workers' Paper* in June. The central committee worked toward the creation of a unitary organism of workers. Thus conceived, the corporation is not only a union for professional defense and an organization of political representation but also a group for economic activity. Attempts to create work establishments in the 1830s have already been seen. From the idea of workshops to aid strikers, financed by the entire corporation, the transition was gradually made during the course of several months in 1848 to the permanent association of production of the entire profession.

Each workers' corporation for production was quickly formed, and at the end of December 1848 the Chamber of Work was created, composed of delegates of the associations, and which was essentially a general union of associations of workers. Its tasks were multiple: corporative action, development of the association movement, and political representation. This established the link between the workers' will to restore the old corporations (but limited to wage workers alone) and the socialist ideas of the association and the right to work.

In each corporation the workers elected one commission, which dealt with wage matters with the employers' chambers (sixty of them in 1848), placed the unemployed in the national workshops, opened and managed the production association of the corporation, and took all political measures and the defense of the corporation. Here too the functions were multiple and virtually undifferentiated.

This kind of corporative organization into collective workshops under all the workers had to lead to a national collective economy with state coordination. In a word, corporative organization was destined to create other types of social relations, a socialist society. In this schema the production association is the workshop of all the members of the corporation, "all working there for the good of all." "The association of work," writes Gossez, "is one of the pieces of this *total* workers' organization that the workers of 1848 conceived." A central committee of workers' associations would have to represent all the associations, aid them, develop them, organize the exchange of products between them. This "administration of things" dear to the Saint-Simonians was prefigured in the far past: the corporations would form the government by themselves.

Such was the audacious project of 1848. In practice they were only certain of the first steps, some hundred professions alone being organized at the dawning of the June days. Even later on when all efforts along these lines were threatened, it was still intended that the association of production must not only ameliorate the lot of its members but must contribute to the general emancipation of the worker, and that for the alert worker the association was only an apprenticeship in the direction of business and not a goal in itself. Making himself the interpreter of the desires of the workers, Louis Blanc declared:

> It is necessary that the thought of the worker, that the efforts of each worker have for a principal goal the enfranchisement of the entire working class. It is necessary that, in each association, they see not only a means of ensuring or augmenting the well being of the associates but a means of preparing, through solidarity, to establish among the diverse associations the general emancipation of labor.[12]

Thus the association of production appears very different from what it was to become at a later date under the blows of repression, and later still, when liberty for labor unions permitted other forms of struggle. These workers' corporative associations must not be confused with the cooperative establishments of some workers that were legion under the Second Republic and which proposed only amelioration of the lot of their own workers. In October 1851 the Almanac of New Corporations counted 190 associations. Among the more numerous were the hairdressers (44), cooks (28), and bartenders (26). It was not a question of associations of socialist inspiration. Simple commercial interest led to the birth of others that Nadaud evaluated at 300 in 1851.[13]

After the June days the workers' movement found itself leaderless, disarmed, and its spirit broken. This explains the lack of resistance to the coup d'état. From a unique form of association through corporations they had to return to more limited goals and to the constitution of small, isolated cooperatives. This type that was to remain characteristic of the French associations of production.

On July 5, 1848 the National Assembly opened a three-million franc line of credit on the proposition of Corbon, to be used in large part for this type of isolated association. Associations proposing to organize a corporative shop were brushed aside. On the contrary, besides the cooperatives, associations between workers and employers were favored and the funds permitted some employers to face the economic crisis and the managers of cooperatives to become petty employers.

The June Days and the Start of the Repression

The June days not only broke the spirit of the workers' movement through the death or deportation of the militants, but obliged it to return to a clandestine existence. From the dawn of the June days, a series of legislative measures had limited the right of association. From the beginning of the revolution the Republican front was disunited, making the opposition between the Socialists and the bourgeoisie appear irreducible.

> People had fought for them in 1834, in the affairs of April, but after 1848, these workers dared to ask for the organization of work, the right to work, the abolition of taxes on drinks. They even went so far as to propose a new social economy. Then the workers appeared in a new light. It was necessary to combat them in order to save society.[14]

Once the red specter was evoked, repression was extended to the Republican groups also. Hence the decree of July 28, 1848 on clubs, distinguishing four categories: (1) clubs whose formation was free under the condition that they be open to nonmembers, that their minutes be drafted, that no one discuss therein "any proposition contrary to public order and to good morality, or tending to provoke . . . denunciations against persons, or individual attacks." "Public order" meant "social order," for as the report declared, "public order means family and property"[15]; (2) secret societies, which were forbidden; (3) circles which had no political goal and which could be created freely; (4) nonpublic political meetings which required permission from the municipal authority.

Relations between clubs were forbidden. The law of June 19-22, 1849 authorized the government to prohibit clubs and other meetings during one year. Then, the special powers permitted it to renew the law (up to the coup d'état), when the decree of March 25–April 2, 1852 rescinded that of July 28, 1848—save regarding matters concerning secret societies—and revived those concerning associations and meetings, articles 291 to 294 of the penal code as well as the law of April 10, 1834.

The National Assembly evidently deflected the Left from its path; the minister of progress was brushed aside; the minimum wage rates had only a short-lived application; the decree regarding minimum duration of work fixed by the Commission of Luxembourg was revoked November 9, 1848 because it was "noxious" to national industry; and as we have already seen, the grants from the three million francs for associations were distributed with preference to the associations that had representation of capital and labor, and to the isolated cooperative groups.

The Constitution of 1848 proclaimed equality of relations between employers and employees, and the law of November 1849 gave the same definition to employers' coalitions as to coalitions of workers, and sanctioned them in the same fashion. Nevertheless, the workers' coalitions were still poorly thought of, not only for political reasons but also because they were held to "ruin national industry, leading to work suspensions and passing industrial command to strangers."[16]

The societies of mutual aid did not hesitate to serve as refuges to resistance societies. They continued to be authorized by the law of July 28, 1848. Numerous mutual associations thus camouflaged secret Republican societies, in a close working relation and in contact with the central committees established in Paris or Lyon, and with the exiles in Switzerland and London.

Meanwhile, mutual associations were submitted to precise rule by the laws of March 8 and July 5 and 15, 1850. They could be dissolved if they deviated from their goal or managed their funds badly. In addition, each year they had to submit their books to the prefecture, like an accounting for the use of aid funds. Thanks to these dispositions it was possible

> to provoke the dissolution of pretended mutual aid societies that deviated from their goals and would be a cause of misgivings for authority and for good citizens. Those among them that refused to obey the order that could dissolve them would have to be prosecuted and punished by penalties provided by Article 13 of the decree of July 28, 1848 against secret societies.[17]

In imposing controls on the mutual associations, the law placed them directly under the thumb of the administration,[18] under the discretion (little changed) of the same functionaries and magistrates already in office under the July monarchy, who applied the laws with the same perspective as in the past. These were the groups and small associations of production which permitted a number of clubs and resistance societies to remain alive, and that served as a refuge to threatened militants of the workers' movement — functions that they have not lost today![19]

FROM THE REACTION OF THE EMPIRE TO MODERN ASSOCIATIONISM

The Reaction of the Empire

The June days had decimated the working class, which could not stand against the Empire; in addition, the separation of 1848 between the workers and the Republican Party was to be accentuated in the future. In all domains the government created laws by edict that restricted the rights acquired in preceding years. What follows is a rapid review of some of these dispositions in regard to organizations of workers.

Mutual Associations. By July 5, 1850, the National Assembly had refused to record the unemployment allotment as one of the goals of mutual associations. The authorized mutual associations could administer their own affairs freely (decree of July 28, 1848) but were required to communicate on demand all documents to the prefects (decree of June 14, 1851). In 1852 an endowment of ten million francs was created for the mutual associations and a decree of March 26 prescribed the creation of one society for mutual aid per commune, placed under the authority of the mayor or the curé. Finally, a ministerial circular gave instructions to the prefects not to authorize aid in case of unemployment: "In any case, you will not approve the promise of aid in case of unemployment: this condition will not only be a cause of ruin and demoralization, since it will tend to encourage laziness and pay to labor a bounty for insouisance, but it will carry the germ of all strikes and the experience of coalitions."

Associations of Production. At the beginning of the Empire they were subjected to strong repression. The directors were arrested, their banners torn down. Gossez notes that of 299 associations of production in France, only 15 survived.[20]

Prud'hommes. On March 21 the emperor reestablished the councils of *prud'hommes* at St.-Etienne and Lyon and, on June 1, 1853, a law specified the operating conditions: the councils were to be composed of one-half employers and one-half wage workers. The workers kept the right acquired in 1848 to elect their own representatives and to be elected. On the other hand, the emperor named their presidents and vice-presidents.

Other measures were taken, such as the reintroduction of work passes. But in spite of the reaction to annul it, the spirit of organizaton subsisted: the auxiliary unemployment funds were clandestinely reconstituted and the militant elites again formed and guided protests and spontaneous workers' strikes. Little by little the repression calmed, and a more liberal phase of the Empire was announced.

The Liberal Empire

Prosperity led to a certain relaxation in the attitude of the government toward the working class. Under the Second Empire, France industrialized rapidly, even though it was still only a nation of artisans in 1848. The population concentrated more and more in the cities, agriculture improved its methods of production, industry concentrated, railways covered the country creating a national market and reinforcing industrial concentration, mechanization developed rapidly, the huge stores and credit establishments came into being.

The face of the entrepreneurial class had still not changed much. In 1872, 80 percent of employers were still former workers and 15 percent of them the sons of workers.[21] But the situation was not slow to change:

> It so happens that under the reign of Napoleon III we have business carried on by the last generation which is of popular origin . . . , the social classes become more impervious, capitalism has acquired by its own magnitude an inflexibility that renders more and more difficult access by the worker to the status of big entrepreneur.[22]

There were also some political reasons behind the thaw in the attitude of the Empire toward the workers. Having adopted a politics of free exchange on the economic level, the government found itself alienated from a part of the industrial protectionists, and because of the intervention of French troops in Rome, a part of the Catholic bourgeoisie. Consequently it sought the support of the working class to compensate for its losses. In 1862 the emperor pardoned twenty typographers who had been condemned to prison for striking, and in this way recognized the right of coalition (i.e., to combine or unite, in a general sense).

The law of May 25, 1864 manifested these new dispositions: it suppressed the offense of coalition. The right to strike was then implicitly recognized since coalition ceased to be an offense. The suppression of the law of Le Chapelier was just a matter of time. Only the intent to bring about a coalition was to be punished: it was an offense to infringe the liberty of labor by threat or violence with intent to obtain adherence to a coalition. Protection was given to workers not in a coalition who worked during a strike.

Even if the right to strike was recognized, the right to meet and the rights of association were still forbidden. But how to form a coalition without meeting? In reality the law of 1834 remained in force. Nevertheless, after 1864, meeting authorizations were given more freely and the law of June 6-10, 1868 only demanded previous authorization for meetings having a political or religious goal. Other meetings were made subject to a simple previous declaration signed by seven people and filed with the prefect.

Professional associations were tolerated officially during the 1860s. But the law of 1864 created confusion and necessitated still more laws to make them sufficiently precise.

> The situation of the striker was found more precarious still, if one imagines that the laws about meetings were then subject to all sorts of hindrances and that unauthorized associations remained prohibited. Now, how can a coalition be formed without taking counsel together? And if a coalition lasts, does it not become an association? Is there anything more than a matter of degree between the two? The reform remained incomplete and the possibility of using the new arm freely was problematic.[23]

On the labor union level, the *Manifesto of the Sixty*, published in 1864 and signed by sixty workers, affirmed the necessity of a workers' representation in the Chamber and took up again the resolution of the labor union chambers. The manifesto was inspired by Proudhon, and led the government to pronounce itself in favor of tolerance of the labor union chambers (ministerial report of March 30, 1868). This recognition spared the workers from forming societies of mutual aid dissimulating resistance societies. In all the trades and somewhat everywhere, the chambers took a stand on the goal of obtaining agreements on wage rates and collective contracts with employers. In 1869 the Federal Chamber of Workers' Societies was formed, uniting forty professional associations. The workers' commission of delegates to the exposition of 1867 and the International Association of Workers encouraged the labor union chamber movement. We shall briefly trace the evolution of these two organizations.

The Delegates to the Expositions and The First International

In 1851 some worker delegates chosen by employers had been sent to the exposition in London. The idea was taken up anew in 1861 in relation to the forthcoming Universal Exposition of London in 1862. With the support of the emperor, the Workers' Commission of the Exposition was constituted, whose goal was to hold elections of delegates. Parisian delegates, numbering 183, representing all listed bodies, left for London in 1862. There they met delegates from labor unions who were at the time already strongly organized, with a central organism, a press, permanent agents, collective contracts, and, notably in London, a union council.

Upon their return, the delegates demanded the creation of labor union chambers bringing together the more well-informed workers of each trade and before informing the authorities, deputies, and ministers. Such was the dominant idea, even though the chambers were to have other functions: mutual aid, resistance, professional education, and creation of workers' associations of production for ownership and management of the means of production.[24]

The idea of the labor union chamber was not new, but the workers profited by putting it forward because of the relative liberty they enjoyed as delegates. What was new was the international contacts established in London. Some delegates did not return to France and, in 1864, laid the foundations of, and adopted with the English, the regulations of the International Workingmen's Association. Marx was a part of the provisional committee. At the beginning of 1865 an office was opened in Paris.

In 1865 the first congress of the International was held in Geneva where the French supported the Proudhonian thesis of free cooperation by opposition to those who reproached them for supporting state control. Also on the program were questions of work legislation (hours, women and children), cooperative work, unions, the necessity of opposing Russian despotism in Poland, the relations of standing armies with production, the influence of religious ideas on the political, social, and intellectual movements, and so on. From the outset the International took a position on the multifunctional association through its discussions on questions foreign to work itself.

The following congress took place in Lausanne in 1867. There was opposition there between the French and Italians, on one side, and the Belgians, English, and Germans on the other, between the theses of Proudhon and those of César de Paepe, who proposed that the first stage be the socialization of the land, followed by the canals, roads, railroads, and then banks. The congress in Brussels in 1868 saw the same opposition, but that of Basel in 1869 sanctioned the success of collectivists theses over those of Proudhon. After the Commune, the International did not show any great activity and disappeared in 1876.

In France, on the occasion of the International Exposition of 1867, the idea of worker delegates was again brought forward and the government instituted a Commission to Encourage Labor Studies. The entire working population elected delegates, 316 in number representing 112 professions. The reports of the delegates again took up the demands of the labor union chambers. After the exposition, a more restrained commission continued to meet in Paris and held eighty meetings spread over two years. This commission was in part responsible for the administrative tolerance regarding union chambers.

The delegates to the congress of the International as well as those to the Commission of the Exposition were influenced by Proudhon. The entire movement rested on the principle of collaboration with employers toward amiable solutions: revolution must come not only through class antagonisms but by their reconciliation.

Freedom of Association

Between 1876 and 1884 several projects regarding liberty of professional associations were discussed in Parliament. The law of March 21,

1884 recognized not only the isolated labor union but also local combinations among different trades and federations of trades and industries. Nevertheless, the modern labor union is a voluntary organization of private law, by opposition to the older corporations under public law (the sworn trades were not voluntary: it was the sole form of association permitted and was obligatory to the people of the trade; the corporation was a public service with privileges and obligations).

The law was completed by addition of the law of July 1, 1901 on associations and that of March 12, 1920 conferring complete juridical capacity on labor unions (except entrepreneurship). The law was meant to lead only to the development of syndicalism; the workers' associations of production were considered utopian and even dangerous. In the spirit of certain of its promoters, some indeed seemed to expect the associations of production to flourish. Thus in 1898 Waldeck-Rousseau expressed this wish:

> I have the profound conviction that the capacity to receive and employ capital savings, profit from experience, represent an incontestable solvency, the professional unions must become generators of workers' associations, decisive agents of the grand evolution which is, in our eyes, the solution of the future: the accession of the wage earners to industrial and commercial property.[25]

The labor unions always took account of the existence of two different functions: defense of professional interests and production in cooperative association. In addition they feared that in letting themselves go into commercial activities, they might forget those ends which were not then at stake.

Economic life was almost ahead of social legislation: if the law had been voted thirty years previously, it is probable that a different direction would have been possible, but in the development of capitalism oriented more and more to large units, there was no other place for the association than in the domain of small businesses requiring little capital and in production that was more or less artisanal. It was this path that the production cooperative was to follow.

In addition, the law promulgated previously had to meet with the favor of those innumerable societies of mutal aid which formed resistance societies, and of cooperative associations in the years 1860-70 which had the same ideal of the multifunctional corporative association. In 1884 it was too late: the Marxist cause had virtually won in France, since the Congress of the International in 1869. More and more, the principle of class struggle replaced the ideals of utopian socialism.

A great number of production cooperatives were still to be created, especially at the conclusion of strikes. The members of the strike committees associated when they could no longer find work. Meanwhile, syndicalism rapidly abandoned the solutions of association and cooperation, that it judged utopian, to demand nationalization, state management of productive forces, and the transformation of capitalism into a state economy. It was around such issues that the great debates of the following years took place. At the labor congress of Marseilles, in 1879, new directions were witnessed, as the following statement shows.

> The congress, considering that production and consumer cooperatives can only ameliorate the lot of a small number of the privileged, of a small proportion . . . , declare that none of the cooperative societies can be considered a powerful enough means to achieve the emancipation of the proletariat.[26]

Development of Syndicalism and the Parties of the Left up to the Time of Their Unity

From the 1870s the question of the relationships between labor unions and parties was posed. Although the two first workers' congresses (Paris 1876 and Lyon 1878) remained moderate, purely concerned with occupations and hostile to the intrusion of politics (they especially discussed labor union chambers, councils of *prud'hommes,* associations of production, cooperatives, and so on), the third congress, at Marseilles in 1879, saw the majority rally to socialism founding the Federation of the Socialist Workers' Party of France. It was a class party and its program was developed by Marx, Engels, and Guesde. In addition to the amelioration of the lot of laborers, it posed as the final goal the socialization of the means of production. Two years before, in 1877, Jules Guesde had created *Egalité,* and it was notably through this journal that Marxism became popular in France.

To compete with the socialist Federation, a number of labor union chambers created the Union of Syndicated Workers' Chambers of France[27] which held its congress in 1881 and 1882 on the margins of those of the Federation. But the Union lost the field, for it divided into pure syndicalists—limiting themselves to demands on wages and conditions of work—and cooperators, in other respects equally hostile to the collectivist of the socialist Federation and who saw in the Union only a stage toward workers' production associations.

The socialist Federation also experienced internal struggles and, in 1882, the Possibilists, behind Brousse, left the party and founded the Federation of Socialist Laborers of France. Their program, if it agreed with Guesdism as to ultimate goals, differed from it in posing permanent intermediate goals around a minimum program of immediate ameliorations. Reformism had entered the scene.

The Guesdists remained alone and the socialist Federation took the name of French Workers' Party. In 1886, it took over the party of a corporative organization, the National Federation of Syndicated Workers, which became only a branch of the party and suffered from a lack of autonomy.

The confusion between politics and syndicalism seemed to bode ill for the labor unions, which were ceaselessly torn by political conflicts. There soon developed a current of thought that aimed to place labor unions above partisan struggle. In 1890 some elements detached themselves from the possibilists of Brousse and founded the Revolutionary Socialist Workers' Party, or Germanists, from the German name of their leader. Fiercely opposed to state control, they were inspired by anarchist thought. For them, workers' organizations must become the owners of social property, but in the immediate situation they would leave the labor unions their autonomy. It was by their inspiration that was born, in 1892, in competition with the French Workers' Party, the Federation of Labor Exchanges in France.

The National Federatic n of Syndicated Workers had just escaped from Guesdist control. Their basic ideas were opposed: the Federation leaned toward the general strike as a means of taking power, while the French Workers' Party wanted to achieve revolution through parliamentary political action. The directors of the Federation of Exchanges put their quarrels to profit and developed a program of corporative action independent of political action. This program advocated the concentration of labor unions on the local level in exchanges (constituted like local unions) and on the professional level in federations of trades. The program was favorable to the general strike, purely economic, and exclusive of all political action.

In 1894 a common congress took place between the Federation of Exchanges and the National Federation of Syndicated Workers, and the following year there was founded through fusion of the two the CGT, partisan of the general strike and opposed to the seizure of a political party. The Exchanges achieved separate status, but their federation was absorbed in 1902 by the CGT which united local regroupings as well as organizations of trades. Labor unity was complete. It was necessary to wait several years to see similar unity among the workers' parties.

Under anarchist influence, the CGT pronounced itself in favor of direct action: the working class must regulate its affairs by itself, without representatives, even in Parliament. Other anarchist methods were advocated, such as the boycott, the general strike, and sabotage. By the same token the Germanists wanted to destroy the state and not simply to conquer it like the Guesdists. Under anarchist influence, they opposed collectivism which entrusted social property to the state. For them, political action only aimed to satisfy personal ambitions.

In 1901, the Possibilists, the Germanists, and some departmental socialist federations founded the French Socialist Party, in the face of which the Socialist Party of France was set up by the Guesdists and the Blanquists.[28] In 1904, thanks to the international socialist congress in Amsterdam, the fusion between the two parties was decided on and in 1905 the unity was accomplished by creation of the SFIO.

In 1902, the CGT comprised 56 exchanges,[29] 29 federations of trades, and 373 unions. Between 1902 and 1912 the federations were transformed into federations of industries. In 1902, at the Congress of Unity at Montpellier, 121,000 adherents were represented. By 1912 there were 600,000.[30] The years between 1902 and 1909 saw a strong increase in syndicalism. From 1909 it met its first great crisis, the relaxation in the effort of the working masses, for which the general strike and revolution were too long in coming.

On the ideological level there were two conflicting tendencies: that of the pure syndicalists who were anxious only regarding their professional demands, and that of the anarchists who affirmed the value, exclusive of union action, of scorn of the state and parliamentary political action. It was from these two currents that was born revolutionary syndicalism, antistate, antipatriotism, and antimilitarist—and independent from the parties.

The SFIO could not be suspected of reformism, and avowed itself to be decisively revolutionary. An agreement then became possible with the CGT, and in 1906 the question was posed at the congress of the CGT in Amiens. But the collaboration could not be brought about and it was reaffirmed that the labor union alone could pass from resistance group to production group after the success of the general strike.[31] The resolution of the congress, "syndicalism is sufficient by itself," remains celebrated under the name of the Amiens charter.

World War I and especially the October revolution upset the painfully acquired balance and in 1920 at the congress at Tours, a schism was produced in the SFIO regarding the Third International. The Communist Party was founded, with its union parallel, the CGTU.

Cooperative Associations

Cooperation offers us an excellent example of differentiation of functions and acculturation to the values of the global society. Although the beginnings of the cooperative movement were situated in the past century, as early as the eighteenth century there had been composite associations that were at once workers' cooperatives and religious fraternities.[32] For example, the Fraternity of Tailor Brothers, formed by religious workers, was functioning in 1657.[33] Owen knew of similar ones in England. "In 1884 Friedrich Engels himself still referred to such experiences in his propaganda in order to prove that communitarian life is not only possible but beneficent."[34]

Besides these semireligious groups there were other examples of worker cooperation: in Scotland the weavers of Fenwick associated in 1761 to purchase the appliances of their trade in common,and eight years later extended this to food purchases. The same thing happened in Lyon. In 1824 Robert Owen left for America where he founded New Harmony, thinking that the multiplication of such colonies would little by little liquidate the old society. The same year Fourier wrote to Owen to offer him his own plans and services.

> Whether it was a Fourier phalanstery or a Robert Owen community the institution of these autonomous microcosms was certainly the panacea of the debutant inventions. But by their fiery preaching both Owen and Fourier excited an emotion in the working classes of England and France, an enthusiasm essentially favorable to the blossoming of associations of socialist inclinations. It is this idealism, especially thick in the doctrines of the two famous socialists, this enthusiasm for the idea of association, that provoked the discovery of the cooperative mechanism.[35]

But there was a dissidence in the Owenist movement that was destined to have a strong resonance in classical cooperatives. The current centered around Dr. King and his paper *The Co-operator.* The objective was to create consumers' cooperatives whose final goal was to stimulate, thanks to accumulation of profits, production cooperatives very near these communities, the "harmony villages" wanted by Owen.

> When capital will have become sufficiently important, the society will be able to buy land, live there, cultivate it, establish all the manufactures that it needs and provide sustenance, habitation and clothing for all. Then the society will call itself a community.[36]

Several hundred attempts, 200 to 500, according to various authors, were made in the years 1828-34; almost all disappeared, some because of lack of preparation by responsible members, and some because of chartism which at the time drained the forces of the worker movement. At about the same time in France Michel Derrion, a Fourierist, founded a consumer cooperative in Lyon, called the True and Social Commerce. The shop prospered at once and brought a return to the customers in proportion to their purchases. Three years later police harrassment, economic crisis, and the favor given by workers to production associations or republican societies terminated this endeavor.

In 1844 at Rochdale, near Manchester, the celebrated pioneers of the cooperative movement opened the first cooperative store of the modern type. This new type of cooperative marked an adaptation to conditions of the moment. Although the society preferred by King anticipated an accumulation of profit to transform itself later into a harmony village, the coop of the Rochdalian type offered immediate advantages to purchasers based on the price of goods and on a refund. The idea of common funds for the future community then disappeared and there remained only a certain percentage based on sales to be used for purposes of education.

The influence of the Rochdale cooperatives was found in all countries, and in France beginning about 1864. But even from 1848 to 1851 a lively cooperative efflorescence was noted in France. We have already mentioned the development of production associations (around 250 in 1849). Consumers' cooperatives were also created here and there, in a less spectacular fashion but perhaps more deeply rooted. The provinces were more fertile in this regard than was Paris for this type of cooperative. The statutes anticipated that accumulated profits would not be redistributed but reserved for social transformation objectives. After the coup d'état of December 2, 1851, the consumers' cooperatives again nurtured some resistance societies as did the mutual associations and production associations. This exposed the coops to repression, and of the hundred that existed under the Second Republic, the rare ones that survived owed their health to clandestine operation.

As we have seen, from the time of the liberal phase of the Empire, the workers' quest was oriented toward union organization. Cooperation tended to be supplanted as the center of interest, although the congress of the International discussed it in 1864 (London), in 1866 (Lausanne), and in 1868 (Brussels). Marx, in particular, recognized the value of these experiences but also the limit of their span and of their possibilities for social transformation. In 1867 French legislation gave them a statute.

In 1870-71 the cooperative movement was disintegrated by the war, the siege of Paris, the defeat, the repression of the commune. The years that followed saw a clean break between the cooperative strand and the political expressions of the labor movement. In particular, the third congress of the Socialist Workers' Party of France at Marseilles in 1879 condemned cooperation almost completely, an exception being made solely for cooperatives with political objectives. The resolution of the congress affirmed that "none can be considered as powerful enough means to arrive at emancipation of the proletariat," but that these associations could nevertheless render services for propagation of collectivist ideas. This position gradually led to a proclamation of neutrality in religion and politics. In spite of this condemnation, cooperation experienced an impressive growth in the years that followed, especially from 1885 to 1894.

In 1884 the production cooperatives created a national federation that grouped twenty-nine associations. The following year, consumer cooperation took a similar step at the instigation of the group from Nîmes, which was to become celebrated as the School of Nîmes. The congress of consumer cooperators met in 1885, representing eighty-five out of some hundreds of coops in existence at the time. An organism analogous to that of the production cooperatives was set up. It later took the name of Cooperative Union. The union was divided between the economism of the managerial types who saw in cooperation nothing more than a business venture, and the militant revolutionary collectivists.

The cooperative formulas remained under discussion within the movement. In particular the question of allocation of surplusses was not always settled: Must they be distributed or put in reserve for creation of production coops? The discussion became an issue in the International Cooperative Alliance, founded in 1892. The partisans of profit sharing, hence of a certain form of association of production, collided there with the partisans of wholesale operations, that is, of wholesale stores that would purely and simply integrate production workshops under the everyday rule of the wage workers. The School of Nîmes made common cause with the English Christian Socialists to impose the profit-sharing clause onto international consumers' cooperatives. This option was in turn judged too bourgeois by the French socialist cooperatives, nonmembers of the Union, and who founded the Exchange of Socialist Cooperatives in 1894.

There were, then, two national federations of consumers' cooperatives. A strike at Carmaux in 1895 brought their differences into the open. The Socialists supported the strikers and under the leadership of Jaurès the Exchange acquired national socialist acclaim. In 1912 socialist cooperation, defended by Jaurès and A. Thomas, future animator of the International Labor Office, concluded a unity pact with the Cooperative Union. The united Congress of Tours, the same year, created a new organism, the National Federation of Consumer Cooperatives (FNCC). Nine hundred sixty-two cooperatives were thus federated and a single wholesale store replaced those that each federation had previously created.

Employers' Organizations

It was necessary to await the twentieth century to witness the strong development of employers' associations. Meanwhile, since 1859 employers' union chambers were created by trade, industry, and region. In 1864 under the influence of a Saint-Simonian, Léon Talabot, the Association of Heavy Industries was created; it long remained the most powerful grouping. The association brought together 350 out of 430 blast furnaces that existed during that era.

The metallurgy and mining industries long remained in the avant-garde of employers' organizations. Dolléans and Dehove show that this entrepreneurial concentration has not only been a response to the concentration of workers but has been rendered necessary for economic and technical reasons. It comprises three aspects: economic (struggle against foreign competition, for example), social (housing, mutual aid societies in opposition against strikes), and commercial (sales agencies). In 1919 the Confederation of French Production was created. In 1936 its statutes were modified and gave birth to the General Confederation of French Employers, precursor of the CNPF.

NORTH AMERICAN ASSOCIATIONISM: INTRODUCTION

Voluntary associations are such habitual components of the North American landscape that they have been studied relatively little.[37] We have, in the past century, an admirable field of study in that the industrial revolution unfolded in a new milieu, without a state tradition, and at a time when the doctrines of laissez faire saw no limit, when the influx of manual labor from Europe, of peasant origin, repeated and even accentuated the consequences of industrialization.

In Europe, and France in particular, the industrial revolution unfolded in a strongly structured society that was under the weight of traditions that were associationist, charitable, and juridically strong. Even emigration to cities did not change these ancestral ways altogether. The passage to the United States, however, broke all moorings to such traditions and surrendered without defense the troops of industrialization to those who claimed the country. Although France experienced a more rapid development of its industrial revolution thanks to the complicity of a strong central power, in the United States such a power was only constituted later, once the economy was established.

A series of phenomena seems to act differently or even be absent in some countries. Among the most important to recall in order to comprehend the differential development of associationism are the following:

- While the industrial cities of the old continent witnessed a population increase throughout the past century, the rural exodus was progressive in proportion to industrial needs. In the United States this rhythm was incomparably more rapid and around 35 million persons immigrated in less than 150 years.[38]

- In Europe migrations took place in a single cultural context and men created in the city almost the same institutions they had left behind in the country—the differentiation between urban and rural lifestyles only emerging later and more slowly. To the contrary, in the United States the immigrants disembarked into a totally different milieu that in no way recalled their previous way of life.

- In the Old World, especially in the country, "natural" hierarchies subsisted, oppressive sometimes, but never refusing help in case of need: the church, the local community, and so on, still well established in a feudal aristocracy. In the new country, none of that existed and the hierarchies established themselves only gradually.

- While the rural exodus posed problems in European cities, they were not comparable to those of American cities, where the local government was weak, where the division of powers between the states and the federal government left much initiative to the states, to localities, and to the citizens themselves.

- The émigrés who left the cities of the coast for the interior, the frontier, felt still more the need to unite to make up for the lack of all legal regulation and even, once constituted, the local governments took and maintained greater powers than those known in Europe.

- In the Old World, the new industrial workers encountered comrades speaking the same language and having the same mentality. In the United States even if immigrants gathered together by nationalities, the majority not only had to speak another language but had to be versed in different languages and get along with men of different mentalities.

- In the European Catholic countries the churches filled several functions that the Protestant churches of the New World tended to devolve to separate groups. In addition the Protestant ethic tended to dissociate religious activities from professional ones and the norms of conduct were left more to free choice. Man was, hence, free to both deliver himself to the worst human exploitation under the cover of efficiency and liberate himself from guilt through philanthropic activity, or combine the two. This absence of rigidity in moral conduct gives this specific tone—where hypocrisy is not applicable—to the American way of life where business colors philanthropy or philanthropy is strangely commercial, where the most sordid interests are reconciled with moral principles.

- In Europe, the rupture with the family milieu experienced by the immigrant to the city has never been as complete as that of the émigré to America from his family in Europe. Material insecurity and psychological isolation, the impersonality of social contacts in the new cities and with varied populations, obliged immigrants to recover in associations a little of that fraternity, that human warmth, a rhythm of life more familial than that of the city.
- In Europe, the principles of economic liberalism tended to be tempered by existing social structures and by recourse to the state. To the contrary, in the old English colonies, entirely open to the audacious initiatives of capitalism, yet entirely suspicious of public powers and commercial regulations, only unity and mutual aid could resolve some of the problems of adaptation, of adjustment to this new country.
- In the United States the associations witnessed no legislation nor any power hostile to their development.

The definitive reasons for such a flourishing associationism were American liberalism and the lack of a strong state. Obliged to shift for themselves, to unite, the immigrants attempted to preserve their customs and values by means of associations, while they adapted to their new environment. The earlier immigrant population, already established and having a more secure economic footing, found in the association the means to give charitable aid to less privileged newcomers and to provide them models of conduct. Social work later had to separate itself from this paternalism of the better-off classes and to give to the popular classes the means to acquire the standards of life that they considered desirable.[39] The dominant religion, Protestantism, influenced the other religions to create lay groups more or less independent of the church to which its members belonged.

The basic reason for the immense development of associations in the United States has been the number of different ethnic, religious, and economic subgroups. This fact also explains the lesser development of these groups in the Old World. To different degrees, with less sharp contrasts, this is the reality of all the rapidly industrialized countries. In the United States the contrasts have been less strong because there was a country to discover and conquer and because of the number of people competing for the tasks.

To attempt to paint a complete picture of American associations would be an almost impossible task. Not only are the materials still lacking, but in addition a great number of associations have never acquired a formal character which alone could leave traces. So, we will limit ourselves, as was done regarding France, to follow some selected strands such as the associations of immigrants and the charitable and social work associations. We will also follow, insofar as it provides a comparison with the materials presented regarding Europe, the first steps of socialism and American unionism. Rather than retrace the history of each of these in turn, we have preferred to divide the material into periods.

AMERICAN ASSOCIATIONS, 1800-70

The great waves of emigration commenced after 1815, once the seas had been pacified. In his fine book Oscar Handlin describes in a moving manner the diverse phases of the transplantation of the émigrés. Their lifestyle and mentality had to be adapted to a new environment as soon as they had left their villages. In their old world villages—the émigrés were mostly of rural origin—kin relations had a determinant function in the human relationships and fixed the position, rights, and duties of each. Marriage touched not only the interested parties but a great part of the village because of the links of kin and lands. Modes of life, hopes, plans—all rested on stability, on the hypothesis that there would be no radical changes in landed property, in the number of inhabitants, and in the relationships that held the village together.

Scarcely had the immigrants arrived in the New World when their old attitudes and norms were challenged. Those who had some success, who found work and an independent situation were those who rid themselves of prejudices, who elbowed their way forward and thought only of themselves. "Therein was the significance of the unwillingness of the peasants to undertake the journey in the old traditional communal units."[40] They preferred to face the voyage alone, each one on his own. "Somehow they had been convinced that the village way which had been inadequate to save them at home would certainly prove inadequate away from home."[41]

The most painful feeling was solitude. In his own village the émigré had been surrounded by familiar beings and things. Now he found himself surrounded on all sides by anonymous beings who were indifferent to him, and his life itself was impersonal. "Loneliness, separation from the community of the village, and despair at the insignificance of their own human abilities, these were the elements that, in America, colored the peasants' view of their world."[42] Their natural reaction was to reinforce their ties to religion. Not only were they still tied to their faith in the country of origin, but the New World and their isolation provoked the need of faith. So they turned toward their church as the first means of identification. But their foreign ways set them apart from the American churches. They then reconstituted the church of their native country rather than filling the pews of an American sect.

Religion serves to reinforce old ideals, old values. But it is not solely a question of faith and principles, for funds are necessary to build chapels and pay ministers. The immigrants had no experience with these questions for in their own countries the churches were generally the beneficiaries of the rents from their lands or of grants from the state. In the United States, to the contrary, there was not any established church, or a church protected by the state. Each sect was free and in competition with the others. This competition among them also obliged them to renounce overly strong discipline or punishment of troublemakers, and because of this their credo was not severe. Even the Catholic church was shaken by these new conditions and schisms were produced in it, for the centralizing spirit, order, and discipline could not be maintained in all their force. Evidently other religions witnessed schisms as well. The Lutheran church saw the birth of a number of distinct churches among the Norwegians, Danes, Icelanders, Finns, and Germans. Even the Jews, however habituated to being considered dissidents and adapting themselves better to American conditions, experienced schisms.

A milieu that lacks cohesion renders conservation of old values difficult, and even if after enormous sacrifices the immigrants succeeded in rebuilding their churches, those who came after them did not find there the spirit of their fatherland and in turn founded still new sects. In the new churches the new arrivals found only the formal aspect but not the lifestyle. Those who preceded them had lost the deepest bases of their existence, the intimate meaning of things.

> Yet there was no alternative but to continue as before to hold on to what was left, the form; to resist where possible any change in that. Their religious life accordingly grew rigid; they became far more conservative than those of their fellows who had remained in Europe.[43]

But religion was not the sole means of breaking the isolation from the environment. Scarcely had the immigrants arrived when they sought out someone who could aid them, with whom they could fraternize. The result was a proliferation of more or less organized associations. The extremely miserable housing conditions in overcrowded and unfurnished buildings favored spontaneous forms of solidarity, which were manifest in aid between households in sickness, death, unemployment, and childbirth.

The men met in bars and saloons. There they celebrated family events, according to the customs of their homeland.[44] These celebrations and these public places gave birth to informal, spontaneous associations, without statutes, without written rules. But soon these groups had need of a separate place of their own. The roles within the associations were allocated: a treasurer was placed in charge of common funds for mutual aid, members were elected to distribute the aid in homes, and so on. The society for mutual aid was born, just as it was born at the same moments and under similar conditions in Europe.

As everywhere else the first function of the mutual association was help in case of death, first for burial (it was necessary to pay to be decently buried, for the little village cemetary did not exist any more) and later on help to survivors. These innumerable mutual associations that were constituted among groups of immigrants lasted unpredictably, according to the honesty of the treasurers. Some dissolved due to unemployment. Sometimes the reserves proved to be insufficient. Others became strong, thanks to the prudent and qualified administrators who ran them and to those of their members who made themselves recruiters among new immigrants. With time the mutual associations extended their efforts to facilitate the first steps of immigrants from their countries of origin. In addition they opened hospitals, orphanages, and homes for the aged.

The mutual societies had to restructure themselves. The rules and statutes were inspired by the American limited liability company, comprising a directing council, a president, a treasurer, and a secretary. Other associations took the form of the secret society and, after 1850, orders and chivalric groups of all sorts spread everywhere.

> The magnetic element at the core of all, however, was always the oportunity for sociability. With the occasional association dedicated to intellectual and physical self-improvement, these provided the means by which men got to know each other. The balls and picnics had the additional virtue of raising money; but their true end was sociability. And the event that excited greatest enthusiasm was the parade, a procession which enabled the group to display before the whole world evidence of its solidarity, which enabled the individual to demonstrate that he belonged, he was a part of a whole.[45]

American schools were open to children of all origins. They threatened the solidarity of immigrant groups and a number of mutual associations opened their own schools. Few among them succeeded in collecting sufficient funds. There were, nevertheless, schools for Germans, for Poles, for Jews; but few survived. By contrast, it was only necessary to have a few hundred readers to have a newspaper in a native language which became the mouthpiece of the group, in which the unknowns of the new country were explained in simple terms. In addition, from the 1850s the popular theater enjoyed great success among immigrants. The Germans, Italians, Jews, Irish, Greeks, Poles, each had their own theater.

In the big cities, all these associations were born very rapidly. The demographic base was sufficiently large to maintain all the associations of all national origins. To the contrary, in agricultural zones, the church tended to be the central point of village life. But if he took up the typical American form of association to preserve the old culture and if groups organized themselves around the dominant values of their ethnic group, the immigrant who entered into a society of mutual aid, who read the paper of his nationality group, who went to the theater, adapted himself at the same time to typically American institutions that were not imported from his fatherland. But he also fell back on his own group and rejected the society of the new world. Such an ambiguity could not be prolonged forever and as free association was not opposed in America and as the voluntary initiative was honored there, the immigrant groups little by little took cognizance of this liberty and reconstituted other nationality groups of greater moment. Born spontaneously from need, the immigrant groups came little by little to surround all immigrants of the same language. Although from the start the common origin and the same religion constituted a reason for adherence, habitation on the same street of New York or Boston and the same language became the more important motives.

The lack of participation in the power structure of the society explains also the growing number of associations in ethnic groups. The leaders of immigrant groups were often political émigrés but they had few profound affinities with those of peasant stock. From 1850 to 1880 anarchist socialist groups tried to attract immigrants to them, but without great success, for political problems were not present in the consciousness of the immigrants. For them, the state had always been something hostile and their political interests were strictly local and municipal, and only the second generation acquired a global vision of the state and of social mechanisms.

As in Europe, the first steps of socialism took utopian form. The utopian thinkers, shocked by the misery and the inequalities that constantly surrounded them wanted, we would say today, to test the hypothesis of more fraternal relations among men by experiences in isolation. They thought that once a success in new human relations came about in a limited context, the experiment would snowball and that all society would be transformed in its image. Thus, during the 1840s, a great number of communist colonies were created in the United States. Brookfarm is the most famous, and the elite of thinkers of the epoch were more or less linked to it: Emerson, Thoreau, Nathaniel Hawthorne, William Ellery Channing, George Ripley, and others. Owen tried to create New Harmony in Indiana, between 1825 and 1828. In 1843 a North American phalanx was created at Red Bank by a group of New York idealists. The majority of these attempts were to fail miserably. It was hard to found socialist colonies in the midst of a hostile milieu and ruled by entirely different principles. There were some successes, where the community was religious and where the authority of the group exercised a severe control on the private property of the members.

But these attempts did not touch the majority of the immigrants. Nevertheless, they were not without echoes and the fundamental discussions stimulated by them constituted one of the sources of American socialism, that were to come to fruition between 1880 and 1900.[46]

AMERICAN ASSOCIATIONS AT THE END OF THE NINETEENTH CENTURY

The population of the big cities increased enormously all during the nineteenth century. From 1840 to 1870, the population of New York increased by half each decade; between 1840 and 1900 it grew from 312,000 inhabitants to 3,437,000. Chicago knew an even greater growth, going from a mere 4,000 in 1840 to 1,700,000 in 1900.

The country not only saw a continuous wave of immigrants break on its shores, but, within each city deplacements continually took place as well. Each person wanted to leave as soon as possible the foul lodging that had been his shelter from the time of arrival. Often the immigrants won a new quarter under the pressure of still newer immigrants speaking unintelligible tongues and displaying bizarre customs. Thus the same houses were successively occupied by Irish, Germans, Italians, Poles.

Each removal again threatened the existence of associations and prevented their crystallization. On the contrary, a transformation was at work there, for another reason: many of the associations had been directed by the wealthier émigrés or by the politicians who were not of the same social class as the members, and who often saw in the societies the means of their own ascent. Under their lead, the societies could not maintain themselves in the founding state. In addition, under the pressure of their own organizations, spontaneously created groups escaped, once organized, from the control of the mass of their members. Little by little a nucleus of directors was formed, more clever than the rest.

But the immigrants of the "base" changed also. Gradually they learned English and adopted the customs of their new country. Mutual aid societies broke forth. In New York a German mutual association, preoccupied by need for funds sufficient in case of unemployment or of numerous deaths, reached an accord with an insurance company in 1868. The agreement between the association, the Hildise Bund, and the private company, the future Metropolitan Life, the largest insurance company in the world (1951), signified the decline of the mutual aid associations. Strange contribution, this, of an old small society of émigrés to great capitalism on the make. Such will always be the fate of associations that undergo institutionalization of what was once spontaneous and voluntary.

The immigrant press also submitted to changes. The second generation, instructed in English language schools, did not want to make the effort to learn to read in a foreign language. From the end of the century, J. Pulitzer, editor of a German paper, succeeded in imposing his paper, the *World,* in the same way that William Randolph Hearst conquered the American-born Irish. These mass circulation papers took up numerous characteristics of the immigrant press, which they preserve still today: taste for the sensational, space given to associations and to local events, detailed counsel on delicate questions, and so on.

Finally, the theater underwent a decline under the competition of the moving pictures when the mass immigration ceased. In the theater and in the cinema personages were no longer German or Polish but were generalized and became part of the American patrimony.

> In the strange world of lonely men, the immigrants had reached out to each other, eager in the desire to have brothers with whom they could dwell. In the fluid and free life of America, they found the latitude to join with one another, to contrive institutions through which they could act, means of expression that would speak for them.
>
> But the same fluidity and freedom ultimately undermined the societies, the press, and the theater, that at the start they encouraged. While the immigrants, through those institutions, were adjusting to the American environment, the American environment was adjusting to their presence. An open society offered ample scope for mutual give-and-take.[47]

The second generation was no longer preoccupied with preserving ancestral customs and it was in this generation that the immigrants began to participate in the life of the country. The political problem was indeed foreign to the immigrant: of peasant stock, for him the state had only been a source of fiscal exploitation; he had never thought (except the French) that he would one day be able to control it. In addition his contacts with America left the impression that the state was everywhere the same; his contacts with immigration officials and with police had convinced him of it.

To the contrary, the second generation, to whom the schools had taught the structure and functions of the state, began to play a decisive part in politics. What is more, politics constituted the sole means of obtaining success for the sons of immigrants. They remained poor, but they had their numbers going for them. Whence the phenomenon of the boss, or the intermediary between the immigrant group and the powerful (business, police, public powers). The boss remained closely linked to the immigrants; he was one of them and was the unique recourse for all nonspecialized people, for a good part of the employment in public works was reserved to him as the public representative of the foreigners. Thus the immigrants' associations acquired a new function, the pressure group.

> The local issues were the important ones. Whether there should be new public bathhouse in Ward Twelve, whether the city should hire extra laborers, seemed questions of no moment to the party statesmen. To the residents of the tenement districts they were vital; and in these matters the ward boss saw eye to eye with them. *Jim gets things done!* They could see the evidence themselves, knew the difference it made in their own existence.[48]

The fact that the immigrants were irremediably bound to their condition, that no one aided them, also explains the emergence of the political boss. The union organizations were closed to foreigners and to nonspecialists, and the efforts of radicals, extremists, socialists, and anarchists to organize the immigrants politically or by means of unions did not succeed.[49]

The most powerful socialist organization up to the start of the twentieth century was the Socialist Labor Party. As in Europe numerous schisms marked the parties of the Left, and it was necessary to wait for 1901 to see the regrouping of a part of the labor and socialist forces into the Socialist Party.[50] Meanwhile, the socialist organizations had achieved little hold on the immigrants. Certain associations began to interest themselves in the affairs of the larger society and perceived that electoral pressure could have some effects. But they utilized these forms of pressure for nationalist ends: in the 1850s, some federations took place between associations of the same national origin, and from 1880, gave birth to numerous leagues, orders, and alliances. Often fidelity to national origins led to nationalism. Thus, during all of one century the Irish sustained struggles for the independence of Ireland, German groups demonstrated against the Empire in 1870, Italian associations against the monarchy, and the Jews actively collected funds for zionism.

Numerous charitable associations proposed to come to the aid of the immigrants and during the depression of 1873 some efforts at philanthropy took place. Nevertheless, in the majority, these associations denied the existence of poverty. They preferred to speak of pauperism, that is, of a character fault that was responsible for the condition of life of the poor. The accent was therefore placed on human contacts with the aim of preventing the poor from falling into pauperism, or to remove them from it. It was thought that if pauperism were to spread that it would constitute a menace to social order.

Business and philanthropy were moreover kept separate and gifts made to the poor provided from accumulated riches, from the fortune, rather than from the profits of industry. Above all, it was a matter of course, that in any case the gifts made to those who suffered from the industrial system did not lead to any control over the system on their part. The reactions to this approach were not always good, families refusing the help and demanding justice in place of charity.

An approach of very different origins was that of the settlements. They found their origin in England, where the conditions of life, described by Carlyle, Kingsley, and Ruskin stimulated the interest of numerous universities. Having asked counsel of Canon S. Barnett about what they could do, a group of students from Cambridge rented a house and proposed to settle in a workers' area; in 1884 the first settlement house, Toynbee Hall, opened its doors in London.

> A settlement is a colony of members of the upper classes, formed in a poor neighborhood, with the double purpose of getting to know the local conditions of life from personal observation, and of helping where help is needed. The settler comes to the poor as man to man, in the conviction that it means a misfortune for all parties and a danger for the nation, if the different classes live in complete isolation of thought and environment. He comes to bridge the gulf between the classes.[51]

In the United States the first settlement dates from 1886, the Neighborhood Guild in New York, later called the University Settlement. In 1897 there were 74 settlements and 103 in 1900. But the settlement is a more costly organism than a simple charity, and that is perhaps one reason for the rather feeble overall result in the twentieth century, around 800 total at the present time.

The charity associations resembled the settlements in organizing aid by districts and through personal contacts with families. Friendly visiting joined settling—by the two processes it was thought that the poor would absorb a little of the culture and the ideals of those who approached them. In 1877 a first try at the organization of charity took place, in Buffalo, on a basis that approximated that of the settlements. The city was divided into districts similar to French police *arrondissements*. The visitors to the poor divided up the districts. Similar attempts later took place in Philadelphia and Boston. Collaboration among the settlements tended above all to avoid duplication, and to make common cause for social demands of the municipalities.

The accent placed on personal contacts, permitting each to comprehend the problems of the other and to arrive thus at better social relations did not disappear from the methods of social work and remained a credo of American social and political life. Little by little poverty came to be considered as a total social phenomenon with general causes. From the beginning of the twentieth century, the idea of cooperation with the poor came to be accepted by the charity associations.

Nevertheless, if the most miserable fraction of the proletariat, the lumpen proletariat, was as easily accessible to philanthropic organizations as the most comfortable portion, that is, those who wanted to elevate themselves socially and to change their social class, it remained true that between the two extremes was the working class that preferred to organize itself. In fact, Handlin remarks, the most detestable enemies of the immigrants were the functionaries to whom they had recourse when in need of assistance. These social assistants of the public or private organizations, very sure of their own social and personal superiority, did not succeed in integrating the immigrants into American life.

Meanwhile, other forms of associations must be cited; they too gradually contributed to make of the arriving masses a more homogeneous nation. In this regard, adult education, so lively today, played a considerable role in the integration process. Its influence seems, moreover, to have been exercized more in the rural milieu where the immigrants settled down than in the great urban ports of arrival or the intermediate cities of transit. Cultural associations were organized during the first half of the nineteenth century. In 1831 the lyceum movement was created and around 1835 more than 3,000 cities possessed groups that met weekly for a conference and discussion.[52] After the Civil War innumerable associations were created with more or less similar goals and methods (the YMCA, the fraternal associations, and the Boy Scouts in 1910). The Chatauqua movement was created in 1874, and in a few years covered the country with a network of cultural circles and an organization of correspondence courses. The idea of the correspondence school was then taken up by the universities who created home study departments.

The massive immigration of the years 1880 to 1890 impelled the public authorities to aid the universities to organize evening courses in Americanization for newcomers. The idea of University Extension made its way and in 1892 the University of Chicago created the first of its outward-oriented departments, which took such an important place later in the activities of community development. The content of instruction of these departments enlarged constantly until it extended to all aspects of the lives of the inhabitants. Here again institutionalization was preceded by a broad movement of private associations.

THE PERIOD FROM 1900 TO 1914

During the entire nineteenth century the laws facilitated immigration. In 1882 a law closed access to the country to idiots, anarchists and to polygamists but it did not stem the flood of immigration and it was necessary to await the coming of the war before the pressure of the Immigration Restriction League (founded in 1894) could make itself felt.

The labor movement gave strong support to the limitation of immigration. Although they constituted the mass of the workers, the immigrants were not organized and the AFL, which dominated since 1890, only organized specialized workers. The sons of new immigrants commenced to compete with long-established workers. Sometimes the factories did not accept immigrant manual labor. This competition also made itself felt on the political level, where immigrant groups represented a power that the parties tried to attract.

At the end of the nineteenth century the great melting pot still had not succeeded in fusing all nationalities into a single nation. The immigrants no longer felt themselves European; neither were they yet American. Everywhere people tried to define what a true American was, not only by opposition to the Blacks and to the Chinese but also by relation to the poor immigrants, whose poverty was considered a sign of racial inferiority, and to those who did not want to adapt and remained in closed associations and voluntary segregation. Meanwhile, neither did the American bourgeoisie open its doors nor did the Protestant churches want to see their temples occupied by a crowd of the poor, and all that in spite of the competition with the Catholics, the Jews, and the Orthodox religions. And when the population of a district changed, the churches preferred to close their doors rather than absorb the newcomers. At the end of the century racial theories gave an ideological justification to these tendencies. Although liberated by the Civil War the Blacks were considered as an inferior race, like the Chinese on the west coast, like to a certain degree all that which was not Anglo-Saxon or Nordic. Is it not also strange that the Ku Klux Klan was very powerful in the 1920s? And the Klan represented only one extreme of some very widely shared ideas. Sons were better adapted to the ways of the country than their fathers and "it was this superiority that gave the second generation its role as mediator between the culture of the home and the culture of the wider society in the United States."[53]

Around 1860 the Irish sent four to five million dollars a year to their families in Ireland; at the beginning of the twentieth century all European émigrés sent 140 million a year, the nationalist currents having also contributed to the aid. But the distance between motherland and the émigrés was to increase in spite of the requests for money that they never ceased to receive. They changed, adapted themselves, and all the efforts to preserve their traditions only ended up in reality by adapting them better to the American way of life.

The family, the only institution that had been transplanted from the old continent also began to break up. "Properly speaking, the family no longer had an income; there were only the combined incomes of its members. The larger unit was now a source of weakness rather than of strength."[54] One child left after another, and the father and mother remained alone. And when the necessity arose they found it better to take in roomers, with whom relations were impersonal and pecuniary.

When the man was no longer the sole support of his family he lost authority over it, especially over the children. The reciprocal rights and duties of spouses were no longer reinforced by the community and grew blurred. Children did not owe obeisance to their parents; the school and street life emancipated them. They formed groups with companions of their own age, just as their parents did, and the spirit of the local street group or of the neighborhood competed successfully with the old family customs. These groups proposed new criteria of success. In the 1880s sports became very popular, among the adults as well as among the youth, and the latter found there a means of success. Juvenile delinquency assured other forms of success, especially financial, as did services rendered to the political boss. In fact, these were the sole avenues of success that opened to the sons of immigrants.

All success was concretized by money. Social ranks were not recognized; no man, no family had position in the social hierarchy. Only money conferred prestige, and constituted the measure of all things. Obligations to one another were strictly monetary also: patrons were not tied to any obligations other than the distribution of wages. But the social reformers of the first decade of the century, denouncing political corruption, struggling for temperance, for religious tolerance, for the vote for women, did not reach the immigrants, no more than the anarchists or socialists.

The prestige of the political bosses was not attained by the social reformers. If the influence of the bosses decreased from the beginning of the century it was because the favors they had to dispense were not enough to go around. A fair number of the bosses turned up in the unions, which they attempted to make into political instruments.

The first ten years of the century saw a great development of unionism. The American Federation of Labor went from 278,000 members in 1898 to 1,676,000 in 1904. The Industrial Workers of the World formed with the goal of organizing nonspecialists but their attempt was sporadic. At the same time the great trusts were born and prosperity ended in the crises of 1904 and 1907. Social agitation was very strong between 1904 and 1912 and the strikes of these years entered into the legends of the American labor movement.

This was also the era of the muckrakers—Lincoln Steffens, Charles Edward Russell, and others—who denounced corruption, misdeeds, and the abuses of power by big business. Novelists also illustrated social conditions and attacked the same abuses: Upton Sinclair with *The Jungle,* Jack London with *Iron Heel,* Ernest Poole, and others. Some surveys also illustrated conditions of working life. The first American Christian socialist and secular socialist literature appeared under the names of John Dewey, Charles Beard, Charles Steinmetz. Thorstein Veblen and Lester Ward published their sociological and economic contributions. Finally, some social workers such as Jane Addams, Frances Perkins, and Florence Kelley attempted to reach the real, profound causes of poverty while bringing amelioration of its existent status.

An innumerable intellectual elite studied the problems of the industrial revolution and its social consequences. The Rand School of Social Sciences and the Intercollegiate Socialist Society were founded. Some socialist dailies appeared in New York, Chicago, and Milwaukee. The Socialist Party reached 16,000 members in 1903 and 118,000 by 1912. Socialist Victor Berger was elected to Congress.

In spite of ideological differences, this increase in the strength of socialism seems to show a certain unity. But, as in Europe, it was to be broken by World War I. Even previously there was a conflict between the moderate socialists—Hillquit, Berger—and the extremists. As in France, the first were parliamentarians and the second—William D. Haywood, leader of the IWW, for example—were strictly unionists and counted more on economic action and even, like the CGT in France, on strikes, sabotage, and the general strike. In 1912, Haywood was ejected from the committee of the Socialist Party, which excluded sabotage and violence from its programs.

Equally, from before the war, the social workers and a certain number of intellectuals separated from the Socialist Party in order to support the progressive programs of Theodore Roosevelt and later supported the candidacy of Woodrow Wilson for the presidency. The war provoked another rupture: the majority of the Socialist Party was opposed to the entry of the United States into the war in Europe and the party lost members for this reason.

It was during this period that the Socialist Party received the most help from intellectuals and social workers outside of the party. Even if they were in the future to receive numerous votes in elections, the occasion for building a strong socialist movement in the United States had been already lost at the beginning of the century. This lack of success has received several explanations:[55]

- A new country, the United States presented more possibilities for social ascent than in the countries of the Old World. Geographical mobility was also very great, and when a worker was not content with his lot he could move on.
- The population was very heterogenous, particularly before 1914 and as has been seen, the immigrant groups, a majority of them of peasant origin, were impermeable to socialist propaganda.
- Although the Socialist Party had always affirmed its faith in democracy, the bourgeoisie had disparaged its ideals.
- The union movement on the whole remained very weak before 1914, and Gompers's AFL was strongly antiparliamentarian.
- Finally, the presidential system was not and is not favorable to the intermixture of a third party in presidential elections. Even socialist sympathizers hesitated to give their votes to the socialist candidate for fear of seeing the most reactionary of the other two candidates elected.

Parallel to these developments, a strong growth of social work associations took place. By 1913 there were 413 settlements, and local federations of settlements were created after 1910. In these beginnings the personnel of the settlements was constituted of volunteers or of people of good will without any special qualifications. They were not received with such scorn by the families that they visited, as was directed to the professionals.

The situation was similar with the numerous social associations that were created after the depression of 1907. They increasingly oriented themselves toward the organization of the entire locality, and proposed not only the coordination of charitable aid but also of the activities and groups of all the community. Several surveys were taken during these years in order to know the conditions of life of one locality. That of Pittsburgh, 1907-08, concluded:

> It is not making gifts of libraries, expositions, technical schools and parks, but by the reduction of the work-week by one day in seven and the reduction of the working day, by the increase in salaries, by saving human lives, by the prevention of accidents and by elevation of the standards of life that the profits might return to the people of the locality from which they have been realized.[56]

The promoters of these surveys were the social workers. They hoped in this way to arrive at recommendations and plans for amelioration.

Sometimes, in their conclusions they joined the critiques of the sociologists, in the knowledge that it is vain to want to resuscitate in a district or a community a life similar to that of the traditional village. In addition, they denounced the ever present tendency to place the emphasis on the district when the problem arose outside of it.

In this period the organization of social work, "community organization," was considered as a panacea for all social evils. The tendency to work with little groups, to stress personal contacts, to work with leaders, was already noticeable; all practices that were studied later on by American sociology and social psychology.

The charity associations, the settlements, and the school centers gave a start to the American social work movement at this time. The school civic center movement developed rapidly and represented an attempt to get citizens to participate in communal life. Nevertheless, leisure took precedence over civic and cultural affairs. The school centers were supported by the municipalities, but in the long run they depended on the political parties which sometimes opposed them or thwarted their civic actions.

The associations that aided the school centers were middle class and the endeavors tended to start out in middle class neighborhoods. In fact, the school centers very often took on a paternalistic character, and only rarely were the attempts spontaneous and democratic. And once the formula succeeded it was soon adopted everywhere in a standard manner.

The two basic ideas behind the school centers, creation of a permanent communal assembly place and self-financing or public financing, represented, in fact, a double advance over the charity organizations and settlements. In 1911 there were 428 school centers in 48 cities; in 1913 there were 629 in 152 cities. After World War I the movement ceased and the centers gradually decreased in number. No one spoke anymore about civic participation, the social workers abandoned their great ideal, an ideal of strong humanistic, even socialistic character and set themselves on a path of refinement of methods, of organization and coordination of forces; all this, it seems, to the detriment of the content and long-range goals of their actions.

During World War I the school centers joined in with the Council of National Defense, a federal organism for the mobilization of local and national resources. There was work in the hospitals, campaigns for aid to soldiers and assistance with their reintegration into civil life, and so on. On the local level, the defense councils created councils of all social work organizations in which all citizens were members. Delegates elected by the citizens were sent when requested by superiors of the Council. The plan was a success because of patriotic sentiments and war-time fraternal feelings.

Practically, the councils constituted social agencies or community welfare councils for coordination and representation to the municipalities. Parallel to the defense councils were the War Chests, organizations charged with financing local social activity programs. In many cases they gave birth to Community Chests, organisms with the same function, but permanent.

Another important factor in the evolution of social development was the intervention of the federal government at the start of the war. In 1914 the Smith-Lever Act gave a structure to the agricultural extension movement and established cooperation on research, teaching and agricultural education between federal, state, and local institutions. Each state had a college of agriculture and each county was covered by county agents.[57]

The last years of the nineteenth century and the first years of the twentieth presented currents of ideas still very near to those of Europe. The humanism and the reformism that united social workers and socialists led them to conceive of the state as an instrument of social welfare. Robert Wood wrote in 1905:

> Industry, like culture, as progressive as it could be in certain domains (and perhaps exactly because of this progress) has only a partial and inefficacious conception of what is in the last analysis the sole problem: the properly proportioned and distributed welfare of the entire community. The new profession of social work has for its object to put this end and this goal back in its proper place in politics, in industry and in culture in contemporary life.[58]

The settlement of this epoch, like the school center, aimed at goals more distant than the district and the neighborhood in which it was located. Like Barnett's settlement, that of Jane Addams addressed itself to all the city and to all the nation. The problem orientations that were developed there were national rather than local. The men who devoted themselves to the work were principally from the theological faculties and the women (a majority of the promoters were women) won through it a function in society. Some settlements were at that time centers for the feminist movement. These ideas were the deeds of a generation of pioneers. With the generalization of societies for social work after the war, these superior individuals were lost among the large numbers of social workers who created a profession in which generosity and enthusiasm supplanted the lack of method and experience. In fact, the postwar era was marked in this domain by the influence of psychiatry and its applications to social relations. Institutions such as the settlements limited their activity, and often their thinking, to the boundaries of their neighborhood. Certainly this limitation of the zone of influence and this enhancement of the quality of interindividual contacts, this improvement of techniques of intervention, improved individual capabilities, but it also left the responsible members of these associations entirely unfurnished to cope with the problems of worldwide scale that were raised by the crisis of 1929.

AMERICAN ASSOCIATIONS FROM WORLD WAR I TO THE CRISIS OF 1929

The war united the xenophobes, and in 1917 a law was promulgated that limited immigration to those who could read and write. The real goal was to limit immigration to North European countries, the Slavs and the Italians being mostly illiterate. In addition, after the revolution of October 1917 the first were ranked with the Bolsheviks and the Italians with the anarchists.

In 1921 and in 1924 immigration quotas were fixed in proportion to the residents of each country. The great wave of immigration was henceforth terminated. From 1915 to 1950 the number of immigrants never passed that of the single year of 1907.[59]

These laws firmed and hardened the separations between the different nationality groups and the diverse economic strata. They amounted to a denial of the right of certain ethnic groups to become American. These restrictions favored the development of immigrant associations.[60]

On the social level the conception of the Community Council gradually took shape, an organism composed of delegates of local organizations. The definition of "community" has never been very clear and its limits coincide more with those of zones of action of organizations than with juridical, administrative, or sociological boundaries.

After the war the councils set to work in the great cities. As has been seen, they were born in organizations of charity and kept some of the same functions, such as elimination of duplication, development of professional standards for social workers, and cooperation between organizations for better satisfaction of needs. The council had no power over its member organizations, in relation to whom it could act only by their recommendation. The federations for joint collections of funds also date from this postwar period. Between 1922 and 1928 the number of chests increased from 49 to 297 and the funds collected grew from $23,656,000 to $63,397,000.[61]

The social work movement gradually separated itself from the charity organizations that placed the emphasis only on the family and not on the community. These family-oriented movements also developed community activities (housing, for example) and interested themselves in problems of health, infancy, and juvenile delinquency. Later, specialized agencies were created for each of these problems.

The school centers diminished after the war. The interest in this experience, even if it has failed, lies in its participative character, both civic and political. The centers did not become popular organisms of participation under municipal management: financed by the city, they were not autonomous and their recreation activities outweighed their civic activities. On the other hand the old districts changed a great deal and the new arrivals, speaking a new language, were not integrated into their new city and their new neighborhood. Political discussions and local affairs did not meet with success: the barriers of race, of religion, of national origin, of class, were still too strong.

The Cincinnati experiment, which aimed at this participation in local affairs by citizens who were both residents and members of a trade also failed.[62] This was, nevertheless, a most audacious attempt for it proposed to make of the citizens themselves the masters of the social politics of the city and not simply people who submitted to it. Accused of being socialist, the experiment had to be abandoned.

The current forms of social work were created in the 1920s. The prevention of pauperism took a definitive place in the organization of the community. The content of organizational programs was established and one has the impression that, consequently it was only a matter then of coordinating the programs better and of creating new approaches and facilitating contacts between social work professionals and the beneficiaries of this work. This last point still returns to present day agendas as if the gap had not yet been bridged. As to the values of this work, they were not to be questioned again, in any case up to the end of the 1960s.

THE CRISIS AND THE YEARS FROM 1929 UNTIL THE WAR PERIOD

The crisis struck and a few years later Franklin Roosevelt was elected president. Signs of the times: the socialist vote increased to 900,000. The unions witnessed an increase in effective membership to 15 million in the 1930s.

The New Deal adopted many of the reforms that the socialists had requested, such as pensions and retirement, unemployment insurance, minimum wages, length of work, collective contracts, public works, housing at moderate rents, and progressive income tax. Many progressives abandoned the Socialist Party for the New Deal. In a very real sense all of its program had been realized. The decline of socialism in

America followed the social accomplishments and popularity of Roosevelt among the workers, as well as existence of a favorable atmosphere for reforms in place of more fundamental changes in social structure.[63] During World War II the socialists sustained the politics of the government while continuing to demand social property and democratic control of the monopolies. Meanwhile, the numerous associations of older émigrés and the associations of autochthones (émigrés' descendants for a certain number of generations) remained divided. Few of them survived the war, because of the unity with other citizens brought about by the war, and the attendant prosperity.

In spite of the Soviet Revolution, the majority of the Socialist Party held to its pacific and parliamentary line of action for a cooperative-socialist society. In 1911, the extremist faction founded the Communist Labor Party which died out very quickly, and the Communist Party which went through several phases of development and from which were bit by bit disengaged certain current small groups of the extreme Left.

The membership of the Socialist Party declined during 1912-22 because of Bull Moosism, Wilsonism, the war, the October Revolution, and the schism with the revolutionary unions. The union movement also saw a sharp decrease in membership: from 4 million before the war it fell to 2.5 million because of several lost strikes and because of the combative politics of numerous patrons. Several unions then oriented themselves toward political action and founded the Conference for Progressive Political Action which supported the presidential hopes of Senator La Follette of Wisconsin in the election of 1924. La Follette received 5 million votes thanks to the support of the AFL. But these progressive forces failed to unite in a single powerful party of the socialist type. What is more, the prosperity that the country experienced up to 1929 did not help the socialist cause. It was proclaimed that capitalism had resolved the problem of crises and the unions experienced difficulties organizing labor during this period of full employment. In the 1928 elections the Socialist Party collected only 267,000 votes and Republican Herbert Hoover was elected.

There were 15 million people unemployed in 1933. Nevertheless at the beginning of the crisis there was a tendency to consider unemployment as a form of pauperism, of personal incapacity to adapt. During the first years of the crisis, the unemployed depended entirely on private organizations. Then, in 1935, the Social Security Act insured wages in public works undertaken by the government like employment insurance and other social advantages cited above. Several forms of voluntary aid were attempted, such as the idea of block aid tried in New York, which proposed to assure work to at least one person in a block of buildings thanks to voluntary contributions in cash.

Unemployment favors juvenile delinquency, and it was during those years that a true attempt was made to resolve the problem. Delinquency is caused by large amounts of geographical mobility as well as by unemployment. Several programs of delinquency prevention were begun in which both parents and adolescents were invited to participate. In these projects an attempt was made to place decisions and control in the hands of the residents themselves rather than with the inhabitants of the more respectable areas. From these projects were born the coordinating councils, which had the goal of coordinating the activities of organizations dealing with the same problems, or working in the same neighborhood, or the same district.

The settlements experienced much difficulty in this period. Neighborhoods had changed, and the new inhabitants were not always favorable to the activities and goals of the centers. In addition, the new poor did not accept quite so docily the aid of the social workers—they knew what frustrated them, and that it was not the aid of the social worker that could help them. The settlements then turned toward the promotion of associations among residents of their areas. The school centers were also in difficulty. The parties opposed their civic participation work, and commercial leisure was much more attractive than the events organized in the centers.

All organisms of social work attempted to adapt to the conditions created by the crisis. Councils of social agencies developed. New neighborhood organizations sprang up, but experienced a contradiction in the conditions that faced them, between aid in personnel and funds that came to them from the coordinating councils, and their desire for an independent existence; between their desire for grass roots participation in planning, and control over their activity.

The 1930s saw the end of the ideal of civic participation and of social integration. The social organizations became more and more organisms of social welfare and less and less pretended to be defenders of civic participation. This was the form of acculturation to the dominant values of the society that announced the optimism and conformism of the postwar years.

During the war the full employment in the war economy of women and sometimes of adolescents created new problems. The war experience led to much regrouping of activities and of organizations. Groups associated themselves for fund raising and organized annual campaigns through the United Appeals. In 1941 the Office of Civilian Defense was created in order to facilitate cooperation between the federal powers and the state and local governments for civil protection, maintenance of morale in wartime, and in order to mobilize participation in the war effort. More than 11,000 local defense councils aided in the effort of coordination of these social organizations. At the end of the war a great many of these councils survived to become community councils.

These accomplishments show one of the aspects of collaboration between the state and the private voluntary organizations. State aid from taxes supported the efforts of private organizations, and the community councils worked in close cooperation with local governments. The financial aid of the local governments and of the state continued after the war. The social legislation of this period provided for financial aid and henceforth the private agencies confined their services to areas not yet assumed by the government programs.

In the domain of adult education, financial aid by the state to local organizations and institutions increased and announced the multiplicity of its interventions in the years after 1945. In the period studied here, the most important work of popular education carried out by the federal powers was without doubt the educational programs of the Tennessee Valley Authority.

THE POSTWAR YEARS

In spite of postwar prosperity and sometimes because of it, a series of problems were posed for the thinking and action of American public powers and the numberless American associations. First, the population went from 76 million in 1900 to 151 million in 1950, and increased especially at the age extremes. The country was obliged to construct more schools and to occupy itself with the lot of the aged who in addition risked being isolated because of the decrease in family ties. Second, even if the mean annual income of a family reached $4,700 in 1956, 16 percent of the families earned less than $2,000. A fraction of the population suffered very low standards of living in the midst of general prosperity.

The Southern states had the largest underdeveloped zones and it is not surprising that a third problem of the country derived precisely from these inequalities of development: the strong current of Northward migration. The stream was comprised of Blacks who also sought to flee oppressive racial discrimination, and mountain people of Tennessee and Kentucky rejecting their isolation and their exhausted lands. There was an equally massive arrival of the Puerto Rican subproletariat in New York, and by contrast on the west coast, the agricultural manual laborers from Mexico, the wetbacks. Like the immigrants of the century past, these new categories of immigrants had the tendency to settle in the cities and preferred industrial to agricultural labor.

The flight toward the suburbs by the White population before the massive arrival of the subproletariat of various origins constituted another important problem. The center of the cities tended more and more to be abandoned. Besides the fact that the conditions of housing were deplorable and the overcrowding intolerable, the displacement of populations led to certain problems of local administration and a constant redistribution of public services. In spite of segregation of the less favored parts of the population by streets or by districts, racial and intergroup tensions did not dimish.

In itself the growth of the suburbs created problems. That of transport is perhaps the most spectacular and the one that has the greatest impact on the daily life of the suburbanite or of the exurbanite having to transport himself to his work in the center of the city and return each evening. Growing urbanization (175 cities of more than 100,000) and the expansion of the city into the countryside (in 1957, 27 percent of the country lived in suburbs) constantly modified the physiognomy of the country. To that we must add the displacement of industry and its location in regions of less dense population by consequence of the necessity of automation, the resulting displacement of manual labor, and more generally the adaptation of a population to an annual increase of 3 to 4 percent in national income.

These economic and demographic phenomena are expressed by an astonishing mobility—in the eyes of Europeans—of the population. One-fifth of all families changed addresses each year. This mobility and interior migration in the time of war (creation of new industries, war industries) contributed to erase differences of national origin and the little islands of local culture. The old associations of immigrants that were so flourishing in the 1920s and 1930s did not reconstitute themselves again, and belong to the past.

Under the influence of these factors, it is not surprising that the community encountered different realities than those of preceding times: the inhabitants are only attached to other temporary residents like themselves or to people they work with. Interests are divergent and multiple, by the chance of professional contacts or residential district; the sentiment of belonging or indentification to the city has vanished; communal power is the resultant of an equilibrium of interests rather than that of political participation of citizens.

Individuals search in the associations for an outlet for their participation needs and perhaps a consolation in that solitude so eloquently analyzed by Riesman. In Europe, where meanwhile conditions of life are also uncertain, low mobility engenders a certain security: for many years the housing, friends, objects, the quarter, the work, remain the same. To the contrary the American sees the universe that surrounds him change with each of his displacements. Perhaps this is one of the reasons for that insecurity which is the motive to join with others in formal and informal associations. In the less favored classes religious groups seem to best fill these needs for participation, for identification, for security.

But the majority of these societies are strictly unifunctional and only hold the individual by an aspect of his personality. He is not satisfied to grow within it alone, and he does not attach himself profoundly to a single group, quits them easily, passes from one group to another and never really identifies with any one. Hence, the reliance on little groups and the family of which we have spoken in the first part, or his participation in new groups, reflecting upon the fundamentals and the styles of life of the American society or, better, of the consumer civilization that it has created.

NOTES

1. For France, I have followed especially Edouard Dolléans and Gerard Dehove, *Histoire du travail en France,* 2 vols. (Paris: Domat Montchrestian, 1953 and 1955); Etienne Martin Saint-Léon, *Histoire des corporations des métiers,* 3rd ed. (Paris: Alcan, 1922); Joseph Drioux, *Etude économique et juridique sur les associations* (Paris: Librairie Nouvelle de Droit et de Jurisprudence, 1884).
2. Twenty pages on the Roman and Germanic origins of French associationism are omitted here. The discussion of Germanic origins of associations has generated more heat than light, especially in the late–nineteenth-century discussions. The best easily available discussion is Sylvia Thrupp, "Gilds," *International Encyclopedia of the Social Sciences,* 17 vols. (New York: Macmillan and Free Press, 1968, vol. 6), pp. 184-87. (Ed.)
3. Arnaldo Cherubini, *Dottrine e metodi assistenziali dal 1789 al 1848* (Milan: A. Giuffrè, 1958), p. 92.
4. Dolléans and Dehove, pp. 235-36.
5. A section on workers' associations is omitted here, pp. 74-75 of *Vers une Sociologie des associations.* (Ed.)
6. Celestin Bouglé, *Socialismes français* (Paris: A. Colin, 1933), p. 96.
7. Cited by Dolléans and Dehove, p. 173.
8. "Decidedly," write Dolléans and Dehove, "the Third Estate knew what it was doing in proclaiming liberty, but it had taken care to assure that it could not hurt itself and liberal capitalism had henceforth the field free before it" (p. 166).
9. Rémi Gossez, "Circonstances du mouvement ouvrier; Paris, 1848" (Paris: ms., 1951); idem, *Les Ouvriers de Paris,* vol. 24 (Paris: Société d'Histoire de la Révolution de 1848, 1967).
10. Gaston-Martin, *La Révolution de 1848* (Paris: PUF, 1948). English-language catalogues list the author as "Martin, Gaston." (Ed.)
11. This contestation is so true that still today certain members of communities of work speak of the "dictatorship of the intellectual."
12. The banquet of 25 November 1848, cited by Gossez.
13. Martin Nadaud, *Les Sociétés ouvrières en France,* p. 131.

14. Iouda Tchernoff, *Associations et sociétés secrètes sous la Deuxième République, 1848-1851* (Paris: Alcan, 1905).
15. Ibid., p. 11.
16. Dolléans and Dehove, p. 20.
17. "Circulaire du ministre de l'interieur de juillet 1850," cited by Tchernoff, p. 20.
18. Fascism returned to the same politics. Cf. Albert Meister, *Associations coopera-tives et groupes de loisirs en milieu rural* (Paris: Editions de Minuit, 1958).
19. At this point six pages of the original text in *Vers une Sociologie des associations* are omitted. They concern examples of the treatment of associations at Lyon, taken from a court report of January 1850. (Ed.)
20. Gossez, *Les Ouvriers de Paris,* p. 320.
21. *Journal Officiel,* 19 November 1875, p. 9466, cited by Dolléans and Dehove, p. 293.
22. Georges Duveau, *La Vie ouvrière sous le Second Empire* (Paris: Gallimard, 1946), p. 415.
23. Georges Scelle, *Le Droit ouvrier* (Paris: A. Colin, 1929), p. 221.
24. Dolléans and Dehove, p. 304.
25. Ibid., p. 383.
26. Cited by Georges Bourgin and P. Rimber, *Le Socialisme* (Paris: PUF, 1957), pp. 84-85.
27. The French is Union des Chambres Syndicales Ouvrières de France. (Ed.)
28. In 1881 the amnestied people of the Commune founded the Central Revolutionary Committee which became a socialist party open to all under the leadership of Edouard Valliant.
29. In its beginning the CGT comprised two organizations: the exchanges or local federations and the federations of trades. With time a certain centralization intervened. At the start of their existence the Labor Exchanges had to be placement agencies but this goal rapidly was transformed into a second and they became local citadels of workers' organizations, with the status of union locals; in 1918 in each *département,* a departmental union was created beside which the labor exchanges subsisted but with an attenuated role.
30. Dolléans and Dehove, p. 412.
31. The member could nevertheless belong to a party provided that he did not introduce politics into the labor union.
32. See in particular the study of Henri Desroche, "Coopératives, communautés et mouvement ouvrier," *Communauté* (1953): 6-8.
33. Cf. J. Godard, *Travailleurs et métiers lyonnais: Les origines de la coopération lyonnaise* (Lyon: n.p., n.d.), p. 20.
34. Desroches.
35. Bernard Lavergne, *La Révolution cooperative* (Paris: PUF, 1949), p. 175.
36. *The Co-operator,* cited by Desroche.
37. Since the time this was written the situation has been remedied somewhat by the founding of the Association of Voluntary Action Scholars (in the United States) and IVAR:VOIR (International Voluntary Action and Voluntary Association Research Organization: Organisation Internationale pour la Reserche sur les Associations et l'Action Volontaire, headquarters in Brussels. The field of American voluntary association studies is surveyed in Constance Smith and Anne Freedman, *Voluntary Associations* (Cambridge, Mass.: Harvard University Press, 1972). (Ed.)
38. Cf. Oscar Handlin, *The Uprooted* (Boston: Little, Brown, 1953).

39. Sidney Dillick, *Community Organization for Neighborhood Development—Past and Present* (New York: Woman's Press, 1953), p. 198.
40. Handlin, p. 61.
41. Ibid.
42. Ibid., p. 108.
43. Ibid., p. 142.
44. See the description that Upton Sinclair gives in *The Jungle* of the marriage scene of Jurg. Upton Sinclair, *The Jungle* (New York: Airmont, 1906).
45. Handlin, p. 177.
46. There had previously been a socialist movement that began with the exiles from the revolution of 1830 and 1848 in Germany, but it was absorbed in the struggle against slavery and by the civil war. Another current formed around the International, transferred to New York from 1872 to 1876, date of its dissolution.
47. Handlin, p. 200.
48. Ibid., p. 211.
49. The attempts at unionism were a failure: "Indeed the immigrant who had been at home in his own mutual aid society was dismayed by all these efforts to turn his joining into something else." Ibid., p. 196. He often left these larger groups and returned to his own neighborhood to establish spontaneous small groups in it.
50. In 1895 the Socialist Labor Party, after a vain attempt to take over the Knights of Labor, organized the Socialist Trade and Labor Alliance, in competition with the AFL and the Knights of Labor. But because of these union problems the party divided and a faction founded the Socialist Party of the US. It allied with the Social Democracy group that had been organized shortly before in the Midwest (this was the group organized by Victor Berger, the socialist leader from Milwaukee) and with the groups of Eugene Debs. Of Alsatian origin but born in America, Debs had organized the train conductors, and between 1880 and 1893 made a very strong union of it. He subsequently organized the nonspecialized railroad workers into the American Railway Union. In 1898 Social Democracy emerged on the scene and Berger and Debs formed the Social Democracy Party. In 1900 Debs ran for president of the United States, becoming allied with the Socialist Party of the United States, and in 1901, all these forces united into the Socialist Party.
51. Werner Picht, *Toynbee Hall and the English Settlement Movement* (London: G. Bell, 1914), cited by Dillick, p. 27.
52. The lyceum movement began in 1826 in Derby, Connecticut, but was organized nationally in 1831. An international organization was contemplated but not achieved. (Ed.)
53. Handlin, p. 229.
54. Ibid., p. 229.
55. Cf. Harry W. Laidler, *Socialism in the United States* (New York: League for Industrial Democracy, 1952), p. 26.
56. Cf. Edward T. Devine, *Pittsburgh the Year of the Survey* (New York: Survey Associates, 1914), p. 4, cited by Dillick, pp. 45–46.
57. Cf. Joseph Di Franco, *The United States Cooperative Extension Service* (New York: State College of Agriculture at Cornell University, Cooperative Extension Publication No. 7, 1958), p. 28.
58. Cited by Albert J. Kennedy, *The Settlement Heritage* (New York: National Federation of Settlements, 1953), p. 28.

59. Handlin, p. 293.
60. Under these conditions, it is not astonishing that many Italians took a position in favor of Mussolini, in whom they saw not so much the head of fascism but one who had shown the whole world the power of Italy and had known how to impose respect for the Italians, a respect they had not enjoyed in the United States. A great number of Germans established in the United States likewise saw in Hitler the avenger of the anti-German climate of World War I. The Jews, under the weight of attacks by the Klan, Henry Ford, and racist organizations, felt that they had not found in the United States the free country of which they had dreamed, and sustained Zionism.
61. Dillick, p. 91.
62. Ibid., p. 80ff.
63. In addition the coming of Hitler provoked a new schism in the Socialist Party. In spite of the communist propaganda that demanded unity against fascism, the Socialist Party reaffirmed its democratic character. One faction separated off and finally rejoined the communist ranks.

4

IDENTITY OF MEMBERS AND PARTICIPANTS

Many inquiries have been effectuated on the social and personal characteristics of association participants. These works will in time permit responses to the questions: who are the leaders of the associations; who are the members; and also, who are the nonmembers, those who refuse to adhere or to participate?[1]

This chapter is based on an analysis of studies done especially in the United States and in the countries of Western Europe. The traits of the association participant that they permit us to elucidate above all concern the western militant, although the data from a study on militants of a socialist country, Yugoslavia, show that even in this different socio-cultural context militants possess the same social and personal characteristics as those of our countries.[2] Although not yet supported by other research, these first results tend to confirm the convergent tendencies in participation within the two great types of industrial societies.

GENERAL HYPOTHESIS ON SOCIAL PARTICIPATION AND SOCIAL CHANGE

The general hypothesis that can be formulated on participation in associations is the following:

1. *Social change and modernization disorganize and even destroy* (as is, for example, the case during the period of industrialization of our societies) *the structures of sociability of individuals.* As in some Piedmontese associations, old groupings are impoverished, the village community, the parish and the family, which previously constituted the structures for contacts with others, and that dictated ways of living for the individual (in a word, his sociability), these groupings are impoverished and even disappear in the end.
2. *Associations are the structures and the means by which individuals and groups manifest their sociability.* This second proposition does not prejudge the type of manifestation that the association will develop in response to social change, for example, associations for resistance to the new economic and social structure, isolation of the association by the creation of a marginal community and so on.

3. *Social change does not affect all individuals and all social groups with the same intensity.*
4. *Individuals and groups that feel social change most intensely create more associations and participate more in them.* This fourth proposition of the hypothesis will permit deduction of the particular hypotheses that follow. Note that we confine ourselves here to formal participation.

The association, insofar as it is a voluntary recruitment grouping, is a creation of modern industrial societies. One finds, certainly, associations before the industrial revolution, but they tended to have a somewhat different character than the modern association: the trade guilds or fraternities limited their recruitment rather strictly to the members of the profession, and their rites made of them more or less secret societies; in addition, these societies altogether concerned only a part of the population, that part engaged in the artisanal sector or in commerce. The rest of the population, and it was the majority at the time, had no occupational activities that led to association and lived elsewhere than in the cities.[3]

During the industrialization phase, the number of individuals submitted to the influence of change increases abruptly and enormously. This influence is nevertheless carried out in an uneven fashion: thus the traditional institutions, especially the family, resist change, and in surroundings where they resist more, the individuals participate less in associations. It is especially the case for workers of peasant origin whose families have only recently established themselves in the city or near the factory. Elsewhere where these traditional structures of sociability have already been weakened, as is the case in the cities, the traditionally urban professional categories see more of their members participate (the printers, for example). This hypothesis envisages one of the phenomena, urbanization, that generally accompanies industrialization, but in a period anterior to industrialization.[4]

PARTICULAR HYPOTHESES: FACTORS IN PARTICIPATION

A certain number of particular hypotheses can be deduced from the general hypothesis and are verified by the research analyzed.

1. The fourth point of the general hypothesis predicts a greater number of associations and a higher degree of participation among individuals and in groups created or developed by social change. This applies particularly to urban milieux and to occupations of the tertiary sector. It can be deduced from it that the individuals and groups belonging to these new activities make more effort to create the specific new structures of sociability that these associations constitute. We also note that these new

activities created by social change tend to be of a nonmanual character. We can therefore propose the two following hypotheses.

1a. *The newer the occupation, the stronger the social participation.*

1b. *The less manual the occupation, the stronger the participation.*

Certain occupations have been and will still be typical of the activities of the tertiary sector for a long while: merchants, agents, free professions, and so on. All have as a common character that they are independent and in competition with others: in consequence, we can reason that the individuals who occupy such positions must feel with more intensity the need to create new structures for their sociability. Therefore:

1c. *The members of the independent professions participate more than the others.*

These three aspects—absence of tradition, nonmanual work, independence—also characterize the most remunerative occupations of our society, and much research has shown a strict correlation between social participation and importance of income. A classification of occupational activities may be made that separately identifies the part of each of those variables and its correlates.

TABLE 4.1
Occupational Classification by Sector and Activity

Activity	*Examples*	*Sector*
T M D	Farm workers, manual laborers	Traditional—primary and secondary
T M –D	Traditional artisans, peasants	
T –M D	Clerks, traditional employees, petty functionaries	Traditional—tertiary
T –M –D	Lawyers, notaries, free professions, traditional commercial	
–T M D	Industrial workers, manual laborers	Modern—primary and secondary
–T M –D	New artisans, repairmen, installers	
–T –M D	Engineers, executives, employees	Modern—tertiary
–T –M –D	Industrialists, business heads, directors	

Note: T = traditionalism; D = dependent; M = manual. Minus sign = less; no sign = more (i.e., plus implied).

The hypothesis on which Table 4.1 is based, restated in terms of the code used here, is that participation is increased as one passes from TMD to -T-M-D. This has already been verified in certain specific instances, for example, TM-D/TMD; T-M-D/T-MD, and so on. Research to come must verify other relations to the end of giving a consistency to the entire table.[5]

Table 4.1 permits, therefore, the hypothesis that the most active participants and leaders of associations will be recruited by preference in these later categories. Meanwhile it is also advisable to take account of types of associations. Here are some examples: in an American inquiry, the merchants and members of the free professions were considered leaders in the domains tied to their profession, although public functionaries tended to be seen as leaders whatever their domain (industry, recreation, health, and so on.) Leadership tends therefore to be specialized according to profession. The same conclusions were reached in a French study of the underrepresentation among militants in cooperatives, which was explained by the tendency of worker militantism to be oriented toward union rather than cooperative action. As to coop militants, the majority of them are functionaries, employees, teachers, and retirees from these three professions (and therefore nonmanual workers, clever with the pen). As for artisans and merchants, it has been shown that their strong participation was due to the advantages that they anticipated in it for their professional occupations.

Meanwhile we note that it can happen that the high accessibility of certain associations and the high degree of local consensus as to the necessity of their action favors participation of all social and occupational classes. This is what has been established in certain studies on associations for local development. One cannot let this fact pass in silence, even though it may perhaps be due to the exceptional situation that created the consensus.

As has been said, the professions registered at the bottom of the table are the best remunerated in our societies. Being well-off is considered here as an attribute of the occupational position and it is not surprising that inquiries have shown that the more well-to-do participate more and have more chance to be leaders and officers. The standard of living has also been found to be correlated with participation, as indicated by such measures as degree of comfort of the dwelling, quality and age of furniture and household equipment. In fact, the nature and quantity of consumer goods, considered as indicators of the accessibility of the family to certain social positions, sustains even better correlations with participation than income or profession alone.

Possession of consumer goods seems to strongly affect women's associations; it was, beside other social characteristics, one of the criteria of recruitment, and played the same role as indicator of success for the housewife as type of profession exercised for her husband.

Among farmers, the size of area exploited is related to participation.

As might be expected, the larger the area the stronger the participation and the more positive the attitude to cooperatives.

These several research findings are only some examples permitting illustration of the kind of relationships implied by the three hypotheses indicated above.[6]

2. In traditional society prestige is more attached to the social position of the family or the occupation than to personal efforts of the individual. Prestige there is transmitted, and not acquired by the individual. With social change, the institutions that maintain the hierarchy of social positions disappear, as does the prestige attached to these social ranks. Personal effort alone is the source of prestige, or, what amounts to the same thing, the accumulation of a fortune from the effort, plus other means of consuming it. In this case, prestige can be transmitted. Finally, there is one other type of prestige that is difficult to transmit: that acquired in sport, politics, and associations.

The research analyzed shows relations between each one of these three sorts of prestige and social participation: sometimes participation varies with nonacquired prestige (for example, seniority of residence), sometimes with accumulated and transmitted prestige (a fortune), sometimes with nontransmittable prestige (leadership in associations).

In our modern society, increasingly uniform in appearance, and where habits and other means of consumption are no longer sufficient to separate and classify individuals, belonging to such and such an association becomes a more certain sign of the position of an individual in society. We can act on the authority of certain inquiries in supposing that the search for prestige is an important aspect of sociability, and that in this sense, social participation is a means of satisfying this search. Whence the two following hypotheses.

2a. *The more individuals are affected by social change* (the greater the distance that separates them from old forms of social prestige), *the more they seek the social prestige given by associations.*

2b. *The stronger the aspiration to social prestige, the stronger the degree of participation in associations.*

Analysis of research work on participation is not yet sufficiently advanced to conclude that these hypotheses have been verified. It is nevertheless very useful to formulate them because of the link that they will establish between research in the domain of social mobility.

As in the preceding section, here are some examples drawn from research on prestige and participation. These studies tend to show that the individuals to whom high prestige is attributed have the feeling that others expect them to be active in associations. In rural America this is the case of merchants, members of the liberal professions, and farmers with high incomes. To the contrary, individuals with low incomes and little prestige have the attitude that their participation is not necessary, and ultimately, not wanted. In other terms participation and nonparticipation might be expressions of individuals' sentiments about their superiority or inferiority in the locality.

The study of relations between prestige and participation leads to conclusions rather similar to those formulated regarding income and socioeconomic status. To level of income, which translates evaluation of a position in the hierarchy of positions, corresponds the popular judgment of the prestige attached to each occupation. In this perspective we can expect rather strong correlations between income and prestige, although there are other elements in the composition of prestige than the single socioeconomic status. Such seems to be the case in surroundings as homogeneous in their aspirations as American rural environments previously evoked, and which have shown positive correlations between prestige and participation; and as has been already seen, between income and participation. In these same environments it has equally been shown that there is a correlation between prestige and religious participation. Of course things can be different elsewhere, and it might be necessary to also investigate other milieux than those already studied. For example, environments in transformation, in which prestige founded on rank and on personal effort are opposed, that is, in which there is ascribed and achieved prestige.

Social ascent that sanctions membership and leadership in certain associations constitutes one of the driving forces of social change in our modern societies. And associationism is one of the evidences of the more or less rapid functioning of this force. Thanks to the influx of leadership candidates, the associations survive and multiply by ascent to responsibilities, based on outside recruitment and by splitting-off of associations as in the case where there are too many candidates for a limited number of directorial posts.

3. The level of education is among the independent variables that are generally found to be significantly correlated with participation. The same result is found with level of information which we consider a better measure than simple years of schooling, especially among workers' groups where militants and officers are in general self-educated. The school in effect gives a minimum of knowledge and some techniques to utilize in order to renew and enrich this information; what finally counts is the use that is made of these techniques (by means of reading, courses, and so on) in adult life: that is what is here called level of information.

Analysis of research on the question shows that participants, and above all very active participants, have at once levels of instruction and information higher than the members in general. Thus, for example, one study made in an American rural area even arrives at the conclusion that persons who have benefitted from four years of university have forty times more chances of taking responsibilities than those with no university training. There are, however, some exceptions to these regularities: although American studies show a consistent relationship between participation and level of instruction, one German study shows to the contrary that persons with a university education tend to live in seclusion and to not participate very much in daily life.

As we have already seen above, it is therefore necessary to take account of the type of grouping. Thus, in the case of certain union groups, attendance at meetings does not vary with level of education. The linkage of participation–level of instruction would appear above all in noneconomic associations.

It is, to be sure, in taking responsibility that level of instruction is important, because of the fact that many tasks of officers boil down to writing and office work. The overrepresentation of the nonmanual professions in the officer category has already been indicated. It has been remarked that there exists a norm or expectation that those with higher education take an active part in associations.

Other components of level of information may include adult education and training in the occupation. The relationship between participation and technological competence in rural America may be explained in this way, where it has likewise been noted that there is a correlation between newspaper reading and participation in formal groups.

4. Numerous studies have shown a difference in the social participation of men and women. This result does not lead us very far in the comprehension of the phenomenon of participation unless it is integrated in more general theoretical structure. In fact, variations in participation according to sex are best explained by the following hypothesis, which is also deduced from our general hypothesis.

4a. *The sexes are not equally affected by social change, and the one affected more participates more.* Such a formulation is not simple formalism, and such a hypothesis can account for different models of participation, at first glance contradictory, between men and women in different associations according to circumstances and sociocultural milieux.

Some examples of the results of inquiries in an American rural area reveal that churches and religious associations register more female participation although economic and professional associations witness higher male participation. Women participate more in associations for social sanction and reinforcement of traditional norms, while men participate more in associations of social change, centered on direct material progress. Female participation, and in general participation in social sanction groups, tends then to reinforce norms of traditional sociability that were current in the church, the family, the neighborhood. In this sense these associations are the prolongations of traditional institutions gradually impoverished and eliminated by change.

Recently, some inquiries have completed the picture by showing that if men participate in a greater number of associations than women, the latter give more of their time to the activities of their groups. In addition, women seem to be more stable in their affiliations. Despite appearances, the question of a stronger participation of men is far from being evident, and even on such a problem that one could consider to be relatively simple research is still necessary.

5. What has just been said on the subject of variations in participation according to sex is valid for that which concerns variation according to age. The following hypothesis can be deduced from our general hypothesis.

5a. *At the moment of life in which social change is the greatest, social participation is the highest.* This hypothesis can account for the variations in participation demonstrated by research: increase between the ages of 15 and 19, corresponding to the adaptation of the adolescent to changes of environment, departure from the family, and entry into a profession or the beginning of college; a lower level between ages 20 and 30; and a very high level between ages 30 and 55 to 59 corresponding to the most intense period of professional activity.

The period of most intense professional activity generally coincides with a certain phase of the family cycle, measured by ages of children. It can also be shown that it is the families having children both above and below ten years that participate most in associations. It is generally during their most active professional period that individuals have their children in these age categories. Then, with advancement in the family cycle, the individuals tend to participate less and to take fewer responsibilities.

The data on the family cycle, like that on ages, can therefore be reduced to sociooccupational data. It is in this way that the weak participation of the unmarried young, the childless married, or married with preschool children can be explained.

From some data on older people it can be seen that the system of stratification and isolation of the aged from the occupational structure combine to create a decrease in formal participation. Low socioeconomic status and retirement combine to produce weak participation: these two factors are more closely linked than age alone to the decrease of participation, for individuals of high socioeconomic status do not see their participation decrease so much with age. In other words, a high income, and equally, a high level of education favor participation of the aged. Certainly age affects some types of participation more than others: participation decreases more rapidly in interest groups than in religious groups, and the motives for adhesion of the young are in general more complex than those of the old.

In consumer cooperatives the militants are generally older than other members. In agricultural cooperatives it has been found that the young are less favorable to coops than their elders, though there are among them fewer diehard opponents. Here we may again apply the hypothesis on the disinterestedness of the young regarding cooperation, the aging of its cadres being only the consequence of the disaffection of youth and the lack of new candidates for offices.

There are, however, some contradictory research results, notably concerning participation in unions. According to these results, participation in meetings is higher among the unmarried, the divorced, or the married without children, and the unions play a role of family substitute for them. Another study, however, finds no links between family status and union participation.

Finally, participation can vary according to socioculture surroundings. The research cited is mostly American and cannot be extended to less modernized surroundings, in which participation in associations is reserved exclusively to the head of the family and where spouses—and sometimes women in general—are kept apart from the life of the group.

6. The characteristics examined up to this point have been biological and involuntary (age, sex), or social and more or less voluntary (occupation, level of information and so on). There are, nevertheless, other factors to consider that are social but involuntary. Among them, adherence to groups and to milieux that the individual has not chosen to belong to, and which have influenced him from his tender infancy: his social class, his religion, his race or ethnic group, his minority group, and so on. Certain of these groups are moreover voluntary (religious groups, for example), but they are envisaged here under their involuntary aspect, that is to say, when the individual is born and raised as a member. In such a case the person's voluntarism is limited to the possibility of leaving the group or to not participating in it. It is, nevertheless, well known that one can only superficially escape the hold of such groups, whose influence is so profound and so far off in childhood that it continues to be manifest for a lifetime.

The particular hypothesis that can be directly deduced from the general hypothesis concerns the process of social change and its cumulative effects in the course of time.

6a. *The more the involuntary groups to which the individual belongs have been affected by social change, the stronger his voluntary association participation.*

To begin with we shall examine religious group membership. The empirical data are generally in agreement that voluntary participation is stronger among Jews than Protestants, and stronger among Protestants than Catholics. But it is still necessary to show that these three religious groups have not been equally affected by social change. Happily this work has been done by Durkheim, in his studies on the variations in suicide by religion. Merton has formulated the hypothesis of Durkheim: (1) social cohesion aids individuals psychologically subject to anxiety and sharp tensions; (2) suicide is a function of unrelieved tensions to which the individuals are subjected; (3) Catholics have more social cohesion than Protestants, religious institutions having maintained more strength among the former; (4) in consequence, suicide can be expected to be lower among Catholics.[7]

This type of explication does not aim only at linkage of two domains of sociological study, participation and anomie—tending thus to reinforce our network of hypotheses on participation—but also increases our comprehension of the phenomenon of participation, considered as adaptation to social change, in the same fashion as suicide was considered by Durkheim as a sort of nonadaptive behavior.

Our theoretical schema on participation would be greatly strengthened if the following hypothesis was verified: individuals who commit suicide participated less in associations, other things being equal. A study on suicide of widowers has been recently published, in which it was found that although widows suffer the same suicide rates as married women the same age, widowers have a higher rate than married men of that age group. This finding led the authors to study local integration and participation. It appears that widowers who commit suicide had fewer participation links; they had abandoned their occupational life and had no local participation, or they counted on the participation of their spouse, whom they considered as their link with the community. The death of his wife isolated him completely. By contrast, widows were much more involved in networks of contacts and of participation before the death of the husband.[8]

Social participation according to racial or ethnic origin has also been made the object of empirical research. The data collected in the field confirm the hypothesis that the group or the nonvoluntary environment that has been the most affected by social change sees a very great voluntary participation of its members. For example, in the United States participation of Whites is greater than that of non-Whites; participation of urban non-Whites is stronger than that of rural non-Whites, and so on. Research is needed, however, to the end of isolating the influence of certain added factors, such as degree of ruralism, or of religion.

Traditionally, all the involuntary groups considered here (religion, family, local community, and so on), tended to maximize their hold on the individual. In this sense, they were all groups with totalitarian pretentions,[9] claiming to completely mold the personality of the individual, imposing their *Weltanschauung* on him. As such, they were equally very jealous of their power over the individual and did not hestitate to struggle against outside or compelling influences. Such groups have not entirely disappeared in our more industrialized societies and it is very important to recall these characteristics in order to comprehend survivals such as parochialism, family spirit, group cohesion in local areas, and so on—all variables that are commonly found in research on social participation. One knows moreover how present such "determinants" of social participation are in developing countries and how much they can stand in the way of community development work, animation, and creation and good functioning of cooperatives, of unions and other associations.

The more the totalitarian influence of these involuntary groups is eroded by social change, the less capable they are of resisting new changes. This is particularly true of the family. Empirical studies have regularly shown that the sons of individuals with strong associationist participation are more likely to have a high level of participation. In other words, the active participants in an association are more likely than nonparticipants and less active participants to see their kin or members of their family group participate actively. Regarding cooperatives, where this relation has also been verified, researchers have even spoken in this regard of "family traits." Whatever the name given to the phenomenon, the empirical data render evident the fact that the more involuntary family group has been affected by social change, as indicated by the high participation of parents, the less it tends to conserve a totalitarian hold on its members and the more it encourages their participation, giving rise to new social change.

7. Ecological factors have often been analyzed in relation to participation, in the same way that social change has been put in relation to industrialization and urbanization. The two latter phenomena are not always linked and the empirical data suggest the following hypotheses: the more pronounced the urbanization, the stronger the participation; the higher the degree of industrialization, the greater the participation.

It is tempting, however, to renounce these general categories and come back to the Durkheimian concept of social heterogeneity in order to study the different degrees of participation. In fact, voluntary associations have often been described as means of adjustment for individuals to an environment in constant change, marked by conflicts of groups and values, in constant mobility, in growing heterogeneity (urbanization and industrialization being only composing elements of this social heterogeneity). This heterogeneity increases the sensitivity of individuals to the process of change; from this we may deduce the following hypothesis.

7a. *The greater the degree of heterogeneity of the social milieu, the higher the level of social participation.*

This hypothesis has been confirmed by empirical research and contributes to the explanation of different types of participation according to the degree of heterogeneity of the environment (for example, the greater participation in social sanction groups in homogeneous environments, and the greater participation in groups oriented toward change in heterogeneous surroundings), but also renders account of the perpetuation of institutions and traditional structures of sociability in certain homogenous subgroups, more or less segregated, but entrenched in the most heterogeneous environments (for example the weak associationist participation and the persistence of traditional family models in certain working class districts of our most industrialized cities, European as well as American).

The concept of degree of heterogeneity leads us to more subtle analysis of the environment than the simple correlations of data on participation with indices of urbanization or of industrialization. Equally, it permits us to link the domain of research on social participation to anterior research done on the celebrated Durkheimian types of solidarity.

8. In the preceding pages the association has been considered as a response to change, and research shows that individuals submitting more to the influence of these changes participate more in associations. In the same order of ideas we can also suppose that the individuals who are the most open and the most favorable to change participate more. Here, the causal factor is an attitude and no longer a personal characteristic or a situational variable.

Little of the research evoked until now has verified the hypothesis that attitudes favorable to change were linked to greater participation. By contrast, the two following hypotheses have frequently been verified.

8a. *The greater the degree of information the stronger the participation,* a hypothesis already mentioned above, and:

8b. *The greater the degree of information, the more favorable the attitudes regarding social change.*

From these premises, we can deduce logically that:

8c. *The more favorable the attitudes regarding social change, the greater the social participation.*

As noted above, this last hypothesis has received but little empirical evidence. On the other hand, it can be verified indirectly and partially (in the agricultural world only) by the two transition hypotheses that follow.

8c′. *The greater the degree of adoption of new agricultural practices, the more favorable the attitudes regarding change.*

8c″. *The greater the degree of adoption of new agricultural practices, the stronger the participation.*

Starting from 8c′ and 8c″, we can logically come back to 8c. This means of verifying hypothesis 8c merits some comments. It shows how empirical data that seem foreign to the domain of social participation can be utilized in order to enlarge the network of our hypotheses and how they permit reinforcement of internal coherence of all the system of hypotheses. We add that hypotheses 8c′ and 8c″ have been frequently verified by investigations.

We should also note however that hypothesis 8c is only verified in part, for the rural population only, a population in which the adoption of new practices has been studied intensely. The adoption of new practices and methods ought to be studied in other surroundings in order to permit us to more completely verify hypothesis 8c.[10]

The analysis of research of the kind evoked in this chapter permitted us, in our inquiry in rural Argentina, to study systematically the relations between the perception of change and participaton, as well as the relations between this perception, this participation, and innovation. To this effect, we recorded information that established the existence of change, attitudes toward change and the ability of things to change again, aspirations to change, the inevitability of change, behavior involved in change, and so on.

For each of these points, an attempt was made to specify the appearance of these changes: the individual conceives them, and in the case of behavior, realizes them, at his personal level, or at that of his family, or of the environment in which he lives, or to the contrary, places it in a broader context, at the regional or even national level.

CONCLUSIONS

The analyses retraced here are still very partial due to the fact that interpretation of the work on participation is still in process. In addition, the inquiries combined here are quite different as to their methodologies and as to the types of associationist groupings in which participation was studied. Thus the conclusions that follow are tentative and of a theoretical and practical character.

On the theoretical plane, the construction of a middle-range theory of social participation on the basis of a network or system of logically interconnected hypotheses seems to necessitate the following three tasks.

First, an effort to make more precise the base concepts, particularly that of social change. Besides a conceptual effort this task necessitates at one and the same time historical studies on the process of social change in our industrialized countries and studies on rapid change in countries currently on the development path.

Second, an effort to make explicit the postulate that lies behind the general hypotheses considering participation as behavioral adaptation to change. This task requires particular attention to the other types of participation distinguished above (spontaneous, instigated, and so on), and to the disappearance of traditional models of sociability (point one of the general hypothesis).

Third, an effort of research leads simultaneously to different levels of abstraction. The preceding pages are an effort of generalization from research, and because of that tend to bypass without comment the complexity of different types of associations studied, the incompatibility of certain of them, and so on. Such a level of abstraction cannot be reached without recourse to data collected in innumerable concrete groups—only these very specific data will permit an ulterior generalization. In addition the multiplication of limited observations must be encouraged, including inquiries and monographs on very diverse groups. All these partial materials constitute the raw material necessary for the fabrication of the final theoretical product.

On the practical plane, research on participation can guide animators, the experts in matters of cooperative creation, community development workers, and so on. It can, in particular, permit them to better comprehend the resistance to participation in societies not yet having set their change in motion. The essentials of the analyses to which we have devoted this chapter show that participationist behavior is the prerogative of a rather limited group of individuals (at least in that which concerns active participation), informed, disposing of certain resources, sufficiently distant from traditional sources of prestige to feel the need of new social evaluations, living in heterogeneous environments, and so on. All these factors are, on practical grounds, conditions of success of animation of groups and of associations proposing basic development, local communities or other groups of popular recruitment. To neglect them or to ignore their importance can in the long run lead to the failure of the institutions created and from which, at all levels, much is expected.

NOTES

1. It is necessary to indicate briefly here the problems in gathering research materials in this domain. The studies are numbered in the hundreds, but are not integrated into a common theoretical framework susceptible to reinterpretation or construction of hypotheses for future research. The distinction proposed by Merton seems useful in the characterization of what is needed: a theory of the middle range. (Note shortened—ed.)
2. Albert Meister, *Où va l'autogestion en Yougoslavie?* (Paris: Anthropos, 1970).
3. There were no associations, in the modern sense of the term, in the preindustrial era, though there were groupings that resemble our definition. There were discussions in certain milieux that anticipated industrialization, and it was in these areas that associations would probably be found later on. (Note shortened—ed.)
4. If the hypotheses that follow were to be verified, we might conclude that urbanization without industrialization weakens the traditional structures of sociability, but we would not know whether industrialization is necessary to give the *coup de grâce* to the weakening of these institutions. (Note shortened—ed.)
5. The independence/dependence character (-D, D respectively) of the profession has not been utilized regarding Yugoslav militants. Data nevertheless confirm the role of the other two factors.
6. The bibliography here has been reduced to the minimum. Some of the following references will permit the interested reader to inquire further. Robert E. Lane, *Political Life: Why and How People Get Involved in Politics* (New York: Free Press, 1965); Lester W. Milbrath, *Political Participation* (Chicago: Rand McNally, 1965); Albert Meister, *Participation, animation et développement* (Paris: Anthropos, 1969).
7. Robert K. Merton, *Social Theory and Social Structure* (Glencoe: Free Press, 1951), p. 93.
8. This paragraph was a note in the original. (Ed.)
9. Which is not to say that they were necessarily authoritarian or formal. These three dimensions do not necessarily overlap. Moreover the word *totalitarian* is not employed here in the pejorative sense: it simply indicates the tendency of a group to mold the personalities of its members.
10. Two paragraphs on agricultural innovations omitted here. (Ed.)
11. Meister, p. 112.

5

ORGANIZED AND SPONTANEOUS PARTICIPATION

Research on participation in associations reveals the existence of small groups, and special kinds of participation that often have nothing to do with the goals of the associations and are sometimes even in contradiction with them. Besides what I have called organized participation, we are in the presence of spontaneous participation which, distinct from the first, does not require structured staffs, or operates on the margins of the organizations or sometimes even against the staff. For example, in a residential city our inquiry showed that collective services (child care, group purchases, sewing courses) are often neglected by housewives who prefer to gather with neighbors to render each other the same services on a nonorganized and less formal basis. In work communities[1] there is a similar tendency regarding transmission of information: although special meetings are periodically organized by the officers, a good part of the information members possess comes to them through other channels, especially word of mouth. In the agricultural machinery cooperatives studied in Northern Italy, the peasants preferred to come to mutual agreement for rental of a tractor rather than use the tractor of the cooperative.

These studies have nevertheless not penetrated below the behavioral level of organized participation to analyze informal and spontaneous behavior. The pages which follow have as a goal the discussion of some concepts useful for an analysis at this microsociological level.[2] I will first examine some aspects of the structure and functioning of small groups, which is where this behavior occurs, then some problems bearing on leadership of small groups. Then I will turn to the position of small autonomous groups that constitute themselves in the midst of large associations, and the facts relative to their evolution and transformation into more formal structures. It will then be possible to analyze some of the transformations in the global society and their implications for small groups, and to inquire as to the social significance of research in this domain and the extension of these findings to practice and action.

THE CHARACTER OF SMALL GROUPS

The characteristics of small groups have been arranged under the following rubrics: recruitment, needs whose satisfaction is sought in the group, interpersonal relations in the group, contacts of the group with similar groups, and social functions of small groups.

Recruitment

Let us begin with the autonomy present in the creation of these groups. They are independent of formal associations and do not owe their origin or influence over their members to an institution of the global society. No affiliation defines or unites them to the activities of other groups; they fear the intrusion of formal groups, ignore their programs of activities, and eventually organize their own even when they find themselves mixed in with some association activity. Small groups have low visibility, reduced size, and establish themselves below visible social configurations. By contrast to organized secondary groups, they are primary and have person to person contacts.

The degree of autonomy in relation to other groups varies from one small group to another, and has been retained here as a criterion of differentiation. This criterion does not, nevertheless, establish the authoritarian or democratic character of the small group. Created by the members themselves and autonomous as to resources, these groups show a certain scorn for animators who can impose a formal structure to aid them in accomplishing their objectives, such as social assistance to a group of mothers.

Even when created by a large organization with the deliberate end of realizing its own program and extending its recruitment, the small group can sometimes maintain its autonomy and detachment. A certain degree of autonomy subsists to the extent that members remain free to recruit or refuse new members, define the goals of the group, its politics, and program of activities. When an animator comes from outside and does not show himself to be too authoritarian, he is accepted by the group members. These conditions are perhaps difficult to realize, and what follows is more applicable to entirely autonomous groups.

Although in organized groups members belong because of the activities of the groups and become linked with the association through contractual obligations, small groups do not offer such criteria of affiliation and do not rest on such obligations, but much more on interpersonal affinities. The affinity between people who know each other and the agreement to meet together constitutes the motive for creation and often the unique function of the small group. The common activities which can be born from these contacts are considered only an additional value. The degree of pleasure members have in meeting has even been proposed as a criterion of differentiation of groups.

Affinity equally determines recruitment of new members. Those who enter the group are already tied to one or more members and are known by the majority of members. There is no formal principle of membership, but little by little the new member comes to be accepted or rejected. It is the group reaction that finally determines the member's status. Affinity in recruitment leads to groups that are homogeneous as to tastes and aspirations, or socioprofessional or sociocultural points of view.[3] Degree of homogeneity and permeability or access (open or closed group) have been retained as criteria of group differentiation. The minor role of activities in the small group, and in the case in which activities exist, the major degree of improvisation in their production tends to exclude a deliberate recruitment of new members to ensure continuity. These personal criteria of adhesion emphasize member interaction rather than group function. The old proverb "a man is known by the company he keeps" describes well these affinity groups, born of spontaneous choice, resting on emotional expression, and existing covertly beneath visible social configurations.

According to certain authors, particularly those influenced by sociometry, combinations of attraction and repulsion explain part of the favor bestowed on small groups, and also their spontaneous modes of cooperation. By rejecting incompatibles, members come to feel more at ease in informal small groups than in organized groups. The small group forms around the personality rather than on the basis of common interests, and even if the common activities do unite the members, they can better take advantage of their opportunities than in the organized group.

Members' Needs

What are the needs that members desire to see satisfied through belonging to small groups? There is agreement among authors in placing the need for psychological security and emotional stability at the head of the list. The common patterns of rejection and attraction found in cliques tie members together. They find there their most intimate relations during periods of leisure and recreation. Small groups also aid the individual: (1) maintain his feeling of independence, personal integrity, and self-respect; (2) reinforce his personal opinions; and (3) recover his sense of wholeness, put into doubt by the segmentation of formal organizations.

> The function of the small group is that of a mediating mechanism by means of which the individual selects all the experiences he finds significant and

> through which he finds models of acceptable response through the persons he considers important. At the same time the small group aids him in building the image he has of himself.[4]

The individual finds in the small group the support needed for psychological security and emotional stability. These groups become reference groups whose values are accepted and serve as guides for behavior within and without the group. This explains the considerable role attributed to them since the very first studies of small groups, a decisive role second only to that of the family as an indicator of social position in more inclusive groupings. We will see further on the nature of the linkages between small groups and their social contexts.

The motivations of individuals and their attachments to small groups depend on the very free atmosphere that reigns there. Social censure there is at its minimum and almost everything said there is under the seal of confidentiality. The individual must not formulate there any hard and fast position that can tie him down and he remains free to modify his point of view at another time. Even so, there is pressure by others to change his attitudes, and the opinions of the individual may become weak. The individual is accepted in the small group just as he is, totally, recognized and approved as a person, independent of the specialties and capacities he deploys in formal groups.

If the small group permits a freer expression of the total personality of the individual, the latter also feels the need to be associated on more fragmentary bases and in particular for the chance to exercise his qualifications and talents in groups with organized activities. In this sense belonging to small groups and to organized groups are complementary. The two types of belonging and the two orders of satisfaction they procure are necessary to individual fulfillment.

Relations among Members

The principle posed by Kurt Lewin, that the group is a system which is modified, reinforced, or weakened as the result of change in one of its elements, applies above all to the small groups in which interaction among members constitutes the totality of the group.[5] It is in the context of these immediate interpersonal relations that individual behavior must be studied. Three types of interaction have been distinguished.

1. Accidental interaction, by chance of amicable or hostile nature. This interaction recalls the mass type of Gurvitch, sociability that only affects superficial manifestations of individuals present, "while that which they have that is more or less profound and personal remains hidden." In sociometric terms, the isolates, the marginals, would be the individuals who limit their contacts to such fortuitous interaction. More intimate

interaction can be born of repeated accidental interaction and it is very difficult to know at what moment interaction is accompanied by group sentiment. On the operational level this passage to another more intimate type of sociability could be defined by the periodicity and regularity of contacts between members; perhaps at the moment at which they refuse to change their meeting time a group may be said to exist.

2. Associative interaction that is informal and voluntary; the cliques, triangles and squares of the sociometrists. This interaction embraces all the activities of life. It endures beyond simple fortuitous contacts and is personal, direct, and dynamic. Its outcome is a fundamental modification of the personalities of group members. The degree to which members know each other can serve as a criterion of differentiation of informal groups of this type. Other criteria can be the degree of loyalty to the group and the degree of consciousness that members have of the group and its goals.[6]

3. Interaction of the communion type, in which members are tied by bonds of friendship and enthusiasm. It occurs in autonomous groups. This type corresponds to Gurvitch's sociability as "communion," in which fusion and integration attain maximum intensity, "when the Me and the Other meet and interpenetrate to the limit and their less accessible depths find themselves included in the participation of the whole."

It is interaction of the second type, associative and informal, that we will have in mind in the pages that follow. Interaction in small groups is a matter of mutually agreeable choice, but sometimes it is nonexplicit and nonconscious. Mutual aid, if it exists, is spontaneous. Relations comprise all those little things in life "which are such a part of our lives that they appear to us subjectively to be our lives themselves." This affinity colors all these relations, and takes on great importance for the individual, especially when the group does not have explicit goals. These characteristics have led certain authors to speak of these groups as natural, by opposition to interest groups that have been deliberately constituted in order to achieve a goal.

Leadership is acutely aware of or even resents the informality of the group and the liberty that individuals in it have to determine their own roles and manner of participation. Leadership may not fall to any single member, but be divided among all members in turn. Even if the group forms around a strong personality, it is probable that his authority will be so colored by the affinity that there will be no problems of acceptance by members. We will return to this point. Cohesion is another criterion of differentiation of this type of group. Cohesion may be defined as the overall feelings of belonging and identity with a group on the part of its members.

Activities of Small Groups

Although the small groups studied to this point crystallize neighborhood or occupational customs and remain without determined goals, an active sociability is manifest when there is common work to accomplish. This activity appears to vary as a function of the occupational status of members. Small groups composed of individuals of high occupational status are oriented toward leisure activities and activities directed toward the outside (civic or social work for example), while working-class groups turn more toward mixed activities, including leisure, security, and savings (gambling, vacation funds, sickness provisions, and so on). The growth of the group results from its activity. Certain activities for which fees are required (rental of quarters, for example) lead to recruitment of new members to lighten the burden. In turn the recruitment of members tends to ensure the continuity of the group. Growth is a consequence, longevity a result.

The activities of these small groups is often multifunctional, a mixture between affinity of members and goals to be attained. This is the case with innumerable informal leisure clubs. Other small groups, perhaps the majority, remain more nearly unifunctional, without precise activity, with no other goal than the pleasure members find in one another's company. In such groups conversation, the exchange of ideas and commentaries remain the essential element. In time such exchanges can lead to some common activity.

The Size of Small Groups

We have just seen that the activity of small groups is directly tied to their growth and duration. In such active groups there is a risk that the size may increase rapidly and impose transformations on the group. We will study this later on. The remarks that follow concern small groups resting on personal and intimate contacts of members, and whose interaction constitutes their sole goal. The intimacy of the group reduces its dimensions and there is perhaps a limit to its size which permits a maximum of differentiation of personalities and opinions while still maintaining cohesion among members. According to sociometric research, one person could not be in an emotional relation with more than a dozen others, and this number would constitute the approximate maximum size of a "psychegroup" (as it is called by sociometrists).

It is difficult to define what constitutes membership in such an informal group, and the customary use of size to describe a group focuses simply on individuals who perceive themselves to be members. This definition refers only to those with mutual relationships and leaves aside those who hang on to the group or gravitate to it but are not reciprocally linked to other members. This definition is more suited to associative interaction and communion than to casual interaction.

Many personal interactions are very fluctuating, diversified, and spontaneous, at the threshold of consciousness, and thus may pass through the large mesh of our net. Our research instruments are too crude to detect them. Gurvitch's penetrating analysis of forms of sociability shows well the poverty of our instruments of research. Even sociometric instruments furnish us only a cross-section, a photograph, at a level where only a moving picture would be adequate.[7]

Estimates of group size may be valid only for stable small groups, at the moment when group members already realize that they constitute a group, when they can sketch its approximate contours, or at the eventual moment when the question of new members is brought up and the group must be limited to prevent formation of cliques.[8]

Contacts between Small Groups

Communication in small groups is between persons or between pairs. Each individual exercises a certain discrimination in reception and acceptance of information and a certain selectivity in the transmission of information. The scope of these "psychological networks" varies and certain of them are effectively endless and cover broad areas (including telephone and written communications). The length of the net varies according to the nature of the communication (certain rumors are communicated at great distances) and the prestige of sources.

Through each individual member a group is connected to several nets. Rumors, information, influence, prestige, new ideas, and witticisms which flow in each small group constitute the necessary content for contacts among members, the nourishment of their discussions, and the point of departure for elaboration of new information. These psychological networks contribute to give a certain unity of tastes and aspirations to numerous small groups. They have even been called the "crucible of public opinion," for they can be responsible for the forging of thought and judgements into mores and customs.[9]

We do not know what lines of stratification organize the networks and before what frontiers (of class, race, religion, etc.) the nets stop or penetrate too partially to determine this homogeneity of tastes and aspirations for which we would like to hold them responsible. The contacts nets render possible may be limited to small groups of the same organization, such as a large business, a union, or perhaps the same social stratum. When small groups exercise pressure on their members to confine themselves to that one group and oppose membership in all others, as is sometimes the case with adolescent groups, the role of discussion place and crossroads that has been attributed to them is not fulfilled.

When small groups demand only partial adhesion, tolerate other memberships, do not dread role conflicts among members who adhere to groups with contrary values, do not claim any exclusiveness due to social origin of members—when these conditions are realized, small groups can really be places of discussion of the activities of other small groups and organized groups of which their members are a part. In addition, they can even play a role of facilitator of contacts, of coordination, of unification among diverse formal groups. Under these conditions, the members of a small group are able to learn, explore, appreciate what is done in groups represented by those with double membership.

They are alerted to changes and new ideas in other groups and in turn bring these ideas to their own formal group. The relaxed atmosphere of the small group offers optimal conditions for inspiring confidence in interlocutors: discussions are free and information is reciprocal. Thanks to these exchanges, the ideas individuals bring to their formal associations make these small groups authentic means of social change. This is why they have been called ventilation systems between the locality groups (the commune, the district) and its institutions.

The fact that these small groups may sometimes turn inward and sometimes open outward to social changes does not permit attributing to them a particular social value. All the same, their openness and the transmission of social change does not prejudice the quality of change that takes place in this manner. These changes can be progressive or reactionary, democratic or authoritarian, in the direction of social change or opposed to it, and small groups certainly hold no monopoly on social progress or democracy. In the sense that we have considered them here, they are vehicles of information, but vehicles that transport almost any quality of information. It is this problem of the social function of small groups that we shall examine now.

Social Function of Small Groups

As has just been seen, it is necessary to take care to establish a hierarchy in types of groups according to value judgements on what is socially desirable or not. In this sense the characteristics described are neutral and the autonomy of small groups does not guarantee democratic objectives or functioning. Even so, the free atmosphere that reigns in small groups can serve individuals to better appreciate and understand each other, but can also lead to violence against outsiders or pressures against members of the group itself that range from mockery to oppression.

Informal, natural, spontaneous groups probably have no superiority over the rational, utilitarian, and deliberately created groups organized to attain precise objectives. If informal small groups (accidental, associative, communion, psychological networks) seem to be the elementary tissue of society and are very often responsible for the creation and endurance of certain formal organizations, it does not follow that the first are superior to the second. The relation between the small group and the organization is, on the contrary, highly symbiotic.

Studies done in large housing projects have shown the weight of ecological factors in the recruitment and functioning of small groups. The influence of proximity factors has been demonstrated. The same sort of results come from studies of small autonomous groups of juvenile delinquents, studied in reference to the character and appeals of the sociocultural environment and the needs for social ascent of lower-class youths. In such surroundings juvenile gangs have the function of opening possibilities to their members for attaining higher social status by means other than those reserved for the less favored social strata.

Other research has shown the preference of families in a working-class environment for spontaneous association in small informal groups to the detriment of formal participation in large associations. These studies show the dependence of these families on their immediate neighborhood. From such links as these, families find the means to sustain themselves in the face of economic and psychological pressures the outside world exerts on them. As has already been seen, the family, like the individual, finds in these psychegroups satisfactions and fulfillment that adhesion to formal groups does not provide. Research shows the function of informal clubs in the formation of social attitudes of young people, including the development of morality in these interpersonal relations.

These examples demonstrate the weight of the environmental factor on small groups, and show that their connections with other groups and the ecological context must be known to comprehend them scientifically. Conversely, the examples that follow show the influence small groups can exert on their own circles. The importance of small groups as centers in which decisions are taken has been shown. This function of small groups seems particularly important in the determination of political behavior, when individuals are made the object of contradictory pressures from diverse formal groupings. This model concerning decision making in the small group has subsequently been extended to the study of attitudes and models of consumption.

I have shown how information is easily transmitted to individuals in small groups in which the person is at ease, does not have to make an effort to listen to an outside lecturer, where he can ask questions without fear that they will be badly received or that he will be laughed at, or that everyone will speak at the same time, but in which information is transmitted and opinions are formed all the same. The small group is "a basic social mechanism to form public opinion, control local rumors, engender social pressure, transmit news, and develop leadership." It has also been said that the influence of personal contact in groups is fundamental in the formation of social nature and individual ideals.

The social control exercised by small groups was already mentioned. In addition certain studies have shown the correlation between the prestige conferred by these groups and the factors that comprise occupational status. So strong is the relation that a group composed of persons of high prestige actively supporting a certain position can play a role of the greatest importance in accomplishing a collective decision on a local problem.

Innovators must form their own small groups, for formal organizations (themselves old small groups that have gradually crystallized) are often rebellious toward change. Small groups of innovators permit communication among members, correction and validation of points of view. But the isolated innovator or the individual who has too much imagination risks rejection by small groups when the values of the global society are conservative. We lack facts in this domain and studies are needed on the various degrees of adhesion of small groups to established modes of behavior.[10]

LEADERSHIP IN SMALL GROUPS

Leadership does not seem to be very important in small groups. Groups of custom rather than of activities, they display neither a division of labor, explicit rules, prescribed roles, nor recognition by society of a mission or function. These facts do not favor a specific leadership, and members can share the position. These groups also suppose a certain equality among members to which homogeneity of recruitment contributes: if one of the group feels a strong sense of inferiority or perhaps superiority, he withdraws; if inequalities persist, the free climate of the group tends to minimize them, for the existence of superiors and inferiors in the same group limit interaction among members.

It does not follow that small groups are privileged reservoirs of friendship and that tenacious hatreds cannot take root. The latter lead to schisms rather than to development of an authoritarian leadership. It does not follow that small groups are especially democratic but that the superiority of one of the members is recognized and generally accepted, consciously or not, and his orders do not provoke revolt among the others. It is even true that "with certain types of personalities or certain types of situations (tasks to do or threats to meet) the solidarity of the primary group can be disintegrated through democratic leadership." Three types of leadership have been distinguished that correspond to the three types of small groups indicated above.

1. Ephemeral leadership, corresponding to accidentally formed small groups (such as in case of danger, for example).

2. Leadership chosen spontaneously by members of small associative groups. The leader contributes to maintenance of system equilibrium. He is not very apparent, due to the fact that members are not assumed to have to fall into line on an issue and do not submit to any pressure to arrive at conclusions or concerted actions. Such leadership is not often chosen consciously, and the leader is not always aware of his position. He is not necessarily democratic, and the members sometimes want an authoritarian leader, even when their psychological liberty remains intact and they do not experience any constraint. Those who do not feel at ease and do not support dependence on the leader, leave the group.

3. Leadership corresponding to the psychological networks and resulting from judgements that proceed through the chains and create positions of prestige. Here also individuals occupying diverse points in the net cannot be conscious of the leadership exercised by one of them.

These types of leadership correspond only to very small groups, for the more the size increases the more marked the role of the leader becomes. Later on we will take up the matter of the evolution of the small group within the organized group, and we have already noted how the small group is created within the formal group.

DEVELOPMENT OF SMALL GROUPS WITHIN FORMAL GROUPS

We shall begin with the study of small groups born to satisfy certain needs left unsatisfied by formal groups. First we shall examine some characteristics of formal groups, then some aspects of groups created within them.

A Typology of Groups

The differences between small groups and formal groups drawn from research may be arranged as a typology. Although persons perceive themselves as individuals in small groups, in a formal association individuals see themselves as filling determined functions. In large organizations there is an effort to depersonalize contacts between individuals and replace them with contacts between functions. In small groups activities constitute goals in themselves and directly serve the satisfaction of members; in the formal group activities constitute the means to realize certain ends not necessarily tied to the satisfaction of members of the group, or only to that of one party. In the small group expressions of reason and emotion are relatively free, spontaneous, noncontrolled; in the formal group reason and emotion are channeled in view of obtaining prefixed objectives.

Cooperation in small groups is in part implicit and eventual activities are largely coordinated spontaneously. In formal groups cooperation is conscious, organized, and coordinated in view of goals to be obtained, and individuals are conscious of the roles they must play. Cooperation in small groups does not rest on specialization, while the formal group develops precise specialization of activities that are very different from one another. Participation in small groups does not restrain freedom very much; in formal groups modes of participation are prefixed.

Each small group in time develops a number of customary rules and rituals. This is also true in the formal group, but rules and rites there tend to become obligatory and codified, and in addition there can exist an awareness of the need to develop a personality appropriate to the group with the aim of reducing tensions within and presenting a favorable image to the outside. The small group remains a system of private and unapparent relations, while relations in the formal group, through its activities and function in society are more apparent, open, and public.

Although in the small group the leadership is not very apparent and falls to those present, in the formal group leaders are very apparent, draw their authority from a delegation of power much more than from their acceptance by subordinates, are part of a hierarchy, and exercise their power in very limited sectors corresponding to their specialization. If the small group sees regroupings among its members according to mutual attractions, the subgroups that constitute themselves in formal groups are, on the contrary, means of attaining prefixed goals and the division into subgroups is born of the imperatives of the activity.

These several differences between formal and informal groups are matters of degree, and the ultrarational character assigned to the formal group may be only apparent. Such is the case of noneconomic motives that sometimes seem as important as the strictly economic ones. All these criteria of differences must be made the object of precise evaluation in each concrete case. But it remains true that the personalities of these groups and their performances are very different. The individuals who make up formal groups, where "persons become personnel," in which functions take precedence over individuals, cannot avoid psychic tensions and the necessity to struggle against them by the formation of small informal groups. The small groups appear, then, as reactions against rationalization and the depersonalization of the formal group.

The more authoritarian and depersonalized these groups are, the more the risk that there will be born within them small friendship groupings, coteries, cliques.[11] The army seems to represent such a type of group, and it is not surprising that the friendships and solidarity born among soldiers may be the most durable and best resist the ultimate changes and separations of civilian life.

Small Groups within Formal Groups

Several functions of small groups have been recognized that lead to adaptation of individuals to formal organizations. They permit the communication of certain information that does not appear in official documents, but which is of prime importance for the adaptation of individuals to the formal group. In the small group they learn to know how things really are, the why of things, who is in and who is out of power, and all those little things that it is necessary to know in order to accept certain models of conduct and to be accepted by other people.

They provide a certain emotional stability, compensating for restrictions and frustrations of formal systems, molding certain kinds of behavior according to prescribed models. Small groups can cooperate in the maintenance of cohesion and authority in the formal group. In this sense their action is regulative and they aid the formal group to better take account of individual needs. But small groups can resist and take a defensive attitude, ally themselves with other small groups, and as in businesses, gradually organize their resistance through a union. Or they can break up or retire from the formal group (as in the case of schisms), or still another option, retreat into the small group itself.

While small groups are born of the need of individuals to adapt to an impersonal organization, a defective organization can also create them. For example, when it is necessary for individuals to handle situations with ambiguous or contradictory rules, or rules that are impossible to follow, as is the case in certain administrative services in which the task of the employee is impossible if the rules are followed, the small group allows workers to come to a private understanding among themselves. If a superior exercises his role poorly, the discontentment of subordinates can lead them to regroup informally. When a new position is created in an organization and impinges on existing functions assured to other members, an informal resistance group may be formed: the fear and anxiety linked to the appearance of a new position in the group produces a sudden cohesion to protect and safeguard the small group against what seems like an enemy attack. When in an association the gap is widened between the ideal which the group was created to defend and the daily practice that tends to produce the gap, the small groups of dissatisfied members can take precedence over factions and prevent future schisms.

And as recent research in an industrial milieu has shown, the small group can become a counterpower, "having for an objective the reconquest of the power to organize production against the organizational system judged incapable of rationally and efficaciously developing that production." Such a counterpower is manifest sometimes through a slowdown, sometimes through strikes, by hostile attitudes to the command system, and so on. In brief, it is a source of opposition to the power in place.[12]

The variety of situations favorable to the emergence of small groups can easily be imagined. These several examples concern businesses rather than other types of formal groups. But locality groups are equally favorable to the hatching of small groups: a district or a commune are complexes of informal and formal groups in which belonging and loyalty overlap and intertwine. Even in the anonymity of urban life, small groups provide the satisfactions of friendship to individuals, that add themselves to satisfactions that originate from professional competition or which compensate for the failures derived from competition.

EVOLUTION OF SMALL GROUPS

Several authors have produced evidence on the evolution of small groups. Some consider small groups points of departure for all organizations and social institutions. The endless creation of small groups in the midst of formal groups has also been insisted upon: "The formation of natural groups, or of cliques, or of some other name that they may be given, is the natural result of the dynamics of adjustment of the personality, of the need of the individual to realize an emotional stability and satisfying relations with his comrades." In businesses these small groups gradually take on a defensive attitude and form a union. But the union, in growing, discovers the same problems as the business and finds itself prey to conflicts engendered by the formation of new groups.

Following this point of view, everything happens as if formal groups begin through small groups which, having gradually acquired a certain stability and prestige, become institutions. Even small groups of the communion type are transformed: fraternities and sects constitute small groups at the time of origin and will become formal groups in the term of their development. The sociometrist Moreno seems to share this idea when he writes in relation to psychological networks that "the older and the more mature a society, the more the network becomes a super-organization of control."

An original example of such a process of formalization and institutionalization is found in the history of the coffee houses created in England at the start of the popularity of coffee in the 1650s and that became veritable institutions. A somewhat similar evolution has been claimed in the French communities of work where some of the cooperatives have attained a high degree of organization (in terms of industrial production) and have reached a certain rigidity in their functioning. These groups were generally formed in the beginning by little teams of workers.

The passage from informal group to organized group has been made the object of research on informal groups in a district of New York City. The author shows that groups pass through three phases: the collection of individuals, the customary group, the interest group. The collection of individuals corresponds to the accidental interactions of which we have already spoken. At this stage the encounters between members are purely fortuitous and they perceive no special relations among them. Among the factors responsible for the origin of such occasional groups, we can cite proximity, exterior circumstances that lead the individuals to find one another again on a basis of proximity, security sought in the company of others, and personal attraction among individuals.

Research on the sociology of the neighborhood has likewise shown the importance of contacts among families produced by their children. The children constitute the common base on which the relations between families can be established, and to a certain degree, the diversity of contacts of the children could have repercussions on the relations among families themselves. The survival of such accidental interaction and its transformation into a more durable informal group depends on the frequency of external circumstances that bring the individuals together, and the degree of attraction between them.

In the second stage, in small customary groups the members perceive a specific relation between them, but this relation is not yet perceived as a permanent collective goal. At the same time, they commence to attach a certain importance to the quality of recruitment and tend to fix criteria of membership for new members. At this stage there is a marked tendency toward limitation of size by agreement among beginning members; in the groups studied in New York this size varied between ten and fifteen persons. This figure recalls the number of twelve suggested by the sociologists who studied psychegroups.

At this stage organization is almost nonexistent, and is limited to fixing the time and place of meetings and to discussion of the criteria of recruitment. Activities, which are often limited to conversation or simply being together or to routine distractions, do not demand organization or differentiated roles among members.

Meanwhile, more specific activities gradually appear and are responsible for certain modifications in the group. The changes seem to be linked in particular to the occupational status of members, the age of the group, members' affiliations to formal groups, and their previous experience in these groups. The circle of relations of the group expands, the relations between it and other informal groups becomes more intricate, and then relations with organized groups appears. These relations are based upon activities that are less and less centered on the members, are more and more open and of more general importance than the simple satisfaction of the need to be together that is a characteristic of the original group. These new activities also mark the beginning of a certain organization and of the creation of positions that are more or less official.

The passage from the customary group to the common interest group comes about under the following conditions.

- There is dissatisfaction of one or more members with the organization of meetings of the group.
- An unaccustomed experience or frustration forces a change in routines.
- There is a new member who has a new experience to offer old members.
- A suggestion is made by a nonmember concerning a possible goal for the group.
- There is a reaction by members to a new idea or an activity of an outside group common to members.
- There is a discovery of a specific common interest that is chosen as a group goal.

At the third stage the small group gradually becomes an interest group in which the members recognize that a specific relation unites them, and follow an explicitly formulated common goal or an implicitly included and accepted goal. Criteria for recruitment are defined and distinct roles are reserved to certain people. Even if they are tied to formal groups, these small groups conserve a great autonomy and in spite of a certain organization (such as the election of officers, dues, written statutes) they keep, from long established customs that the members have discovered for themselves, a tone of informality in their contacts.

Nevertheless, at this stage the small group become interest group is scarcely distinguishable from the formal group. The processes of formalization and of bureaucratization, against which they must struggle, are responsible for their ever-threatening rigidity. We will not consider these phenomena here; the comparisions between small groups and formal groups made above are sufficiently similar.

It remains to consider some factors in the disappearance of small groups. Among them we may note geographic and occupational mobility factors, such as changes of occupation, of residential area, of post in a factory, and so on. Vertical mobility must also be considered. It tends to show that belonging to a group constitutes a stage in social ascent, for one frequently has different friends at each rung of the social ladder—both going up and going down. In youth clubs, engagements and marriages are sources of dissolution. In small groups that bring families together, new contacts by children as they grow up create new contacts for parents, dissolving some groups and forming others.

Other reasons for dissolution concern activities and the sociability of the group itself. The affinity or friendships on which interaction is based can also be responsible for dissolution: if it dies away, or to the contrary, if it takes precedence over the goals of the group and leads to association by pairs, the small group disappears.

Finally, the inclusion of a small group within a formal group or the development of a formal group from one does not deny its existence as a small group. Such seems to be the case with small groups which pursue social reform objectives and that gradually become the seed of organized groups.

TRANSFORMATIONS IN THE GLOBAL SOCIETY AND THE ROLE OF SMALL GROUPS

The rationalization of modern life, the functionalization and growth of competition in interpersonal relations on the one hand lead individuals to multiple memberships in formal and unifunctional associations, and on the other hand, to the formation of nonformal small groups because of the need for camaraderie and affinity that neither their professional relations nor their memberships in associations can satisfy. The diverse terms of this hypothesis must be made explicit.

It begins from the fact of the bureaucratization of formal groups, which leaves only few possibilities to members to knit relations of camaraderie and to express themselves as persons—and meanwhile associations remark that their assemblies are frequented exactly because of these needs. The success of the common meal that follows their general assemblies must be explained thus. In the same manner, unions, mutual associations and cooperatives become institutions dispensing services such as defense, allocation, and economic benefits, but in which members do not find themselves meeting others on a more personal level. There is then a risk that the natural need for association may not be satisfied in such groups, where belonging brings material advantages but not a rich enough substance for needs of a more emotional character.

In addition, the specialization of formal groups has repercussions on the small groups that constitute themselves in them. They differentiate themselves more and more according to hierarchical and functional structures of the formal group, borrowing technical jargon from this milieu, and not being able to provide the cohesion and unifying force that is sometimes attributed to them. In these conditions, formal groups impose their own coloration on small groups and appear less dependent on them than might be assumed.

In addition, the dynamism of formal groups is stronger than that of small groups which might be cornered in the innermost recesses of the organization or caught in defensive positions.[13] Thus apathy in associations often appears to be a type of response to official programs from on high. In other words, cooperation, or the stimulated participation that formal associations seek is opposed to the spontaneous cooperation of autonomous small groups. The case of juvenile gangs seems to reveal the inadequacy of programs of education, leisure, and so on, of the associations and institutions that the gangs oppose.

The segmentation of activity, the unifunctionality of formal groups—and particularly that of the associations—forces the individuals into multiple and sometimes contradictory memberships. The small groups in which the person participates can in addition resent these identifications and multiple external loyalties. Finally, the formal groups have very often ceased to be closely related groups with frequent interpersonal contacts, and communications between members take written form such as newspapers, notices, bulletins, written orders, and so on, and conversation is replaced by the statement or the conference. Outside these groups, mass means of diffusion take a greater place and even leisure may not provide interpersonal contacts. The influence of small groups is then reduced and they find it even more difficult to exercise their regulative function in formal groups and concentrate on activities that have no larger significance than the simple pleasure that their members have in meeting.

Several sociologists and numerous observers of advanced industrial societies have denounced these transformations in formal groups, the psychological insecurity and individual solitude, the loss of belonging to a community. Their works show that the individual seeks more and more to escape the liberty of impersonality, of secularization and individualism, and attempts to recreate a community in the small autonomous groups very close to concrete and personal needs ignored by formal groups and society in general.

The more ordered and planned societies toward which it appears that our industrial societies are orienting themselves will perhaps see these tendencies accentuated. It is this point of view that is necessary to discuss next. An article by Robert Nisbet can usefully introduce this discussion.[14] The author describes there the military society: a society that is necessarily paternalistic since a single goal, maximum efficiency in the destruction of the enemy, precedes all others and all that oppose it must be swept aside; nothing is left to free choice of the individual and all life is clearly regulated. To the contrary of civil life, the myth of personal responsibility is replaced by the supposition of personal irresponsibility in all matters not covered by explicit orders. Activities of the soldier that can interfere with his warrior efficiency are abolished. Everything that concerns him—food, clothing, lodging—is regulated without his knowledge, in such a fashion that they cause him no anxiety nor involve any responsibility. He unconsciously comes to take them for granted and tends to avoid all curiosity regarding them, curiosity that could lead to free initiatives and confusion. Outside the army, everything is arranged so that his family does not suffer financially from his absence and so that he is not distracted from his military tasks.

The military universe is unified. It offers, what is more, much that civilian life lacks, a sense of belonging. Each one knows his role and the modes of relations with others. In this sense military life recreates the conditions of belonging and responds thus to one of the most disconcerting problems of modern life. The army and war have created very stong sentiments of camaraderie and a sense of group identification which are in striking contrast to the anonymity of modern life, especially in the urban milieu. Many of the impulsions to association that modern civil life represses by its radical egoism are highly appreciated there.

According to Nisbet, something of this spirit, which existed in Europe at the time of the guilds and corporations, and which invaded all the spheres of life, has invaded the consciousness of the soldier during wartime. The military is moreover similar to the medieval hierarchy, and the army, like medieval society, is a community of communities. Privileges and responsibilities are directly functions of the group to which the individual belongs. The principle of inequality between classes is compensated by the rigid equality within each class. The standardization of uniforms is the symbol of identity of individual lives and reflects the solidarity of the groups in which the soldiers live. If to that is added the common dangers, the sense of belonging to a group is the most developed sense of the soldier. And the only moral product of the war is perhaps this sense of belonging and camaraderie. Nisbet even goes so far as to write that the motivations to combat on the part of the soldier are not derived from his perceptions of strategic and political goals of the conflict, but are a function of his need to protect his primary group and to conform to what the group expects of him.

If the formal groups of civil life become gradually more rigid, the role of small groups as refuges for sociability and the need for camaraderie will go on increasing. If all the aspects of the life of the individual are regulated for him by overorganized groups such as work, leisure, culture, housing, security, and so on, whose functioning might be upset by any initiative on his part, and on which his influence would be minuscule, only small groups could satisfy his need for belonging and friendship and aid him to manifest his eventual opposition or his apathy regarding this overorganization.

In this regard, dictatorial societies or authoritarian or totalitarian enclaves in our more free societies favor the emergence of small groups exactly because of their hostility to the free development of associations or to the belonging of individuals to nonrecognized groups. In combatting regroupings other than those that are beneficiaries of its support and in which it wants to enroll the individuals who depend on it, the strong power encourages the creation of small autonomous groups, more or less hostile to it. And these small groups are willing to risk finding a soil more favorable to their development in such a situation of opposition than that in which they share official values.

The accent placed on the small groups as much in social research as by reformers and social workers can be considered as a reaction against overorganization, giantism, rigidity of groups, associations and contemporary institutions. The liberty of associations itself engenders private sovereignties and personal power against which these associations often propose to struggle. Nisbet even speaks of the "formidable restrictions on the rights of the individual and of equality between individuals" because of the liberty of the associations. Their power even surpasses that of the public organisms and they exercise it in a more insidious fashion. "If you want," he says, "to rid your neighborhood of Jews, it is easier to do it as president of the local association than as mayor."

These private sovereignties are manifest in neighborhoods as well as in businesses or in the defense of workers, and all threaten equality between individuals. A total liberty of associations, then, may lead to serious limitations of individual liberty, the social order of associations being exercized to the detriment of the legal order.

Nevertheless these considerations do not signify that small groups are invested with moral superiority by comparison to organized groups. One cannot, for example, subscribe to Nisbet's view that there be a restructuring of formal groups on the basis of small groups: "It is only when industries and unions are constructed to take account of these personal contact groups, and when the articulation, at all levels, of the elements of organizational structure procures effective possibilities of action for individuals and groups who are part of it, that one can expect industrial peace and political stability."

This is going too far with the importance accorded to small groups, and pushing to the extreme the idealistic postulate which says that individuals who are in interpersonal relationships have more harmonious rapport, and according to which the multiplicity of contacts aids in a better reciprocal understanding.

Borne away by their denunciation of the difficulties of participation in associations and bureaucratized and hyperformalized groups, certain researchers (especially in the United States, since these questions have been posed there earlier than in our European countries), have been led to underestimate, and sometimes to even ignore the conservative and even reactionary roles of many of these autonomous groups developing themselves in a strictly homogeneous racial and class environment. Based on affinity and compatibility, many of these groups maintain and reinforce the barriers between individuals and do nothing to struggle against the social barriers that are erected against certain categories of people with whom their members are in daily relationship, as frequent and as routine as those with members of the group. In this regard, racial discrimination can offer numerous examples of such groups. On the other hand it seems that the role of small groups in the functioning of democracy has been exaggerated. Beside the autonomous small groups resolutely engaged in a work of social reform, of cultural, religious, or civic enrichment, how many small groups turn in on themselves and serve only the individual needs of the members of the group?

The real importance of formal structures seems to have often been underestimated in favor of the regulative role of small groups that members form within formal groups. It is thus that the actual cohesion of a factory or of an administration has until now rested, in spite of an eventual concern for human relations, much more on tables of organization and positions defining zones of authority than on the regulative action by small groups on interpersonal relations between members. It is thus, too, that the authoritarian or the democratic tendencies of a formal group (of a factory, by contrast to an association, for example) have repercussions on the sociability of the small groups that make it up, and which see their role and their influence very differently from one group to the next.

PRACTICAL IMPLICATIONS OF RESEARCH ON SMALL AUTONOMOUS GROUPS

The leaders of large social work associations, unions, and communitarian development projects often regard autonomous small groups with disdain; their spontaneity and their intimacy appear frivolous and insignificant. Their role in social cohesion is underestimated, their comradeship is laughed at, their card games and petty gambling scorned. We have, nevertheless seen above that from a base in such activities that general social information circulates and that the groups have a certain influence in the formation of opinions and attitudes of their members. We also know that the programs of formal associations (for leisure, popular culture, political information) directly touch only a minority of the population and that the average adults and adolescents find their social activities in groups completely separated from these formal groups.

Big associations generally ignore these small groups, fixing programs of activities and recruiting personnel to attain their objectives. A few difficulties born from this simplistic approach may be mentioned. Small groups are formed around the personalities of their members rather than around interests or programs of action; and the programs of formal groups which make an appeal to interests have often little chance to be received and accepted by the small groups.

The programs of associations generally address themselves to individuals in isolation and not in their relation with the small groups, or to the small groups as such. The individual often prefers to abstain if adhesion to these programs signifies his dissociation or breaking solidarity with his group.

Small groups are autonomous and prefer to develop their own programs of work rather than follow those designed for them by the associations, of which they can modify only the details. One community development specialist goes so far as to write that "to the extent that the development agencies direct and manipulate the autonomous groups in order to promote their own goals they crush the initiative and the leadership of the locality and put the brakes on social progress."

Few permanent functionaries or animators of associations are prepared to face the complications which could originate from a collaboration with the small autonomous groups which themselves have ideas, and perhaps different ideas, about the goals they wish to reach. In addition, small groups mistrust the lack of a durable interest on the part of assistants and animators from the outside who enter into their group, occupy themselves with it for a moment, then leave in order to make place for another. Whatever may be the preparation and the good will of animators from the outside, a certain ambiguity remains in their role: they may in effect remain constantly divided between their loyalty to their organization and the respect for the autonomy of the small groups with which they work.[15]

Leaders of work programs of associations often place too much emphasis on participation statistics of meetings and activities, instead of intensive work with small groups with existing affinities, and form new ones instead.

Another contradiction has been identified regarding community development. The problem concerns the reinforcement of local power and local autonomy, and the need to fit them into a national plan for social change. The local development plans receive their orientation from national plans and must integrate themselves into plans of a longer perspective. But, at the same time, the planning of technical and institutional change has the effect of softening the local modes of association and diminishing the social controls based on the family, kin groups, and the traditional types of organization. Among the latter, the more or less autonomous groups risk losing their independence and being transformed. Once they work in collaboration with an organism of development, whose activities are specialized and oriented towards material progress, they change their nature and become formal groups centered on a precise task.

These diverse contradictions and sources of conflict have been recognized for a long time and the directors of associations increasingly seek to assure themselves of the collaboration of the leaders of the small groups and to create an equilibrium between formal groups and small groups. More and more, a part of the instruction of these officers includes training regarding the functions of small groups. And it is the small group itself which is created experimentally and serves as the object of analysis in certain training programs.

The tension situations presented here do not concern only community development projects and programs of social work associations or associations for culture and popular leisure, but are found as well in political parties and unions, in which the shibboleths thrown out by high-level directors are sometimes not followed by the little local sections, or in which the locals launch their own actions contradictory to the policies determined in higher places. Cooperatives are familiar with similar difficulties, both in their relations with the solicitations of their federation and in the large cooperative, between the membership base and the elected officials.

The ethnological approach seems to have singled out for analysis the part of small groups in local communities, more than sociology has. In this regard one can evoke the observations made by Irwin T. Sanders on the *sedenki,* or womens' work groups in a Bulgarian village.[16] The author describes the rules that govern these informal work groups. Each woman invites other women to her home to card wool. She chooses those whom she wishes to invite and those whose homes she would like to be invited to later. She rejects those who do not please her or who do not work well.

Sanders remarks that beyond their apparent activity, the manifest function, the *sedenki* are sources of information for the entire village and the centers for dissemination of news and the formation of public opinion. After a work session, each woman has her portion of gossip to digest during several days of conversations with her neighbors who were not there.

Such affinity groups (constituted before their invention by sociometric techniques) are natural channels of information and education that can be used for community development, adult education, and in the formation of new attitudes. This example shows well the practical value of spotting small informal groups in the midst of a locality. All theoretical and practical research done on local leaders begins from these arguments.

The important role attributed to small groups leads to the question of their identification. Groups of low visibility, of fluctuating contours, of more or less short duration in which membership is so natural that the members sometimes do not know they belong—all these conditions render identification difficult and considerable sensitivity is necessary on the part of the seeker and his instruments of analysis to discover them.

One immediately dreams of the sociometric test as one of the more appropriate instruments for discernment of such groups. Its use appears to be rather simple but soon runs up against certain limitations, in particular concerning small groups that are born within structured groups. It is through a geography of small groups that their study must begin: who are they, what do they think, what do they do, what do they want?

But in what measure does an objectivized procedure like a sociometric test, even when employed in an interview rather than in a written questionnaire, destroy the spontaneity that it recognizes as one of the most important characters of the small groups? To what extent is the warming-up counselled by Moreno sufficient to awaken in the members the consciousness of their small groups and permit them to describe the phenomena that they do not ordinarily dare to imagine? Is the language used by our respondents and the words that we ourselves can propose to them sufficiently rich to permit them to express all the nuances of their sentiments?[17]

If the small groups are created, to begin with, from sentiments of attraction and bounded, to begin with, by sentiments of rejection, it is, to the contrary very often simply indifference that the researcher encounters—at such a point that one can ask oneself if this is not the starting variable for whoever preoccupies himself with practical matters of research. The fact that in numerous groups a certain number of members desire to work (a sociometric question) with any of the other members, poses this question in a crucial fashion. Who are these isolates, these affect-neutrals? Does their group not offer opportunities to manifest attraction or repulsion? The indifference that they show evidence of in their choices may be either a genuine distance from the others, or it may be evidence of a profound satisfaction regarding all the members of the group. Do such persons find satisfactions for their needs for affinity outside of the group? Does this indifference hide a lack of the habit of self-analysis or simply defiance or hostility to the researcher? These problems seem important for field analysis and come to grips with, by inversion, one of the conclusions of sociometry: the knowledge that individuals who join and participate in formal groups, the "sociogroups," are also the best adjusted to their psychegroups. In other words, a harmonious life at the level of the small group would precede the development of a sociability of the formal type; and the members of the formal groups would seem to have to be accepted as persons in their small group before being able to tolerate the restrictions and segmentary activities of formal groups.

Up to now we have been led to distinguish, and even to place in opposition, organized modes of participation and informal ways of cooperation. Our understanding of the informal must be developed and blended: what we have learned about small groups permits the supposition that these two types of participation are perhaps not opposed, but concern different contents. The associations whose formal structure depends in great measure on members' free choice, seems to furnish the appropriate structure for verification of any hypothesis bearing on the complementarity and not on the opposition of these two types of participation.

NOTES

1. The community of work is a communal form that had a strong development in France and is different in several respects from the American communes and intentional cooperative communities, principally in its attachment to a particular factory or workplace. It involves worker participation in factory management and partial or complete ownership, plus some form of cooperative community life among workers and their families, not necessarily coresidential, and often urban. The community of work (analyzed further in chapter 7) resembles the Yugoslav self-management or worker council arrangement mostly insofar as the factory is concerned; even there the role of government is quite different, the community of work being essentially autonomous. The most accessible treatment of communities of work in English is Claire Bishop, *All Things Common* (New York: Harper, 1950), now outdated but useful. (Ed.)
2. This is drawn from an article in *L'Annee Sociologique,* 1961, to which the reader is referred for further bibliography. Albert Meister, "Participation organisée et

participation spontanée: quelques études sur les 'petits groupes' aux Etats-Unis," *L'Année Sociologique* (1961):113-61.

3. When they are created on the basis of habitation, proximity tends to reinforce the homogeneity of small groups.
4. Sources are not given in the original for quotes appearing in this chapter. (Ed.)
5. This principle applies much less to big organizations, where the functions and roles tend to be independent of the personality of the individuals that occupy them.

   No sources are given for Lewin. An accessible source in English is Kurt Lewin, *Resolving Social Conflicts* (New York: Harper, 1948). (Ed.)
6. This type of interaction corresponds well to Georges Gurvitch's "sociability as community," in which "the Me's and the others can fuse in opening themselves and interpenetrating on the most intimate level, and their participation in the We can engage their personal depths without this integration always attaining its maximum intensity." Georges Gurvitch, *La Vocation actuelle de la sociologie* (Paris: PUF, 1950), p. 124.
7. I do not deceive myself that such is not the case with almost all our instruments of sociological analysis. Still, the cross-section of time produced by a survey on organized participation groups operates in a time frame that proceeds less rapidly than at the level of the forms of sociability.
8. Two other criteria of differentiation of small groups have been proposed. They are linked to problems of the dimensions of the group: that of the stability of the group, measured by membership turnover; and that of participation, measured by time and effort devoted by members to the group.
9. In this sense small groups constitute excellent structures for group interviews.
10. A lengthy footnote on small-group research is omitted here. (Ed.)
11. For sociometry a clique is defined as a closed formation, without external choices.
12. Cf. Philippe Bernoux, Dominique Motte, and Jean Saglio, *Trois ateliers d'O.S.* (The Hague: Mouton, 1962), p. 139.
13. Such is the case in communities of work in which, in spite of the democratic structure of these cooperative enterprises, the worker base can in certain cases only express itself by apathy, refusal, or spontaneous strikes.
14. No source is given. (Ed.)
15. See "Militants and Animators," chapter 6.
16. Irwin T. Sanders, *Balkan Village* (Lexington: University of Kentucky Press, 1949).
17. Another problem concerns the place of small groups on the informal-formal continuum. This dimension is certainly useful, but the stretch between the two extremes requires explication. At the one extreme, corresponding to the pure informal type, it can be asked if the group situations are still possible, and if the depth of feelings expressed there do not lead solely to dyadic associations. At the other extreme, that of the purely formal type, it can also be doubted whether there are still durable group situations (even in an administration or in the army, nonrational considerations and feelings may invade relations between superiors and subordinates). Natural small groups (by opposition to artificial laboratory groups) to which we refer here are situated between these two extremes and we must locate them on the continuum if we want later on to make comparisons between them.

6

MILITANTS AND ANIMATORS

Up to now the terms *militant* and *animator* have been employed in undifferentiated fashion, according to the usage that the public makes of these notions. In this chapter I will try to make them precise by identifying the differences between them. A typology of militants and animators will be constructed, and in order to focus on the topic, I will equally employ some comparisons between the militant and the economic entrepreneur, and between the animator and the technician. I will also take up the differences already indicated between militants and less active members of the associations.[1]

Several remarks must be made before coming to the heart of the matter. To define the profiles of the animator and of the militant is not to assume that these personalities are fundamentally opposed to one another; to the contrary, far from being mutually exclusive the traits of the one are constantly found mixed among the traits of the other. The method employed is however not less useful, for these ideal types permit us a better comprehension of the real, in which the animator sometimes becomes militant and in which the militant trained in the techniques of handling individuals is transformed into an animator. In other terms, although it may be necessary for the analysis to characterise the two types as if differentiated and even opposed, the reality offers us all the combinations between them, according to the circumstances and fluctuations of the life of the groups.

To attempt to delimit the psychology of militants and animators does not signify that their actions are reduced to psychological phenomena, for leadership and active participation in groups are not sole properties of the individual but the result of interaction between: (1) characteristics of the more active individuals (this is important, for psychological reductionism would lead us to the opposite extreme); (2) the attitudes and the needs of members of the group; (3) the structural characteristics and functioning of the groups; and (4) the relations between the group and the larger economic, social, and political milieu in which it is situated.

In this perspective, the militants, the active participants and the animators are considered at the time as individuals presenting certain personality traits and as expressing the contradictions of their milieu. It is this same conjunction between the personality and tendencies and demands of the environment which give birth to the militant group.

In the same manner that it is necessary to avoid positive or negative evaluation of behavior or to judge them altruists or egoists, it is necessary to avoid reserving the word militant to individuals who are active only in the groups with which we sympathize. Such a value judgement must be separated from our analysis (but not, surely, from our lives as citizens), for we can expect to find militants in groups of the left as well as among fascists; in fact, nothing lets us assume that the qualities and merits that one can attribute to militants are to be found only in these two types of groups. The phenomenon of militantism has nothing to do with group functions nor with attitudes regarding change, be it to refuse or accept it.

The term *militant* is currently somewhat devaluated and is gradually being replaced by that of *animator.* Thus, associations for cultural diffusion spoke, some fifteen years ago, of "cultural militants" although they now employ the expression *cultural animators.* With time the term *militant* has come to be too idealogically charged, while that of *animator,* which seems more "scientific," has emerged. I will not be concerned with these fashions, and will utilize the term *militant* as a category of analysis that could as well have been designated by a letter, without taking up these somewhat pejorative connotations.

These preferatory remarks being posed, it is still appropriate to give a preliminary definition of the militant and the animator. I would also make reference to the types of participation distinguished above, the militant being characteristic of groups of organized or voluntary participation, although the animator is the key man of those of stimulated participation. The animator as militant can originate from a milieu different from that of the group in which he works. While the militant identifies completely with the group, even to the point of acceptance as one of them, the animator on the contrary remains tied to an external institution which generally remunerates him for the task, which is to stimulate participation of members regarding objectives fixed by him and/or his institution.

Historically, the animator finds his model in the curé, organizer of celebrations and parish activities, dependent on a hierarchy foreign to his work situation, and very often, like the animator, respectful of that power and seeking to make people patient with it, to "prepare the cage in which the people live." In contrast is the militant worker and/or revolutionary, a believer himself, but inspired by a different evangel, recruiting or leading in order to upset the social order. In fact, although the animator depends directly or indirectly on the power for his remuneration, and is thus more or less respectful and scarcely able to go further than reform of the power and its abuses, the perspective of the militant is that of taking power.

Historically still, the figure of the militant is linked to the demands of the industrial proletariat. His is the central figure of the past century, to the contrary, the animator has been the dominant figure in questions of participation for only some twenty years; he appears at the moment when, on the whole, our societies have almost resolved demands affecting property, but in which it is still necessary to unite individuals. In other terms, the militant was linked to a society that suffered the lack of having, while the animator is bound to a society that suffers the lack of being.

It was, furthermore, in the cultural domain in which animators were first spoken of, and it is only since the 1960s that the term has been extended, in a concommitant fashion, to the economic changes that led France to enter into the circle of big capitalist countries. So much and so well that currently animators are found in almost all domains, which it will perhaps be useful to mention briefly in order to recall extent and diversity of the phenomenon.

The oldest sector is the sociocultural, first associationist, then public. There were also animators of festivals and leisure events, originated by animators of radio and television games. In the social section, social workers gradually broke with a strict case work approach and discovered community work preceded in that area by the animators of social centers and public establishments of a social character.

The church followed the same route with pastoral animation. Residential districts, and especially the new residental developments and associations and institutions created in them were another field of animation. Businesses themselves, whose personnel functons had already been transformed into management, commenced to feel the need of animation of this same personnel, a new, more seductive form, but perhaps less deceitful, than the older human relations. Finally, the administration, which had already discovered the charm of hostesses, launched programs of animation, notably on the local and regional levels. These programs were designed to improve the images of institutions joining public relations programs of big businesses.

Finally, some new fields were opened during recent years, in particular political animation to begin the organizaton of electoral campaigns that the parties confided more and more to the technicians. But it is above all commercial animation that has had increasingly intrusive effects into daily life, and the most numerous troops of animators, including the animators of big department stores and publicity campaigns, and those who recruit majorettes and organize the festivities on the occasion of opening a new commercial center.

Surely it is other forms of animation than the following, ludicrously enumerated at the start of a special number of *Pour* devoted to animation:[2] *dodo* animation, which benumbs aggressivity and suffocates; *cock-a-doodle-doo* animation, which is demagogic, which delights in particularisms and chauvinisms; *money* animation, which will sell itself to anybody and is at the service of commerce; *hobby-horse* animation, which serves the private interests of animators without regard for the desires of the populace; and so on. As Marc Coulon writes on the subject in the same number, all animation is empathic, but the crucial question is how far it goes. It can intend the simple exploitation of the sensibilities of individuals (that of the night club, for example) or go as far as the awakening of the potentialities of the personality. Animation should integrate individuals and acculturate them, that is, lead them to modify their attitudes and their behavior in the sense that animators and their institutions judge desirable, and at the same time innovate, transform, and even challenge. As a consequence it is difficult to achieve equilibrium between such disparate objectives and the self-management the groups themselves seek.

Such adjustments and counterbalancing are posed much less for the militant, whose system of belief renders him more directive and less anxious about nuances and subtleties of group life. But, just as the militant sometimes tires and loses his combativeness in a post with permanent remuneration, and transfers his loyalty to the institution, it also happens that the animator ceases to be the man of the apparatus and identifies profoundly with the group that comes to consider him as one of its own. In this case he becomes what I call a militant. The ruptures are not often so clean, and numerous fluctuations may be observed between the two poles. It nevertheless seems indispensable to define these abstract types to the end of understanding the oscillations between them that are found in reality.

MILITANTS AND MEMBERS

In research the militant is defined as the active participant of an association, while the participation of the ensemble of the members is evaluated by a series of measures of different aspects of group life, as we have seen in the preceding chapters. The active participant is the one who militates for the group, spreads its image outside the group, recruits new members, takes responsibilities and joins in decision making. In other terms, he contributes to the life and the orientations of the group.

By contrast to this *contribution-participation,* the remainder of the members, in various degrees, are much less active. On the whole, these members identify with the group, much more than they contribute to decisions (*identification-participation*). According to one study of American union militants, the militants often see the other members as lacking the capacities which are their own: initiative, competency to take responsibilities, and autonomy. And if these same militants invoke the blessings of participation of the common member, they are not strongly convinced that this participation will lead to better decisions, a stronger participation seeming to them especially necessary for the morale and good climate of the group. Such a conclusion seems applicable to numerous associations, whose officers constantly complain that the base is not sufficiently trained and not mature enough to take responsibilities, or so that responsibilities could be given to them. That is, nevertheless, not the question, although we will see that the militants seem to be characterized by a will to power and a certain authoritarianism.[3]

In somewhat schematic fashion, the profile of the militant emerges from a number of studies on factors in participation. By relation to the other members of the group, the militant benefits from high occupational and socioeconomic status; his level of information is higher and his sources of information are more numerous; he has more chances of being in the most productive professional years (between ages thirty and fifty), it is likely that he originates from a family whose members also participate actively; he has known a certain geographic mobility and finds himself on the path to upward mobility; finally, from the point of view of his personality, he would be an extrovert, he would not be anxious, would be an optimist, autonomous rather than conformist, marked by a strong opposition to fatalism, active rather than passive, and endowed with a facility with words.

MILTANTS AND ENTREPRENEURS

The idea of the entrepreneur putting into practice technical innovations and exploring domains of activity still lying fallow has taken birth in and concerns a capitalism of small units, in which the entrepreneur worked with his own resources or with those which he had been able to mobilize himself. Associationism appeared at the same epoch and it can be said that associations and enterprises are two aspects of the phenomenon of liberal development.[4] Militantism in associations of all types (unions, cooperatives, parties, and so on) appeared as a channel of social promotion for individuals deprived of capital facilitating their installation as small patrons, above all from the moment at the start of the Second

Empire, when the capitalist concentration much less frequently permitted the promotion of workers to heads of enterprises.

In the first period of liberal development, entrepreneurs and militants presented many common traits: the success of the entrepreneur owed to his flair, to his sense of business, in the same fashion as the militant recruits members and fills his meeting hall thanks to this tactical sense, to his talent for seizing the opportune moment to launch this action or that demand. Moreover both are very anxious to not let themselves be outdistanced by the competition which imitates their actions: the entrepreneur surrounds his management and his technique with secrecy, and the militant strives to denigrate the ideas of the groups that would like to steal his members. The one and the other are thus jealous of their productions, whether of a material or an ideological content, such as appears in the declarations and publications of the group. Their jealousy is in the same scale as their appetite for gain, and neither hesitate to do the most humble tasks—delivery of merchandise or distribution of tracts—in order to guarantee the success of their initiatives. And in the same way as the business head struggles to not be absorbed by a more important enterprise, the director of a group refuses fusions with similar groups; even if he publicly proclaims that a union of forces would be necessary for the triumph of an idea or of a demand, he prefers to remain the chief of a little group rather than the officer of a section in the unified group.

In what measure can one extend to the militant what Max Weber said of the entrepreneur,[5] who wants to draw nothing for himself from the riches (or success or power, in the case of the militant), save the irrational sentiment of having accomplished his duty, his mission? In this perspective, either one might be characterized by the desire to succeed, to run risks, to innovate, persuaded that changes in things or in men results from personal will. Both would be determined from within, by beliefs that are deeply internalized from infancy; they would be inner-directed in the meaning Riesman gives this term.[6] Both would be sorts of "interior sportsmen," fixing for themselves goals to attain, and whose recompense is simply having attained them. Riches or success would not be so much their motivations—even if they are the result of them—but rather the pursuit of a sort of standard within themselves, a kind of passion. Concerning the entrepreneur, Max Weber goes even further, saying that business and its continued trepidations become indispensable to his life, so much that it is the entrepreneur who is made for his enterprise, and not the reverse. Knowing the obstinacy with which certain militants defend and promote their groups, it is correct to ask ourselves if they are not also creatures of their creations.

ANIMATORS AND TECHNICIANS

Just as the militant is distinguished from the entrepreneur by a high degree of empathy, it can be said that the animator is an empathic technician. Perhaps it is not useless to interrogate ourselves briefly on this point in guise of an introduction to the comparison between militants and animators.

Like the technician that the group hires or consults, the animator remains in some ways outside the group. Even if he becomes a member of it, as is the case, for example, with the engineer in the workers' production cooperative, the members keep for a long time the feeling that they have "paid an engineer." If, to the contrary, he remains a consultant responsible to an outsider institution, the distance from the group is still considerable. Animators, like technicians, are remunerated and their salary depends on the reputation that they make for themselves in the utilization of their techniques, and increasingly, on their diplomas.

Like the technician, the animator can integrate himself with a group, share its values and styles of life, and be accepted by its members. His training even permits him to become an appreciated militant. As I have specified at the start, reality offers us all the combinations and fluctuations possible between the militant, animator, and technician, and it is for necessities of analysis that I insist on the differences among them.

Like the technician, the animator is a specialist, but his specialty is the relationships between people. During recent years, animation has benefitted from an extraordinary influx of ideas, from the academics and outside militants who have made themselves propagators and militants of these ideas. This effervescence has marked the 1960s, during which the methods have been tested, the deontologies gradually made precise, the fields of application delimited. The phase of experimentation currently seems terminated, at least as it concerns social animation (by opposition to commercial, political animation, and so on) and one witnesses beginnings of the habitual processes of formalization and institutionalization of what was informal, voluntary, experimental and often even contested at the start. The creation of subsidized schools, of posts and charges in the process of becoming official, of programs of study and diplomas, of professional codes and so on, all that converges to institutionalize animation, and naturally, to progressively drain it of the demanding, sometimes leftist and contestant character of its earlier years. In other terms, as was also the case for social work some decades ago, animation became a trade, with its statuses and its hierarchies. Professionalism has already made its inroads, with its precise employment categories: distribution animators, monitor animators, animators of special groups (youth, for example), coordinator animators, and so on. In addition, given the omnipresence of public powers in this country, it is already well along the path towards a civil service.

In the term of this evolution, the animator becomes a technician, like the social worker or the agricultural engineer or the manager, permanent employee or consultant, remunerated by the group itself or detatched to serve in the group by an outside institution. Certainly, his technique still does not possess scientific fundamentals comparable to those of the engineer, but it is perhaps only a question of time. This technique is essentially one of persuasion, of handling or manipulation; or, if one is not fond of these terms, which perhaps recall too much the public abuse or words, of group work or pedagogy: semidirective, sensitive, oriented to the awakening of potentialities. An introduction to these techniques can be included in training of other technicians, facilitating their intervention in the life of groups. It is not bad, for example, that an accountant learns to explain his accounts in a more attractive and pedagogical manner to the nonspecialists who make up the associations—even if, paradoxically, his power over them is reinforced because of it.

Animators and technicians both have professional statuses, receive remuneration for their contributions to the group, have their careers or their advancement linked to norms of promotion outside the group, must hold an equilibrium between their loyalty to the organism which employs them and their attachment to or even identification with a group. As we will see more clearly in relation to the comparison between militants and animators, the first are often in revolt, projecting their personal conflict on the group and utilizing it in order to gain personal inner equilibrium. To the contrary, animators, like the other technicians, must depersonalize their interventions, to remain neutral in the conflicts that divide groups, to not take sides; and the fact that they generally succeed in remaining thus in retirement while pursuing their work with the group shows well the control that they have over themselves and indicated that they are therefore not in revolt. Finally, due to their professional status, and also because they are not in revolt, animators, like technicians, are typically at work in groups compatible with the global society, groups which give them the occasion to put their techniques to use while consolidating their careers. To the contrary, as is the current observation, groups involved in conflict generally suffer the lack of technical assistance and their militants are psychologically too much in revolt to receive animators among them who would be only technicians. Technicians who attach themselves to such groups consider themselves militants.

MILITANTS AND ANIMATORS

By contrast to the animator, the militant appears like a rebel, powerless to be what he would like to be, and seeking his own fulfillment in action with others, in devotion to them, in the emotional taking charge of their difficulties or of their suffering. More than empathic, he is really sympathetic, and this sympathy is transformed in possession, in domination, and sometimes in tyranny and jealous despotism. Like the entrepreneur, whom he resembles so much, the militant is an inner-directed, grasping person, sometimes desperately seeking some certitudes that he believes fundamental (God, the good of man, justice), and from which he derives, sometimes maladroitly, his rules of conduct and his choices and his priorities. At the extreme, especially when he is young, when he is not yet wasted by his combat or become indifferent through the exercise of power, when he does not yet have a family that might suffer by his actions, the militant is often a fanatic placing the realization of his goals above all consideration for men, his mind clouded by the ends and blind to the means.

At the other extreme is the animator, certainly not a rebel, especially among commercial animators. His training has sensitized him to the detection of the intentions of others. He is other directed. It is the perception of these intentions of others that determines his conduct. He has internalized sensitivity of detection rather than beliefs or a faith. This is moreover why he has need of a deontology, although the militant is the constant moralist of his beliefs. His empathy is not sympathy, and it permits him to remain neutral in the group that he animates and to not profoundly engage himself with it.

But this animator represents the extreme case, and notably in social and cultural animation there are animators much more emotionally involved in the lives of their groups. One often finds among them militants who are tired or aged and/or whom the need for material security has constrained to fall into line. They remain believers, but they have ceased to be fanatics, they know that the law or justice or the good are not for tomorrow, and they have learned to show themselves patient. They often express doubts on the impact of their actions, but happily for their personal equilibrium, their old foundations of belief rapidly persuade them that, even if their action is limited, it is going in the right direction. They willingly take refuge in the deceit that "it is not necessary to hope in order to undertake."

In the social and cultural animation domain there are, beside these ex-militants, a very large number of young people desirous at the time to aid others, to render themselves socially useful while making a career. By relation to the fanatic militants (it will be understood, I think, that I give no pejorative sense to this qualifier) evoked to start with, these animators are in some ways washed-out militants, who have not had sufficient "guts" to go to the end of their engagement and renounce the material advantages and free time and security offered by a regular job in the animation sector. Although these militants are rebels, these young animators are fundamentally anxious and it will be seen later that their taste for the techniques of animation respond to an imperative of security. The more permissive and egalitarian education that they have received has developed their empathy and a sentiment about their social utility, but at the same time, the surroundings from which they have issued—the middle classes, generally—have marked them through their sense of respectability, by their taste for comfort and for security. Anxious, dissatisfied, emotionally badly adapted, placed at their exit from adolescence in an instrumental and functional world that does not satisfy their need for friendship, they see in social and cultural action a compensation for their inner void. But they are at the same time too exacting on the purity of the engagements that they would like to take and too careful to preserve themselves in order that they give themselves to it entirely, the sort that pass their time detesting what they do and refusing to choose what they could do. It is in these terms that it will be necessary for us to evoke the conflict of loyalty of the animators, conflict between their identification with their group, of which they could become militants, and their attachment to the security that their institution gives to them, whose goal is only, nevertheless, the majority of the time, to realize the least possible change compatible with the status quo. Surely, as time passes, with the years and age and the charges of a family, these animators forget their torments of youth and settle down in the ambiguity of their position. At this moment, they have become true animators. Others, to the contrary, have surmounted their hesitations and have become militants.

In spite of the tendency to professionalization of the trade, it is necessary to establish the fact that there is not at the present time any socially accepted definition of the animator. The public, his neighbors, his friends, sometimes even the members of the group that he animates do not know very well what he does nor his mission. In a society based on the prestige of money, the animator—and especially the social and cultural animator—feels discredited; and the feeling is all the stronger because the petite bourgeoisie from which he originated had been motivated by economic gain, thrift, and the taste for social status. In addition, and especially in little cities and the country, the free time of which he apparently disposes (he works mostly in the evenings) and his liberty of movement brings about the perception that he is a sort of amateur (in the country the veiled peasant aggressively taxes him with laziness), having found an agreeable sinecure in order to escape productive work. For all these reasons, he is profoundly anxious and the only way to make himself secure would be to accept the values of the group that he animates and becomes a militant in it, which poses the problem of his loyalty in regard to the institution that employs him.

The militant does not have these problems, for his system of beliefs is sufficiently solid to permit him to resist the indifference or hostility of his surroundings. The warmth of his relations with the members of the group constitutes a sufficient screen against disrepute and criticism.

To pose the problem of the loyalty of the animator brings us to the question of whether he is a double agent. Paid by organisms, institutions, or federations of groups which, implicitly, often aspire only to limit changes as much as possible and to act so that the intervention of animators is limited to reduction of social tensions and to facilitate the integration of the animated, the animator finds himself restrained from defense of the avowed objective, which is to favor conscious participation, autonomous decisions, and genuine group democracy. Between this goal of his action and that which his employing organism permits him to do, lie the margins of liberty of the animator. Whence the questions he asks himself: the social worker inquires, regarding the maladjusted child, if the problem is not only to know how to provide care but also why there are so many. Others ask why social workers do not organize their clients in place of providing aid to them and enjoining them to ameliorate their relations with husband or children. On their side, animators come to wonder why they constantly seek to make people participate in place of posing the question of the reason for this participation and their role in our society.

In practice, all these inquires cast doubt on the loyalty of animators with regard to their institution. The fact that this question of loyalty is constantly posed to animators is symptomatic of this continual hesitation, that I have indicated previously, between their care for material security and their group identification. Here also their social origin can be advanced in order to explain their respect for authority, their solicitude not to offend their employer. In spite of their frequent leftist orientation, in spite of their training in the social sciences, they respect respectability, this dogma of the petite bourgeoisie, and they will continue to pose this question of their own loyalty, and will never be militants, while being no more than simple assimilators of public contestation.

Another aspect to discuss concerns modes of influence. All militantism is defined in reference to power: the militant wants to keep or gain power in the group or lead the group to the conquest of an exterior power. Whatever the group in which he moves, whether labor union, friendly society, or sports club, the militant has a political vision of his action; whether it is a matter of recruiting new members or reviving a council or a committee, or organizing a new activity or taking part in a celebration or public demonstration, the militant always reasons in terms of power; even on a small scale, that of the local group or the section of a larger association, the militant is always a sort of politician who conspires to portion out the different tendencies in a council, who knows how to bluff and maneuver in order to obtain an aide, who knows how to speak and to convince a listener, who knows how to predict when and where the group must be present or represented, and so on.

This technique, for it is one, he has not learned in books, and even if he has completed his training, as for example in a party staff school, what he learned there are some tricks and some guile that he adds to what he already knew and practiced intuitively. For, on the level of leadership technique, he is a self-taught person who has observed here and there and who draws lessons from his failures.

Things are very different regarding the animator, educated in a school or training courses and with a head crammed with the subtleties of group dynamics—he has had to go to learn what the other knows naturally. While the militant is entirely centered on the results to be obtained, the animator is more preoccupied with the means to arrive at them. Defined as "a pedagogical program aiming at participation," animation wants "to favor the flourishing of the individual in his group and to aid him to take awareness of his role in the whole of the social fabric." Leaving aside the goal, the sense and the reason for large and lively social participation, the animator centers on the improvement of communications in groups, on a better employment of time, on a more democratic manner of making decisions. These activities are far from being criticizable; nevertheless, here also, it is necessary to ground them in the reality of daily life struggles for power in groups, and recall the risk that they may be utilized in order to reinforce the power of some to the detriment of their opposite numbers. In fact, the animator always enters into a group on the call of those who control it or claim to control it. There is always an element of play for power. The majority of the time he is conscious of it and this is one of the reasons that impels him to center on means, trying to withdraw from the combat or to not take a position, a sort of Pontius Pilate technician of communication.

This neutrality of the animator is completely illusory, and in practice, he plays the role of an instrument of integration to the views and politics of those who have called him. Certainly, he can make himself believe that his recommendations are impartial, that he leaves the group to decide for itself, that he steps gracefully aside after having aided the members to better pose their problems, that he is nondirective and that he does not exert influence. All that can last for a moment, until the day when the group experiences a crisis (which is rather frequent in associations), when the struggle for power is made overt and all must show their cards.

I have said that the militant scarcely preoccupies himself with the results of his actions, too inner-directed to worry about the opinions that others have of him. By opposition, the animator is more interested by the image of things than by their reality. In the same way that the role of the salesman in a store is less to counsel his customer than to sell him a product that corresponds to the image that he has of himself, and that the surroundings in which he lives expects of him, the role of the animator is to diffuse a culture, leisure, activities, or participation corresponding to the image that the members of his group create of themselves and which the milieu in which they live expects of them. Like the salesman, who has much less need to know his products than the ability to place his customer on the social ladder and to grasp the image he projects, the animator has much less need to preoccupy himself with the nature and the realism of his goals that the group proposes to attain than the feelings of the participants and of their satisfaction in the process of participation. In other terms, he is also more interested in appearances than reality, by the process in play more than by his results. At the extreme, what does it matter whether a group decision be realist or opportune, provided that it has given members the sentiment of having participated, the satisfaction of having deliberated well and the good conscience of having done that which they believe people of their condition and their situation ought to do.

Another domain where great differences can be noted is that of training. Although the militant acquires power because he succeeds in communicating and in popularizing among members his vision of action and of the world, and all that in a dialectic where emotional and irrational elements dominate, the animator enters into the group like a technician placing his bets on rationality, on measures or orientations that he will be called on to suggest being adopted because the group will see their superiority. Whence the decisive importance of the training of animators. Without entering into the details of these kinds of training, some aspects can be emphasized. The newer the domain of animation, the more general the training. To the contrary, in the domains where the trade is professionalized, training becomes very specialized, as for example in social work, in which the accent is almost exclusively placed on case work and with a psychological interpretation of social relations. Such a training has the merit of helping adjust the animators to work that the society expects of them and of giving them technical responses for cases that will be presented to them. I am however more interested in social and cultural animators whose field of action is much less defined and delimited and in which, precisely, the general culture excuses the lack of clarity on ends and domains of intervention; to such a point that one is sometimes justified to ask oneself if there is not a contradiction between the universalism of the training and the specialization of tasks that these animators will later be called on to fulfill.

Sociology and the applicatons of social psychology to the dynamics of groups constitutes the center of training and of pedagogical reflection. Besides the techniques of conduct of meetings, the animator learns above all to diagnose. From this come the innumerable inquiries on districts or neighborhoods, villages and microregions. They are devoted at the time to the goal of knowing the milieu and sensitizing the population to certain problems. Experience shows nevertheless that the populations know their problems better than animators from the outside believe, that they are aware of what they lack, and that they have understood for a long time that the satisfaction of these needs has escaped their control. Thus, in a rural area, to create employment, to create collective equipment, to ensure occupational training, is only dependent on animation in exceptional cases, but rather on the outside powers over which the populations have no influence. As to political pressure on these powers, the animator has not been trained for it and the institution on which he depends generally will not tolerate it. Under these conditions, once the inquiry is terminated, neither the animator, the group, nor the population knows very well what remains to be done. In certain cases the group or the population under consideration goes ahead with activities of improvement, as for example the embellishment of the village or district. In other cases the population, not being able to come to grips with activities of transformation of the surroundings (employment, equipment, and so on) and not wanting to simply "manage the cage in which it lives," the inquiry will have constituted only an intelligent leisure for those who have participated in it as investigators. It will also have served to channel aggressivity into an activity socially recognized as desirable—cultural leisure. This function of channeling dispute is also one of the reasons why institutions ask for so many inquiries and studies of the groups that desire their intervention.

Institutions or groups in which the animator is the central figure have the function of social integration, their strategy is consensual, and minimizes social conflict. By contrast, militant groups, even if their ultimate function is integration, develop a more conflict-oriented vision of society and even accentuate tensions to the end of dramatizing their actions. Although the animator proposes to work with all of a milieu or all of a population and therefore to minimize the tensions within these groups, the militant organizes only a part of these surroundings, whose interests are assumed to be common (the renters against the landlords, for example).

Meanwhile, to the extent that our societies are planned and that the powers affirm their control over social and economic life, the animator tends to be utilized less to defuse and reduce conflicts than to prevent them. A good example of this is animation in rural areas, which intend to adapt the peasantry, and more generally the entire rural area to changes which are soon to be realized in the agricultural economy under the influence of the common market as well as through capital concentration and industrialization of agriculture. In this case, the animators and the groups that they stir up have the function to prepare men for these transformations, to make them ready to accept their ineluctability, to accept the need to emigrate to the city; although this social prevention may go without accidents on the journey, without tensions and disruptions, the possibility for the interests to express their opinions and to participate in eventual proceedings or demonstrations canalizes their aggressivity into controllable paths and converges to realize this change in social peace. Certainly, such an animation could not unfold in this way if the organizations of the rural world had not in advance accepted these orientations to the gradual growth of agriculture and if they did not concur, sometimes simply thanks to their passivity in this work of social prevention.

Animation has then largely extended its field of action. Beginning from assimilation of contestation, which was its first function, it has insensibly assumed a function of preparation for change in the service of those who orient it and plan it. The weakness of the militant movements has singularly facilitated this new role of animation and it can be asked if our epoch is not one of the beginning of the reign of the animators.[7]

NOTES

1. This chapter is part of a larger study on militants and animators that examines the functions of animators in our postindustrial societies.
2. Marc Coulon (no title), *Pour* 18-19 (1971): 133; 20 (1971): 59.
3. This has already been noted in other chapters.
4. See Albert Meister, *Vers une sociologie des associations* (Paris: Editions Ouvrières, 1972), ch.1.

5. Max Weber, *The Protestant Ethic and the Spirit of Capitalism,* trans. Talcott Parsons (New York: Scribner's, 1958), esp. chapter 2. (Ed.)
6. David Riesman, Nathan Glazer, and Reuel Denney, *The Lonely Crowd* (Garden City, N.Y.: Doubleday Anchor, 1953), pp. 28-32.
7. This paragraph concludes the author's *La Participation dans les associations,* and may be taken as a general summation of his views on the subject of the chapter. Albert Meister, *La Participation dans les associations* (Paris: Editions Ouvrières, 1974). (Ed.)

7

PARTICIPATION AND DEMOCRACY IN ASSOCIATIONS

This chapter addresses the problem of power in associations. The interpretations presented here are drawn from a series of monographs on communities of work, cooperatives and leisure groups in a rural area, city residential cooperatives, and studies on self-management (workers' councils).[1] Some of these were youth groups and some groups of older adults, differences that have permitted the study of the life cycle in the evolution of power. We can indeed ask ourselves if all the groups do not pass through the same stages in the functioning of their democratic structures.

The study of numerous groups at different stages can replace that of a certain number of groups considered longitudinally. This approach is practiced by genetic psychology, with the simultaneous study of children at all ages, assuming that the older ones have passed through the stages at which the younger ones are observed.[2]

The results of four separate kinds of studies will be presented. First, a 1956 study on cooperative groups and leisure associations in a rural area of Northern Italy.[3] These groups were created between 1870 and 1880 in a zone constituted of 48 rural communes comprising a total of about 50,000 inhabitants. The cooperative societies were created under the influence of the agricultural crisis at the end of the century. The set studied is comprised of consumers' cooperatives, mutual aid societies, agricultural machinery coops, livestock insurance mutual associations, and so on. A second series of inquiries concerns four housing cooperatives that were part of the Yugoslav system of self-management.[4]

A third study bears on the communities of work. This study was requested of me by their federation with the goal of stimulating democracy in their group. The study was made in 1958, and there were 30 communities.[5] I have continued to work with them up to the present time, which has permitted me to consider their recent development in the last part of the chapter. Communities of work are small groups (of 15 to 200 persons) who, under the stimulus of the resistance movement created industrial enterprises in which property is collective. In other terms, the members of the group are associates who hold capital shares and whatever the number of their shares may be, have only the right to a single vote in the general assembly, with the cooperative principle of one man, one vote. Finally, I shall make frequent reference to the Israeli collectives, the kibbutzim and moshavim,[6] as well as the self-management groups of Yugoslavia.[7]

Although all these studies are about associations of small size, generally less than 200 members, the materials are diverse, collected in different places and at different times, drawn from groups each having its own history and its peculiar problems. In what measure does their evolution reveal common problems, and in what measure can they be compared with each other? Even if the goal of the studies is simply to identify common traits from their diversity, it is necessary to confess nevertheless that the reflections that follow represent only the products of a breathing spell and a time for reflection in the course of a continuing program of research that will be amplified and diversified.

There is another point common to all these groups. Beyond their different economic functions, they each had the will, at the time of creation, and in opposition to their environment, to create cells of democratic life, to bring about or to respect equality among members, and to base themselves on the maximum participation of members through direct democracy. Different factors have prevented the complete realization of these hopes, although the groups remain democratic and voluntary in their structure and generally in their functioning.

The evolution of the forms of participation and democracy can be described by distinguishing four characteristic stages of the life of a group. Two processes must also be distinguished: on the one hand the process of internal evolution of the group, that is, the phases through which they pass from the point of view of collective management and of progressive shrinking of this collective management in the course of their existence; on the other hand, the process of adaptation to the transformations that intervene in the general economy.

Analysis of the adaptation of the association to external economic change was a major concern in the research on cooperatives in Italy and on self-management in Yugoslavia from the very beginning, but less so in the case of the French communities of work. The French research was started well before the profound postwar transformation of the French economy had begun. Certainly we can bring all the judgements that we wish about these transformations in the midst of capitalism, or on their directions, but what is more important is to see in what measure these transformations imply changes for the communitarian enterprises themselves. This is, then, the needed backdrop.

FIRST PHASE: THE CONQUEST

The group has just been created, enthusiasm and hopes are high, the members attempt to persuade their entourages of the soundness of the goals of the group and to bring in new membership. Only the little nucleus of promoters is distinguished from the other members, and the democracy of the group is essentially direct; decisions are made by the assembly of all the members and bear on all the problems posed to the collectivity. The organisms that the group will give itself later on, such as administrative council, commissions, and so on are not yet differentiated. Volunteers step forward for all tasks.

These volunteers are not yet very specialized, and above all appear multiple: the builders do not content themselves with the construction of houses, but they also want to create a veritable network of cooperatives for the benefit of their members, including consumers' cooperatives, laundries, showers, leisure facilities, and nurseries. In a rural setting, the small consumers' cooperatives of Northern Italy wanted, in addition to grocery sales, to support the mutual aid societies with their surplusses, to improve the education of their members, to struggle for universal suffrage and for the right of free association. In similar manner, the first Israeli kibbutzim wanted more than living and working communities, and considered themselves as the first cells of a socialist society. And it was much the same with the Yugoslav self-management groups, self-management being considered not as an end in itself but as the means of arriving at communism.

For the communities of work this first phase can be dated from 1945 to 1948-50. The entire society was marked by the fraternal ideals of the liberation. The men of the left believed in the possibility of constructing a new world, more just, more equalitarian. The communities were born in this climate and seemed like "imperialist" groupings, charged with a message, with an ideology that they wanted to carry to the outside world. Although they were entirely turned toward the outside, so far as this message was concerned, and precisely because of that, they were groups that were entirely turned inward. They were equally very purist and admitted of no rapprochement with any institutions, however similar, unless they had completely the same principles. They would, for example, have nothing to do with the producers' cooperatives nor with the attempts at reform of private enterprise that were rather numerous at the time. Furthermore, occupational activity was considered only as the means of economic support necessary for self-improvement, to diminish the gap between the family and the workshop, to militate, to bring to the bourgeois world a witness of worker management.

Briefly, in all these examples, economic activity was not judged interesting in itself, and there took shape very quickly in these cooperatives, as in all the examples concerning workers, a contradiction between the contempt for the shopkeeper and for commerce in general, and the exercise of a commercial activity by the association itself.[8]

All projects were discussed in the assemblies. Each person had his own opinion and expected to express it. All new ideas, no matter what their nature, were examined with the passion of the self-educated (cooperation has always been and remains essentially a movement of the self-educated). The discussions, moreover, were much more animated as they turned away from daily work or economic activity to the basis of government. Educational activities were not limited to acquisition of useful knowledge but took in civic, political, union, and cooperative matters. The individuals were better able to understand the principles of cooperation and to participate in the activities of the group because they were trained.

But above all cooperation was intended as the creator of new human relations based on equality. Equality, by opposition to the inequalities of the outside world; equality among members so that no privilege was created within the group, and no member could exploit another. The officers were not reelected to their offices and the members exercised a very close control over their activities; their initiative was weak and all decisions taken by the members in assembly. Complicated mechanisms were planned to be sure that equality would be respected: in the first consumers' cooperatives there was some hairsplitting and very frequent controls were exercised over the activities of the managers; in the communities of work internal rules cast the basis of a new morality, and a new wage system was created to compensate superior professional qualifications that included social activities relevant to the ideals of the group. In several communities, remuneration was even more equalitarian. The solidarity that linked the members was warm; the contacts among them (the teams then were rather small) were intense and personal. It cannot even be said that the directors were near to the base; they made up a part of it and were only distinguished by their strong personalities, personalities that were charismatic and which led the others and dominated them, which made them believe that the management was collective when it was simply a question of profound acceptance of their leadership. Because of the equalitarianism of the beginning, all believed equally in collective promotion. I will return to this later on. In summary, during this first phase the belief in the cooperative and socialist ideals—in the broadest sense of the term—was intense and permitted the sacrifices of the members (in time, in hours of work, in lowered salaries), and by the same token, permitted the accumulation of capital and creation of investments. In fact, in believing that they were creating socialism, in militating in and out of the community for the construction of a new society, these men were only in reality constructing their enterprise. It is in this sense that one can say that the historic function of the ideals of collective management was in the end the creation of fixed capital. As we will see, the examination of the evolution of workers' self-management in Yugoslavia permits a similar hypothesis. But a better example in this domain is that of the Israeli kibbutz, of which it is not too much to say that it was erected principally thanks to the militantism and to the hold of equalitarian ideals, reducing consumption in the interest of investments.

Meanwhile, due to their strong equalitarianism, numerous groups suffered from an excess of democracy, each one constantly questioning the group tasks and the activities and inevitable errors of their officers. Economic activity likewise suffered from this cause. Among the first Castors (cooperative building teams) budgetary planning and the introduction of planning in the construction site took place after discussions on the ideal of the city. In the little consumers' cooperatives each member could, at any moment, disturb the seller under the pretext of controlling him, since control was the right and the duty of each member. In the communities of work, meetings that were too long and too tumultous were born of work itself.

Economic activity of the group indeed lends itself to criticism. Efficacity is low and the members complain of a lag between their hopes and effective results. The officers are men of good will rather than specialists trained to the tasks that they exercise and it is the group that pays the costs of their inexperience and their improvisations.

In the communities of work self-financing must make up for the lack of adequate investment in the beginning, and the wages are low. The competition is strong and the margin of profit reduced. One of the members must devote a part, then all of his time to the administration of work. Little by little he completely abandons the workshop and becomes a work coordinator. In the eyes of the others his position has changed: instead of being a comrade, a buddy, he is more and more considered a director. The comrades are desirous of developing the enterprise, are happy to record big orders, even if the communitarian activities must for a time be placed in abeyance.

In summary, this first phase is characterized by the first clashes between a direct democracy jealous of its prerogatives and an economic activity still badly established. The multifunctionality of the groups creates in addition a dispersion of efforts to the detriment of economic activity. Sooner or later, these contradictions lead the group to reconsider its goals and activities, and in particular to make intensive efforts to consolidate its economic activity.

SECOND PHASE: ECONOMIC CONSOLIDATION

Diverse outside influences are exercised on the groups and oblige them to certain adjustments and certain modifications of their original views. Certain of these outside determinants have particularly affected the small Italian rural societies. Such as, for example, the rural depopulation that emptied the villages of their more dynamic inhabitants and in which the cooperatives no longer find either enough members nor enough animators. Or the destruction of local autonomy as the consequence of the development of communications; destruction which renders aleatory the efforts at regulation of prices made by the local societies at a time when the regulation of prices is more and more done at the national level.

On the level of extraeconomic activities, a reduction of group initiatives is produced. Instruction becomes obligatory and renders useless the educational efforts of the societies. The development of night schools, public libraries, and cultural organizations compete. Mass leisure acts in the same manner, to the detriment of traditional activities of leisure and culture of the cooperatives.

Finally, the necessity of survival on the economic level imposes several transformations. In the first place, group organisms are differentiated and specialized. In the first Italian societies, which combined mutual aid, leisure, and consumers' cooperatives, compatible functions that were at first undifferentiated were separated in order to make better accounting of the financial situation of each department. Next, separate administrative councils were created for each of them, although the status of member extended to all three branches of the society; finally, membership itself was separated.

More rational methods of administration, and if one prefers, more capitalistic approaches must be introduced. The mutual aid society must fix contributions according to age of the member, for the propensity to illness is not the same. Equality between members is then found rooted in equality within each age class. For direct lowering of the price of sale the consumers' cooperatives gradually substitute a system of return calculated on profits in a manner similar to the calculation of dividends of the limited stock company. The return then masks the net effect of lower prices for the society, and nonmembers, badly informed, do not take account of the advantages conferred by the status of membership.

As to that which concerns communities of work, one can date this second phase from 1950 to 1960; roughly the entire decade. In the global society the ideals of liberation gradually fell into oblivion. On the economic plane, after the first years of reconstruction and the takeoff of the economy, the countries settled down again into the inherited traditions of the years between the wars, when each professional group, employers as well as workers, hoped to profit to the maximum from an economy in slow motion. Neither of them, in spite of a phraseology occasionally tainted by revolutionarism on the part of the workers, intended or could transform the structure of the economy. Because it could not transform itself, the economy was a little like a gigantic gravy train from which each wanted to get the most possible. Politically, the Fourth Republic scarcely differed from the Third and used social-democracy to carry out its anticolonial struggles: the war in Indochina came to an end and that in Algeria began without encountering much opposition from the popular masses. The latter were divided: Budapest and the XX Congress of the Soviet Party brought into question revolutionary dogmatism and Stalinism.

The communities suffered the backlash from these tendencies in the ambient society. The idealism of the first years gave way to indifference. And it is in the end good that it was thus, for if the equalitarianism of the first years had indeed been necessary in order to constitute fixed capital, on the management level this same equalitarianism and the preponderance of sentiments of association and of camaraderie would be sources of inefficacity and in a certain measure, of lethargy. During this second phase the communities exhibited stratification: the salary scale spread, piece wages and production incentives had to be introduced in order to ameliorate production. Enthusiasm and collective property did not constitute sufficient stimulation. The directors cut themselves off from the base and became business heads, similar to small private patrons; although capital remained collective, it was the presidents-directors who decided the use of it. By reaction against the first phase, the climate of business became purely economic; typically communitarian institutions were put in limbo and the old ideals were criticized or even forgotten. The contrary of the first phase, the communities were no longer closed grouping and opened themselves up to the outside world—but to this outside world, they had nothing to say. They could therefore open themselves to it without fear. The contacts they had with the exterior were moreover purely economic or commercial, and took place only at the directorial level.

The economic base of the groups could not be consolidated without the reinforcement of the executive, the administrative council, and the power of the directors, both elected and nonelected. In the stores of the little rural cooperatives and in the bars of the leisure and popular culture clubs the director ceased to be submitted to the same severe control as in the preceding stage. Moreover, this control proved to be very difficult in practice, and he was bit by bit permitted to sell certain products on his own initiative. And the evolution did not stop there, as will be seen later on. In the communities of work and with the Castors, with time some administrators were trained, and no one could replace them.

In all groups the power of the administrative council increases: the administrators are reelected, their powers increase, the limits placed on their initiatives are weakened. Numerous controls are removed, and they accommodate the rest badly. It is necessary to suppress the controls in order to increase the efficacity of the organization. Reinforcement of the central nucleus is witnessed and a new type of democracy appears, *delegated democracy.* The administrators have become specialists and the group cannot bypass them; in addition, the members of the base have neither the time nor the training to control or even to judge their work. And due to the fact of the low salaries (in the communities of work) or their derisory remuneration (directors of consumer cooperatives), who would want to replace them anyway? How many voluntary groups in the same way find themselves dependent on their president or their secretary?[9]

In the communities of work the salary scale is at once too compressed to attract junior staff from the outside and too broad to not create conflicts within groups. Indeed, with the hire of supplementary workers and the appearance of specialists, equalitarian salaries cannot be maintained and different remunerations appear, according to qualifications. The increase in size itself creates problems: the newcomers are less integrated than the founders, and they have not made the sacrifices demanded at the beginning while they profit from the accumulation of riches produced by the pioneers. Whence, a sort of conflict of generations.

But if democracy has a tendency to become delegated, the delegation of power only bears on certain aspects of the life of the group, in particular on the economic aspects. All that regards extraeconomic activities is still the resort of the general assembly, while those activities that remain under the control of members of the base are gradually abandoned or taken up by public institutions or outside specialist groups. The analysis of attitudes of residents of housing projects regarding leisure or organized cultural activities shows, in addition, how much they are desirous of breaking the narrow circle of their neighbors when they desire to distract themselves. In the communities of work the community activities weaken in the face of priority given to economic activity. From the multitude of tasks that the group proposed to accomplish in the beginning, we pass imperceptibly to a unifunctionality of an economic character.

All these transformations are not without effect on the interest that the members bring to their group and would not have been possible without a weakening of this interest. As we have already seen, the enthusiasm of the majority of the members is battered by the difficulties that the group encounters in the pursuit of its economic activities. The members realize that the tasks that the group must assume are beyond its feeble means and that the advantages that it brings them are tiny by comparison to those that await it. Gradually their interest wanes, the assemblies are deserted. The members are happy to reelect their administrators and give them a vote of confidence.

On the cultural level also, after some conferences, a few lectures, the need for training activities is satisfied. It appears, moreover, that the lower the level of education of the base of membership, the easier it is to satisfy the need.[10] The difficulties of associational life often result in a loss of interest on the part of members. It is true that these problems particularly affect the groups that demand a rather strong participation or in which the roles and obligations of each cannot be defined in advance and according to precise criteria.

Among the small Italian cooperatives (but it is also true in regard to urban associations such as unions and political associations), industrialization and urbanization have weakened the interest of members in their group, separating work life from the leisure of individuals. The rapid rhythms of urban life seem opposed to the complicated mechanisms designed to maintain equality among members, and we can ask ourselves if there is not a contradiction between the rapidity of initiative and decision demanded in our epoch and the respect for democratic sluggishness. The cooperative groups appeared at the time as groups with a slow rhythm, even preindustrial: for each decision it was necessary to meet, to respect mechanisms of control, to give information. The experience of the Yugoslav communes and workers' councils moreover leads to similar conclusions. Their very complicated democratic structures have not resisted the simplification of procedures and the rapidity of decisions imposed by the rapid industrial development of the country.

In summary, this second phase is a period of transition. For the communities of work one can say that it corresponds to the passage from an artisanal economy to an industrial economy. Economic consolidation is not realized without convulsions, and if the group does not die from them, it sometimes remains divided between managers, on the one hand, and militants faithful to the goals fixed at the start on the other. It is in this way perhaps that it is necessary to interpret the high rate of mortality of French producers' cooperatives described in a preceding chapter.

THIRD PHASE: COEXISTENCE

The principal characteristics of this third stage are that the groups have renounced making a stand against their environment, and that delegated democracy extends to all activities. In this stage the groups gradually take up again the values of the global society against which they wanted to struggle in the beginning. Not only have cooperatives had to take up the methods of management appropriate to private enterprise, but the values have changed. The small Italian cooperatives now rent their store to a manager whose activity has been proven impossible to control. The manager in fact acts like the private shopkeeper against whom the society rose up in the first place.[11] In the communities of work local systems of remuneration have been renounced and salary scales fixed by union conventions have been adopted. The members of the city orchestra of the city built by the Castors desired to be paid, thinking thus to gain more public esteem than they would as members of an amateur group. The members of small brass bands and theater groups in one rural setting shared the income from concerts and public events instead of giving them to collective works. In all the groups, as in the global society, the scale of prestige tends to model itself on the scale of revenues.

The household equipment cooperatives that were created in housing projects, like the agricultural machinery cooperatives, no longer constituted themselves on the basis of social goals, not to mention socialist goals; to the contrary, the members wanted to benefit from the advantages offered, to learn how to use the machines or collective equipment, in order to then retire from the cooperative and acquire the equipment individually. In this case, the function of the cooperative was to develop individual needs and reinforce private property, and therefore inequality.

The utilization of the cooperative form of organization with the goal of reinforcement of private property or of private enterprise, as is the case with the agricultural cooperatives and the middle class consumers' coops, makes of the cooperative society one tool among others of economic life. In this way everyone of us can be a cooperator without any implication that we adhere to any particular values. On the one hand the working class has dispossessed itself of one instrument of struggle that it had created, cooperation, and on the other hand, the proclamation of attachment to the working class on the part of the cooperatives, even if they are linked by their origin to the unions and to the parties, is often only a stereotype and represents nothing more. Their general goals remain, certainly, the emancipation of workers and the social transformation of society, but they follow different paths, not coordinated with those of the unions and workers' parties.

The consumers' cooperative movement has seen its recruitment become oriented toward classes other than the working class, and through that its link with the workers' movement has become more tenuous. In addition, even when a rather intimate link still exists between cooperation and the workers' movement, it is not perceived by the larger public. Education has consecrated this state of affairs by treating cooperation solely from the juridical point of view, or marginally in the course of the history of the labor movement.

For the communities of work, the third phase began at the end of the 1950s and extended up to 1963. On a general level it corresponds to the reinforcement of the power of the Fifth Republic, thanks to the end of the Algerian conflict and to the liquidation of its interior enemies; and, especially, this phase coincided with the fixing of new national economic politics, aiming not only at an increase in the rate of national growth, but the entry of France into the circle of great capitalistic countries. On the general ideological level the sentiment that everything is to be built prevailed and men were psychologically available: the old myths were arranged on the shelves of the museums of utopias and the new myths of the society of mass consumption made their appearance. By contrast to this ideological transformation, political transformations were slow to appear, braked by the party apparatuses, by acquired habits, and an objective situation that had not yet changed much at the level of the popular masses. What did change, by contrast, was the division of power at the national level. Syndicalism and the forces of the Left saw their power gradually reduced, and the stability of the new regime inspired confidence in the propertied classes, both French and foreign. Investments increased and the economy became more dynamic. A great part of the salaried cadres progressively detached themselves from the working class in complete transformation: they accepted the juridical amd moral fundamentals of neoliberalism, having need of expansion in order to put their new techniques to use.

In this third phase, the institutions that cooperation had wanted to oppose to those of the global society were impoverished and scarcely existed anymore, except on paper. In the communities of work the interior rule, which was originally the charter that distinguished these cells of the new life from business enterprises of the traditional kind, was transformed into a simple shop regime. Much that was unique was abandoned. Even the distinction that the communities had made between probationary members, postulants, and full members were set aside when industrial organization at the shop level no longer made any difference between member and salaried worker. In addition, the increase in the size of groups diminished cohesion. The need for cultural activities among workers was no longer felt.

The ten or fifteen years of communitarian experience has seen the members grow older, more anxious to instruct their children and to maintain their families. With the lassitude, the need for security has triumphed over the will to hang on to the experience of collective management. It is agreed that this acculturation to the values of the global society has not been made at the will of the members themselves and it suffices to solicit the confidences of the old militant cooperators and workers to convince oneself that this evolution was produced in self-defense.

Things were much the same regarding the passage from direct democracy to delegated democracy. The delegation of authority was made during this third stage of great progress. The general assembly no longer exercised power directly, with the exception of elections and a control of a rather negative type. Indeed, the very complex activity of the officers did not permit to members of the base a regular and efficient control, and too often the officers became obstinate over minor aspects of their activity (for example, travel expenses) without real importance for the economy of the group and especially distant from the general politics of the association which itself ought to constitute the object of control. But the critics were less numerous than at the preceding stage and the members recognized that they could not address all the problems of the life of the collectivity because of their lack of training.

The communities have in effect admitted the limits of their experience and recognized that the suppression of the traditional conflict between patrons and workers has only rendered more painful the antagonisms between directors and directed and between manual worker and intellectual.

But although the directors represented a united and powerful bloc controlling the economic activity of the group, controlling the sources of information,[12] and the power to decide on wage increases and fringe benefits, the worker base was disorganized and the employee delegates were disoriented by the form of the business, where there was no patron to whom demands might be presented and where the atmosphere of work was better than in the private enterprises.[13]

For this is the most certain positive element that becomes apparent from the entire communitarian experience: freedom of expression there is total, contacts with the directors is easy, careerism nonexistent. One of the most positive results of all cooperative experience is that it assures to members and even to salaried personnel a working climate that is better than what they have had in private business.

It is not useless to recall some of the problems in Yugoslavia with what has been called the new managerial class. First, concerning social promotion, it is remarkable that the groups that have occupied us here have permitted the flourishing of their officers. The promotion that had been collectively desired has been made the reality of somebody in particular, the best armed intellectually. And in that there is another source of antagonism. As for the workers of the base, whose occupational level could never be improved much, the community is considered as a business in which one works among friends, where there is a climate of agreeable work and where the wages and the employment security are superior to those in ordinary enterprises. By contrast, the flourishing of the directors leads to the growth in size and production of the enterprise.

Even though they may be drawn from the ranks and trained on the job, gradually, and as their business develops, the directors are progressively cut off from their companions in the shop. With the expansion of the wage scale, their level of life rises and they become acquainted with new consumer goods. Thus, for example, not enough stress is placed generally on the gap that the purchase of a more luxurious automobile can create in surroundings that were once egalitarian. But there is more: because of their functions the officers may be called to leave the business, to rub shoulders with men from other walks of life; by these new contacts they acquire attitudes and tastes strange to their companions of the worker base, constrained to pass their lives in the work shop. This intellectual evolution of the directors represents more than a simple enlargement of the horizons: their position in production has made them distant from their companions and they soon come to sense themselves more at ease in the company of directors of similar private enterprises or in the company of their clients than with members of the community. As has already been seen, their view of the community is not the same any more. For them it has become an enterprise to direct, a cipher to increase, workers to direct. They sense themselves ill at ease in the cultural and communitarian activities that it is their mission to promote and in spite of their attempts at a rapprochement, they are considered more and more as strangers by their comrades of years gone by. In addition, it is rare that their work leaves them the time and the desire to militate. This also separates them from their comrades who reproach them for letting their social and political activities go.

The development of the business and the rational organization of production have widened the gap between those who think and command work, and those who obey and carry out the work. Management, that was once desired to be to the work of all, has become the work of some; the members of a very restrained team, of a directing council grouping chiefs of services. In the midst of a larger council, there emerges a council of administration that brings together officers, and elements from the base group who tend to emphasize the discussion of the problems of the shop and especially those that concern wages. For them, the work of management tends to become identical with demands.[14]

This finding leads us to ask ourselves about the confusion of powers in the midst of communitarian groups and certain cooperative groups. Due to the multifunctionality of these groups, the officers have in effect at once to see to the education and the training of members and to the profitability of the enterprise. Observation shows that these two tasks are contradictory, that an equilibrium between them is rarely attained, that the one over-shadows the other. In the communities of work the human aspects have been relegated to second place, so strong was the necessity to consolidate the enterprise economically, and if, according to the statutes the members have the right to choose anyone they please among them as a principal officer of the community, in practice the business director has always been chosen, and rarely are the qualities of manager and educator found united in the same person.

In addition, though from the juridical point of view, it can seem excellent that an administrative council be composed of representatives of both workers and officers, and that the process of putting these two forces together justifies the expectation of thoughtful compromise and measured actions, but it has not been like that in practice. One point of view almost always triumphs over the other. In the communities of work the administrative council is transformed into a business committee or into a meeting of personnel delegates, just as in certain consumers' cooperatives the members' delegates have sometimes transformed the administrative council into a clients' council. Such tendencies have also come to light in Yugoslav self-management and have led the businesses to excessive distributions of profits to the detriment of investments.

In what measure has the cooperative gamble paid off? In what measure has the consumers' cooperative been able to sell products and at the same time protect the consumer? In what measure has the producers' cooperative been able to satisfy its members on the human level and at the same time develop enterprises? In spite of the lack of systematic studies on this problem, it seems that in the two cases the economic imperatives have had primacy over the goals of education, of training, and in a larger sense, of protection of members. The disaffection of the members and the scant prestige maintained in the public eye seem to indicate the answer. Perhaps this third phase does not establish the end of the evolution, and certain groups allow us a glimpse of another, that of management by nonelected officials, by the salaried administrators.

FOURTH PHASE: THE POWER OF THE ADMINISTRATORS

If it is healthy that in a democratic organism administrators charged with the functioning of a group bring to the councils and committees elements of continuity and thus temper initiatives that are sometimes too audacious or exceeding practical possibilities, proposed by members or their elected representatives, the risk is great that the effective power of the group might pass from the executive to the administration, as it has already passed in the course of preceding stages from the legislative to the executive. And we have shown that such was the case with certain communitarian groups, where even the elected officers in fact depended on the administrative apparatus that it was their mission to direct. For example, it is not generally realized how great is the power of bookkeeping, the thousand ways in which it can oppose itself to the plans of the elected officers, the quantity of information that it is alone able to either deliver or to hide, the good will or the resistance that it can manifest in the execution of a task that is entrusted it.

The complexity of economic life and the swelling of administrative apparatuses (a cause of prestige for those who direct them) has the result that the sources of information and the possibility to obscure, in the manner of organization of facts, the decisions made by the elected organisms, are all in the hands of those who, by career, are constantly at grips with the problems. They are specialists, experts, without whom the functioning of the group would become impossible, and as such, they hold great power. And if per chance their ambition is to pass from the status of technician to that of technocrat, elected representatives, themselves also trained, cannot oppose them with a sufficient resistance.

At this stage, the groups have ceased to respect the democratic schema that they gave themselves in the beginning, and although no modification is inscribed in their statutes, the effective power has ceased to be in the hands of the members or of their representatives. We do not know in what measure this evolution affects all associations. It is moreover a question that it is necessary to pose in regard to this entire evolutionary schema.

SOME GENERALIZATIONS

One can ask oneself whether, starting from the research mentioned above, we are correct to extend its conclusions to other voluntary groups. Moreover, it is perhaps not certain that the evolution toward a shrinking of direct democracy, or what amounts to the same thing, toward a concentration of power, is irreversible. On this second point, it seems that only groups of reduced size can maintain themselves in the direct democracy state; we have even seen a case of turning back to the beginning on the part of a group of consumers who had given their store over to private management and then took it back under their own control. Although rare, this case would tend to indicate that it is due to lines of evolution other than those retraced here, and that in almost every instance the question of predicting how such and such a particular group will evolve remains open.

At this point it is appropriate to make reference to the celebrated thesis published in 1911 by Robert Michels in *Political Parties: A Sociological Study of the Oligarchic Tendencies of Modern Democracy.* Himself an old socialist, Michels especially studied the German labor movement and social democracy, but his references extend to workers' movements of other countries, in particular the French and Italian. He sees in the organization that must necessarily devote itself to party politics, especially the workers' parties which propose the conquest of power, the source of their rigidity, of their conservatism and the oligarchic tendencies which are manifest in them. Whence his famous sociological law: "It is organization which gives birth to the dominion of the elected over the electors, of the mandataries over the mandators, of delegates over the delegators. Who says organization, says oligarchy."[15]

The formation of this oligarchy is not always conscious on the part of the elected leaders. The principle cause, according to Michels, must be sought in the fact that leaders are technically indispensable.

> At the outset, leaders arise *spontaneously,* their functions are *accessory* and *gratuitous.* Soon, however, they become *professional* leaders, and in this second stage of development they are *stable* and *irremovable.* It follows that the explanation of the oligarchical phenomenon which thus results is partly *psychical;* oligarchy derives, that is to say, from psychological transformations which the leading personalities in the parties undergo in the course of their lives. But also, and still more, oligarchy depends upon what we may term the *psychology of organization itself,* that is to say, upon the tactical and technical necessities which result from the consolidation of every disciplined political aggregate.[16]

Michels adds that the formation of oligarchies affects all organizations, be they socialist or even anarchist, because they originate from an organic necessity. Several of these apsects of the evolution of leaders link up with and confirm the facts of the preceding pages.

This convergence reinforces my opinion that a generalization of these research results is possible, and the hope that someday a sort of model or paradigm of the evolution of democracy in associations will be elaborated. We are, nevertheless, still far from it, and studies on different types of associations and on diverse aspects of power must multiply first. It is with the goal of illustrating this point that I present below several results from inquiries on cooperatives, then some of the conclusions of research on union democracy, and finally, some facts on another aspect of the evolution of associations linked to that of power from another source, the change of attitudes regarding money in the Israeli kibbutzim.[17]

There are several studies of cooperatives and many declarations by observers and people close to the organizations that agree with the tendencies indentified above. These observations especially bear on the amount of participation in assemblies, and on the growth in age of the societies and of officers. In Great Britain, for example, participation in consumers' cooperatives did not reach one percent, and participation in elections failed to reach two percent. It is generally agreed that the proportion attending meetings is inversely proportional to the total number of members; the results of our inquiries, from studies of small groups, shows meanwhile that size is not the sole factor responsible for the loss of interest by members and that small societies are also affected by the lack of participation.

The figures on growth in age of members (interesting in order to estimate the disaffection of youth) are also fragmentary and we have but a few studies to cite. One inquiry done in Germany on 5,000 cooperators revealed a mean age of 43; another on the societies of one union of cooperatives in the east of France showed that 43 percent were between 45 and 65 years old; one Swedish study showed that the mean age of committee leaders was 51 and that of members of administrative councils about 52. In spite of a certain renewal in the past few years, it must be about the same with the French producers' cooperatives, for the employees that these groups hire have a tendency to not become enrolled members.[18]

As to the loss of interest on the part of members, it has been made the object of numerous declarations and an historian as sympathetic to the cooperative movement as G.D.H. Cole has not hesitated to see in it the major obstacle posed to cooperative democracy. He noted that "whatever may be the rights of members to control of the societies, there cannot be real democratic control without a lively interest for everything that is done. It is the absence of interest that is responsible more than any other factor, for the relatively slow progress of the movement in recent years."[19] We have seen above that the two factors responsible for the loss of interest in the societies studied were the low economic efficacity and the disappearance of the link between these groups and the other institutions of the worker movement. Are these to be found in the entire cooperative movement?

In matters concerning the economic efficacity of consumer movements, it must be recognized that too often it does not go any further than the distribution of a return and involves neither noticeable price decreases nor any reform of the system of distribution. On the other hand, the range of freedom for action regarding price adjustment is limited and increases in the standard of living lead individuals to less anxiety about small price differences from one store to the next. In addition, fashions, mass publicity, the growing importance of durable consumer goods, and the increasingly strong place of leisure accentuate the loss of public interest in institutions that aim at a reasonable price decrease in articles whose consumption has become so current and whose part in the family budget so reduced that it no longer draws attention. In other terms, the practical action of cooperation, that for which it effectively works—and not its ideological orientations—is today very far from the preoccupations of individuals.

Besides that, as we have seen, overorganized modern life at times favors sociability in small groups, family and favorite haunts rather than in organized groups. It is thus that one notices in urban housing cooperatives a clear tendency to evade organized activities in favor of gardening or hobbies, little informal groups of neighbors or of friends, and individual leisure. All activity that prescribes a certain discipline, and which because of that might recall life at work, has little chance to succeed.

This retreat from organized groups, on the one hand, and the too routine activity of cooperative groups on the other, creates neither the need for nor even the utility of this cooperative education, of which so much is said. We can push the reasoning to the extreme and ask ourselves: even if it were desired, what good would it do for the majority of individuals, being given the conditions of management and the significance of work for these groups? That does not imply that the cooperative spirit is dead, as is sometimes said. To the contrary, the need of union is manifest each time it is necessary to make use of strictly functional organizations that disappear once their goal is attained. Cooperation has perhaps been wrong to count on a need for permanent union and it is not surprising that the cooperative spirit becomes diluted when the cooperative institutions become involved in broader issues.

These arguments lead us to the second factor in the loss of interest—the loss of the link between cooperation and the workers' movement. Branches of a common trunk, cooperation, unionism, and workers' parties have become diversified and each of them finds itself at grips with its own vicissitudes. But they seem to meet with a common obstacle in the disaffection of their members. For them all, the possibilities of consumption brought to individuals by the increase in their standard of living have weakened the spirit of participation and no one sees well today how they will surmount this obstacle, how they will adjust their goals to these new conditions.

The research of Michels served as a point of departure for the work of Lipset, Trow, and Coleman on union democracy.[20] Their study seems applicable to other associations as well, for several previous studies had also shown that the control of power and the passivity of members ends in oligarchy. The conditions for the occurrence of democracy may be listed in abbreviated form as follows.

- Democracy can exist only when there is an equal distribution of wealth and a low risk of rich minorities or demagogues, as Aristotle noted.
- Democracy can occur when units are relatively small and the citizen can observe government directly.
- Democracy is possible when members are not affiliated solely with their own association but also with subgroups within it, serving as channels of communication between members of the central organization and among the subgroups themselves, crystalizing tendencies and organizing interests and opposition.

The research of Lipset, Trow, and Coleman confirms Michels's law of oligarchy. Here are some of their conclusions, in abbreviated form.

- The stronger the autonomy of the local sections, the greater the chances for democratic life in the union.
- The smaller the difference between the status of the leader and that of members, the greater the chance of democracy.
- The greater the attractiveness to the leader of the job that awaits him when his term is finished, compared to other jobs he could get, the more likely he will remain in the union, reinforcing the opposition and the chances of democracy.
- The greater the chance of meeting fellow workers at leisure after work, the higher the interest and participation in union affairs.
- The more diverse the functions of the union, the greater the susceptibility of interest and involvement.
- The greater the interest in work, the greater the chance of participation in the union.
- The more numerous the chances for independent communication offered to the opposition, the greater the chances for democracy.
- The legitimation of the party system in the union, justifying opposition under rules governing conflict, leads to a distribution of power.

- The greater the guarantee of protection of minority rights, the greater the chances of democracy.

Several of these conclusions match the observations made in this book. But perhaps still more than these specific convergences, it is the central point of the thesis of Lipset which merits pondering: to know the guarantee of democracy in an association provided by tolerance of factions and even the organization of an opposition. It is necessary to say that the associations as a whole are still far from holding to such a proposition.

To speak of attitudes regarding money in a chapter devoted to the evolution of power is not as misplaced as it might appear, for these attitudes have been transformed at the same time as the evolution of democracy. In addition, although I will refer here to the experience of the kibbutzim, these groups are far from being the only ones to rise up against the money cult in society and to have tried to suppress its role. Beginning from the Marxist critique of the circuit money-merchandise-money, the idea was to create within this circuit (nontransformable, up to the arrival of socialism on the global society scale) of small collectivities in which money would disappear and in which only the circulation of merchandise would be tolerated. The Israeli kibbutz is a good example of it: although it is linked upstream (for its outside purchases, equipment, and products that it does not produce itself) and downstream (for the sale of its products) in the circuit money-merchandise-money, in the interior, always, money totally disappears.

At the same time as the group suppresses money, it wants to try to realize another hope of socialism, that of the distribution of goods according to the principle "to each according to his needs." As is known, this notion is found at the base of all socialism, in reaction against inequalities due to money in the bourgeois world and in order to perfectly realize the principle of democracy, which supposes individuals to be equal. Up to now, it has received more applications than the idea of the suppression of money, even at the level of entire societies. As to small collectivities, which alone are of interest here, there are several means by which the equalitarian ideal may be approached. One way to start is to distribute, in money or in kind (food rations, for example) equal remuneration to all group members. This system has been tried by numerous groups, certain communities of work, for example. But it is necessary to observe that the principle of "to each according to his needs" is not perfectly realized, for things are equally distributed while needs of all individuals are not necessarily the same. Thus, for example, it is not the same thing to distribute ten cigarettes per day to each member of the group, or to permit each to take from the reserve the number of cigarettes that corresponds to his needs to smoke. This example is not simply theoretical, as we shall see. Diverse attempts have been made by socialist collectivities to put these two notions into operation and it is not surprising that the communes and communitarian groups that are now established here and there have put them to use. I will only consider here the kibbutz, which has wanted to be at once a moneyless society and to respond to the principle of each according to his needs; but which, with time, has had to renounce these two principles in part, and in particular, the total application of the needs principle in favor of equalitarian distribution. To commence, we recall that kibbutzim are agricultural collectives created at the beginning of the century in Palestine by Zionist pioneers. They are groups or colonies which developed the country that later became Israel. The kibbutzim wanted not only to create the Jewish state, but also to be the embryos of socialist society. Within the kibbutz money was suppressed, each worked according to his possibilities and received at will from the fortune of the group, according to needs. With time, however, these principles were somewhat altered and it was necessary to distinguish a certain number of stages.

In an early period, each received according to needs and there was no money in circulation within the group. When a member needed to have some clothing washed, he brought it to the collective wash-house and picked up a garment his size from the pile that had been washed. When he felt the desire to smoke he opened the collective cigarette box and took the number he desired. That went on from 1910 to 1930. The kibbutzim were young and had only begun their work of building Palestine. They were poor and even if they practiced the needs principle there were not yet many things with which to fill those needs. The communism that they produced was a communism of penury.

A second phase was characterized by individual appropriation of certain objects. People no longer went to the laundry to take just any piece of clean clothing that fit, but expected that their own clothes would be washed. Each had his own small personal wardrobe, corresponding better to his tastes, and especially, to his measurements. As in the first phase, clothing continued to be purchased collectively in the city by the treasurer of the group, but in this phase, the treasurer did not purchase by type, but in response to personal tastes.

In a third phase, corresponding to the urban development of Palestine in the 1930s, money first appeared in the kibbutz. Still following the example of clothing, each member received a small sum to cover purchase of clothing in city stores. But money still did not circulate freely in the group itself. It never has circulated there, moreover, but—and this is the essential point—there was more and more money present.

A new phase commenced in the 1940s, with the practice of putting a freely utilizable sum of money at the disposal of each person, for any purchase whatsoever. This was pocket money. One could buy some brand of cigarettes that the commissary had not stocked, or save to buy a radio, books, or something else. At this moment the needs principle was renounced, in favor of equalitarian distribution. The principle of to each according to his need of money would indeed be impossible to apply, for when does the need for money ever stop?

At present, the possibility of individual consumption by members of the kibbutzim has increased and differences have appeared in the comforts of individual habitations, in furniture, in household equipment. In addition, in case of a resignation by a member, a sum is advanced to permit him to begin again elsewhere.

In renouncing the needs principle, it is above all the individualization of consumption that is at issue: from the moment when needs become diversified and when there is a possibility to satisfy individual tastes, the sole way to contain these needs within limits permitted by the economic situation of the group is to root them in a common denominator: money. In other terms, the principle only appears applicable when the group is poor and its members have decided on maximum constraint over personal consumption and thus to suppress their tastes and their preferences, or when the group is very rich and it can really satisfy all needs. No group or society has reached that point and none is likely to, in spite of the promises of the opulent society that this hope will one day be realized. Socialist communism or paradise, these harmonious worlds, forever born by utopia or religion, are not for tomorrow.

At first, though it did not circulate in the group, money was always in a sense present, first as a matter of anxiety, and later in countable form. As a matter of anxiety: to the extent that the kibbutz inserted itself in a larger economy dominated by money, for which it had to produce and whose market fluctuations dictate prosperity and forms of organization of work. Even if all members did not occupy themselves with questions of buying and selling, even if they did not preoccupy themselves much with the prices of the harvests, it was necessary to have an efficient organization to collect the harvest at least cost. Whence the introduction of a division of work and norms regarding yields, that is to say of an economy of time, of a calculus of hours of work and suppression of time wastage. Whether this economy of time is calculated in hours or money makes no difference, its goal in the end is only a response to money problems posed by the situation of the group in the economy. Therefore, constant economic anxiety and rationality, and personally I have never witnessed anxiety for the economy anywhere that matches that of members of kibbutzim.

What is more, reintroduction of money made it necessary to account in one way or another for the advances and sums returned to each member for his personal needs. Each member had his account with the group treasurer, as each of us has an account in the bank or a postal savings account. And—and this is the essential thing—an account that it is necessary to supervise, to see to it that one does not get in debt; thus, to think about money, although it is precisely against this preoccupation that the group had wanted to struggle.

Finally, there is another aspect of the question that I would like to present, on a more general level this time, concerning the position in the larger society of the group without internal circulation of money. In spite of the preoccupation with money of which I have just spoken—and it is not contradictory, for these preoccupations are situated at the member level—the fact that the kibbutz adopted the needs principle led it to a development of collective consumption: not being able to satisfy all the very differentiated needs of individual consumption and the monetary needs of members, the kibbutz has developed specialized collective facilities: restaurants, swimming pools, libraries and so on, all of which weigh heavily on the economy of these groups; and it is known that, on the whole, few of the kibbutzim have a sound economic situation and that a certain number go bankrupt unless they are regularly sustained by ideological solidarity and diverse forms of aid and loans.

Thus, thinking by development of collective equipment to replace or fill the gaps in individual consumption, the kibbutz has gone into debt and created a dangerous economic situation. Not only has it been unable to renounce the money that it must continue to distribute to members, and that continues to preoccupy them, but it has put itself in peril. The fact of wanting to renounce money has finally rendered it more dependent on money. Not only has this type of group possessed neither the knowledge nor the ability to suppress money, but has not known how to accept it.

At the same time that the role of money reappeared, the role of treasurer-accountant became more and more important, in the same manner as we have demonstrated in the communities of work and other associations. At the same time that the concentration of power is witnessed in the hands of some elected leaders, the majority of members of the kibbutz have become disinterested in collective management.

PERSPECTIVES ON RESTRUCTURING

This chapter ends with the examination of some perspectives on restructuring that are posed in one of the movements examined above, that of the communities of work, in which the officers have come to accept the diagnosis proposed above and have attempted to find new techniques of collective management. In fact the communities of work have realized that if they do not want to repeat the evolution of the entire cooperative movement, it is necessary to find, in collective management, bases other than the idealism of the past and the painful repetition of cooperative slogans.

From the start of the 1960s, programs of member education were set up, at the same time as an effort to train informants[21] charged with information dissemination to the membership base. Account is taken of the fact that management can only become collective through gradual training of individuals. Community directors are responsible for all experimentation, but there is already doubt that programs of education may be cut short, that the possibility of promotion from the base is extremely limited, and that the great majority of members do not want such a promotion anyway, much preferring a climate of camaraderie in the business. There is even more: people begin to be aware that belief in collective promotion plays almost the same role as equalitarian sentiments and camaraderie; in fact, the two beliefs reinforce one another and lead to the development of lethargic tendencies, by opposition to expansionist tendencies. The history of cooperative movements shows that if there have been numerous cases of individual promotions, there has scarcely been collective promotion, and it might well be asked why the belief remains so much alive. One of the explanations seems to be that the belief has the function of closing groups in on themselves (to believe that it is necessary to promote from within is in fact to close the group in on itself, because of the limited number of openings): thus the belief forces closure, but closure does not destroy belief. Like all feelings of camaraderie, it plays the role of a mechanism against group expansion.

The courses in worker training for management could not have continued so long without changes in the general economy: at the end of a few courses all would have been trained. But to what oppportunities would such training lead? In the same sense—to what would a better education of the membership base lead, with its graphics and all the audio-visual instruments developed in the hope of a better collective management? To whose profit? To the profit of enterprises that do not grow? It is necessary to recognize that in the absence of expansion, programs of information and instruction only reinforce the best atmosphere of the communities; that is, the association of men, the camaraderie, by opposition to the development of the entreprise. In the last analysis, all this effort may simply reinforce the tendencies to lethargy that good camaraderie inevitably brings, by contrast to opposition to expansionist tendencies that are bearers of opposition, conflicts, and doubts about the ends of man.

I do not want to say that these feelings of camaraderie are not estimable and I understand very well that for many men whose possibilities of promotion are weak, it is much more desirable to pass life working with buddies in a small, sympathetic team, than to become servants of expansion and progress from which they will draw no individual benefit. Many cooperative officers share this view and it is one of the reasons for the lack of dynamism of production cooperatives and self-management groups in general. It is moreover necessary to say that they are not completely wrong: expansion, growth—have they not for their sole effect to increase the ascendancy of some men, the heads, and the weight of the technostructure? After the phase of expansion of the 1960s and especially since May 1968, it is in this way that problems are today posed.

During the 1960s the communities of work were involved in the same expansion as all countries. We recall first some general tendencies: the growing openness of France toward its common market partners intensified competition and led to rationalization and dynamism; political stability and the neutralization of the working forces brought strong American investments, attracted by the high profit levels of an old fashioned economy, and according to the subtitle of an article in *Le Monde,* by a country "where all is to be done."[22] More even than the concentration of business, these openings of the French economy created an expansionist climate which upset habits of thinking and working. On the political level, the Left did not succeed in paralyzing the liberal economy and did not interfere with its expansion. Still existing politically, thanks to its momentum, this same Left had already expired ideologically and its principle proponents, notably the clubs, have, explicitly or not, accepted the economic principles of the postliberal society of huge economic units and mass consumption.

Thanks to expansion, in the majority of cases the communities have acquired financial stability and have become profitable businesses. In the same way the communitarian directors' teams have gradually acquired managerial maturity and are disencumbered of their ideological yokes, and ripe for new experiences, have turned toward expansion. The communitarian groups are largely open outward and the product they offer on the market, of experiences at self-management, is not of bad quality. Certainly self-management is not that which they had hoped to make it, but there exist certain tangible elements of collective management in the teams, drawn from directive councils. As to collective promotion, this slogan has been forgotten, and it is realized that the staff necessary for a politics of expansion must come from outside the businesses. Even if it must come to a halt at intermediate levels, individual promotion in the businesses may be favored by growth itself and, due to the expansionist ideology which accompanies it, the candidates for this promotion at intermediate levels are more numerous than in the past.

The communities of work find themselves drawn along by the general expansion of the French economy. If it must be mastered, and not just submitted to, this movement calls for new orientations and a redefinition of the structures of self-management. In the first place, it is necessary to ask what the word expansion means and in what a politics of expansion differs from the normal politics of business growth. Equally it is necessary to distrust the popularity of certain terms, and at the time, the word *expansion* becomes suspect because of its repetition. In fact, expansion means the challenge of the politics of growth followed during the previous years and is translated by structural modifications in business (adjunction or suppression of activities, fusion, growth in material and human productive capacities), structural modifications supposing a new and considerable outside injection of capital and men, and leading to a modernization of production processes.

The application of such a politics nevertheless encounters great obstacles in cooperative enterprises. Sources of outside financing are limited; the higher levels of administration trained in the leading schools stand aloof from the cooperative world which they reproach for its lack of dynamism and the outdated character of its ideals; finally, the cooperatives are generally concentrated in the domains of activity of the noncapitalized secondary sector and thus very dependent on the sentiments and the will of men who work in it. In these conditions one of the principal leverages for communitarian expansion, and more generally cooperatives, is the regrouping of businesses. But this regroupment also appears more difficult than in businesses which have the status of limited stock companies; in fact, like small family businesses, cooperatives are almost always personalized enterprises, whose directors fear the limitations of power that a fusion or regrouping would bring. That is the essential reason for cooperative atomism, and, more generally, associationist atomism.[23]

Expansion through fusion, or expansion through regrouping, expansion by growth—all these forms of expansion raise these problems and challenge structures and mechanisms of self-management. These problems may be grouped under five headings.

The Problem of Organisms of Self-Management

Expansion and injection of new cadres render still more burning questions relative to the functions of the directing council and the administrative council. Observation shows that the administrative council does not administer and that, when the cooperative enterprise is not of a purely patronal style, it is the directing council that is the true administrator of the society. This inadequacy of the administrative council becomes still worse in an expansionist perspective, when the problems of management are more complex and when the differences between the levels of education of members is enlarged due to the fact of the entry of exterior cadres.

The Problem of Information

In each community, an informant has been named. He is charged to diffuse information concerning decisions of management organisms (especially the directing council) to the membership, to organize consultations with the base and to bring these points of view to the summit. Recruited among the workers, the informant has the function of facilitation of communications from below to on high, and the reverse.

We have seen that collective promotion is a myth which, by reinforcing sentiments of camaraderie, has the effect of discouraging individual promotion by closing the business in on itself. In a perspective of expansion, businesses have, to the contrary, the need for intermediate administrative personnel, and it is appropriate to encourage promotions. This is the group to whom information is aimed, information on the business and the possibilities of promotion that it offers. In this perspective, information is no longer conceived as a parallel communitarian activity sacrificing to the myth of collective management, but as a paying service for the enterprise, recruiting intermediate personnel and society members.

The Problem of Animation

Following developments taken during management training (courses, sessions, and so on) and information transmission, the communities have attempted to train true animators of self-management. Chosen among workers of the base and subaltern cadres, these animators had the task of coordinating the work of informants (two or three, according to size and activities of the business), to prepare and animate assemblies (especially by visual means), and to give training courses to new members.

In an enterprise without expansion, animation is almost useless, its sole function being to regulate those little daily conflicts that come up in the association. In this case, animation is a reducer of group tensions. It happens otherwise in an expanding group, where human conflicts become aspects of the dynamism of the enterprise itself, and where one cannot as much reduce conflicts as to aid in their expression in the appropriate organisms. Animation then assumes another function and becomes a paying proposition for the business and for its productivity.

Information, as well as animation, is no longer considered a relevant activity of the community—by contrast to those relevant to the business—but as a business management activity, as a useful service, paying and paid. The fact that both better serve to integrate members to the views of the directors, than to develop awareness and participation susceptible of becoming competitive, can always be hidden.

The Problem of Integration of New Cadres

The intention is not to claim to make of these new cadres (i.e., basic staff and line officers) cooperators in the sense of the past century, but rather to give them opportunities to put to use the modern techniques that are expected of them. These suppose that the communities would be disposed to receive them over and beyond the usual formulas of welcome. Hence the problem of their integration.

Each enterprise, and even more the collective enterprises, possess a certain number of routines, ways of being and doing, in brief, a personality, a life style. As has been seen, due to their relatively small size, their often difficult history, the personal stamp of the principal director, the communities appear to be very personalized enterprises that is to say, very different from large bureaucratized formalized businesses. Expansion must necessarily transform this very personalized style of life and lead to a formalization of relations between individuals. And therein lies one of the first problems of the introduction of exterior cadres, supports for a politics of expansion.

A second problem touches the association of the men who compose the organization, rather than the cooperative enterprise itself. To choose a politics of expansion is to suffer a blow which can be mortal to the camaraderie of the group, that which makes up the social essence of the community. In fact, expansion modifies and perhaps even kills the community to the profit of the business. It is a risk that has been proven real and that is manifested through personnel departures and conflicts. Even the principal officers are not spared: their relations with their subordinates, whether the workers or the directing committee, become more instrumental, more functional, and even traumatizing for both parties. This functionality and this instrumentality only transpose to the level of interpersonal relations the severe and cold competition of business on the economic plane.

Fusion and Regroupment

Due to their history and their specific type of cohesion, communities and cooperatives have not known numerous regroupings and mergers; expansionism has often been only purely verbal, as in the rest of the countries in this epoch. Regroupings among cooperative enterprises are nevertheless necessary to the extent that these groups are not of such a size to individually make a place for themselves in the market.

From this comes the constitution of some business groupings destined to contribute common efforts at commercialization of products and certain technical and financial services. Such regroupings are similar to those of private businesses of similar size. In fact, the two types often find themselves faced with similar problems, and their responses are in some respects similar.

Attempts to go further in economic union of cooperatives have nevertheless come to grief. It would be a question not only of creating common services, but, in addition, putting in common financial resources for the realization of a sort of holding cooperative, that is, an institution of cooperative planning, playing the same role regarding member enterprises as the planning organisms of the socialist economy. It is here that the Yugoslav experience could be precious; for example, regarding conjoint nomination of directors of enterprises by these enterprises themselves, and the central body representing the totality of the members.

It is indeed appropriate to underline that in a liberal milieu, the community of work and more generally all cooperative enterprise or collective property, is cut off from the plan or institutions of planning and coordination that assume the socialist principles which it resembles. And only one planning institution would be susceptible of making of the small enterprise an element of a veritable self-management section.[24] They are far from it at the present time, yet the community movement can only conclude that mergers and regroupings constitute its last chance. If it does not seize it, its enterprises will quickly rejoin the customary production cooperatives, certain of good work teams, but whose significance in labor history does not extend beyond their creation—which was a considerable workers' witness among small capitalist units, but which represents nothing more today. There is even more: if the current state of small isolated enterprises is not surpassed, it is foreseeable that the efforts of training, information, and animation will sooner or later be abandoned, through fatigue and because they are not truly useful in the midst of enterprises that do not move.

The foregoing discussion on expansion represents what could have been said before May 1968 upset acquired values and before the period of expansion of the preceding years came to an end in the different plans for stabilization and struggle against the overheated economy, before the moment in which the illusions of the new society dissipated.

During recent years restrictions placed on bank credit by stabilization plans have particularly affected the cooperatives, which, due to their origins, have not disposed of significant funds of their own. The most fragile societies or the most dependent on exterior financing have been prey to grave difficulties and several have disappeared. In addition, even among those that have survived, these difficulties have led to placing training programs and animation in abeyance, the officers being more occupied with assuring survival than with promoting participation.

But there is more, in the sense that the depression and moodiness that currently affects all French society have affected the morale of members. May 1968 had prepared them to ask questions on the significance of their experience and the finality of their associations: are there machines to make profits in a limitless growth economy? Is there some sort of retirement fund for members come of age? Or simple material supports for the work of teams of friends? None of these questions has received a response.

The debate on these finalities not being open—the cares of daily life being stronger than the desire to open them—the programs of information and animation may appear to scarcely make sense any longer, if not as a sort of human relations program destined to integrate individuals to the views of their directors. As for the majority of individuals, the problem of the community is simply to survive. For that, no need to ask oneself too many questions, traumatizing as they are; moreover, the society whose directing classes feel the necessity to evade men who ask too many questions, has known magnificently how to produce leisure, consumption, and ideologies which make the rest be forgotten.

In these conditions, it is not astonishing that no liaison has been realized between the communities of work and the new wave of communes and small communitarian groups, which are now forming a little everywhere. One generation, and all of one way of life, separates these two waves of collective experiences in the same fashion that age and issues separated by twenty-five years the communitarian militants from their elders in the producers' cooperatives (who belonged to the cooperative generation of the past century), and from the younger people of the beautiful days of the Popular Front.[25] For the young contestants of the communes, who have scarcely the taste for ancient history, communitarians and cooperators look alike and are all old,[26] anxious about financial stability and comfortable treasuries, integrated into a system in which they have gradually discovered how to create a place for themselves, or even notability, and prudent because of their fear of seeing, due to their initiatives, those in their charge suffer. In a word, they are "types finished for revolution." And to see the new wave plunge into its experiences, attempting to educate an old world that does not want it to, to reinvent the common fund and collective consumption, to find new ways to produce, to discourse on the end of this world and to imagine that it will be born—in a word, to make the same mistakes all over again and let oneself fall into the same snares as the communities of work and, before it, the producers' cooperative—perhaps that is the law, the incommunicability of experience and the necessity of the repetition of error.

It is nevertheless quite possible that each one of these waves might not leave some residue in passing, and if the most recent has only scorn for its predecessors, it does not follow that it might not benefit from some progress that one can inscribe to the credit of its elders: minute progress, certainly, which is perhaps evident in more favorable legislation, or in a more comprehensive attitude in a public already accustomed to this kind of experience. And who knows what more! There still remains to balance the accounts regarding their eventual contributions—perhaps more in terms of the men they have trained (and I am thinking especially of the beginnings of Boimondau, but it is not the only one) but who have gone away and who have taken responsibilities elsewhere.

After the recession of the wave a balance might be struck. If it were to be drawn today, it would appear negative, reflecting the bitterness and the sentiment of nonsense and absurdity that assails us from all sides. The same balance would have been very different at the moment when the star of self-management ascended the heavens of May 1968 and when groups of students listened, enthusiastically, as the communitarian officers spoke of their collective property, of worker mechanisms of information, of attempts at collective management. Between the feeling of setback of 1973 and the illusion of 1968 that all is possible, there is perhaps something more. But it is necessary to wait and see.[27]

NOTES

1. No citations are given here. Sources appear later. (Ed.)
2. A part of this chapter has been published in Albert Meister (no title given), *Sociologie du Travail* 3 (1961): 236-52.
3. Albert Meister, *Associations coopèratives et groupes de loisir en milieu rurale* (Paris: Editions de Minuit, 1958).
4. Albert Meister, *Coopèration d'habitation et sociologie du voisinage* (Paris: Editions de Minuit, 1957).
5. Albert Meister, *Les Communautès de travail* (Paris: Entente Communautaire, 1959).
6. Albert Meister, *Principes et tendances de la planification rurale en Israël* (Paris: Mouton, 1962).
7. Albert Meister, *Où va l' Autogestion yougoslave?* (Paris: Anthropos, 1970).
8. This contradiction had already been highlighted in a parliamentary inquiry in 1897.

9. The shortage of animators in leisure groups corresponds to this lack of administrators.
10. Thus, for example, the number of readers in libraries decreases rapidly three or four months after opening.
11. This evolution seems irreversible, and out of some forty cases, we have observed only one group in which the members have taken back the management of their cooperative.
12. The ability to withhold information becomes an instrument of power for the directors. They have the right to choose the time and place in which information will be given or withheld.
13. In order to counterbalance economizing moves the workers of the base create a business committee and elect delegates from it, even when the size of the business is less than fifty persons, above which size such a committee is obligatory.
14. In spite of a generally satisfying work climate, workers still sometimes strike against the directors they have named. Similarly strikes have taken place in Yugoslav self-managed enterprises.
15. Robert Michels, *Political Parties* (New York: Dover, 1959), p. 401.
16. Ibid., pp. 400-401.
17. Portions of the material from pages 217 and 218, drawn from *La Participation dans les associations,* are omitted here. (Ed.)
18. Production cooperatives are often criticized for becoming ingrown. This is not well founded. Several investigations show to the contrary that it is nonmember workers who do not wish to become members and show little interest in cooperatives.
19. G.D.H. Cole. No source is given. (Ed.)
20. Seymour M. Lipset, Martin Trow, and James S. Coleman, *Union Democracy* (Glencoe, Ill.: Free Press, 1956).
21. A literal translation would be "informers," but the subversive connotation is not intended here. (Ed.)
22. A. Murcier, "Business en France" (*Le Monde,* June 16, 1965).
23. Albert Meister, *Vers une sociologie des associations* (Paris: Editions Ouvrières, 1972). See also chapter 10 of this volume, published since *Vers une sociologie des associations.* (Ed.)
24. The expression "cooperative sector" proposed by cooperative doctrinaires is an abuse of vocabulary. Cooperation does not form a sector in any country; it is only a collection of small isolated enterprises, inherited from the capitalism of small units.
25. It is not surprising that today, when the communitarians feel they have no more message of their own, that they draw closer to the cooperators, whom they have always criticized for having nothing to say.
26. Although the communitarians, most of them in their fifties, are considered the lifeblood of the cooperative organs, where they stand by to take over from the old cooperators who are going into retirement.
27. Here a 15-page appendix to the chapter, on Yugoslav self-management, is omitted in favor of similar material from the author's other works, already quoted. (Ed.)

8

ASSOCIATIONISM AND DEVELOPMENT

The goal of this chapter is to show the conditions and difficulties of the associationist type of development in different societies. We begin with the countries that have not yet started their social change and in which traditional modes of life present obstacles to development of modern solidarities and institutions.

Countries currently on the development path present enormous differences as to the weight of traditional institutions. Certain among them, like the countries of Latin America, began change long ago and have created a national elite capable of taking development in hand, once the necessary internal political, and above all the international transformations render the takeoff possible. The countries of Africa are completely different, scarcely free of colonial domination and still in the first phase of creation of a national elite. In these countries the traditional structures are a very strong brake on the different politics and initiatives of development, and the national elite is very limited in size and quality (very few individuals are educated), still submitting itself to the burden of these traditional structures. The essentials of economic power, and in spite of appearances, of political power, are still in the hands of the old colonial powers. The associations constituted in these countries are most often created at the initiative of the public powers and the participation to which they make an appeal is of the stimulated type.

Another model of development is that of socialist countries. We must refer equally to them here, and the example we will retain is that of Yugoslavia where economic associations, cooperatives, and self-management groups enjoy great autonomy at the very center of national planning. We will see how popular enthusiasm born of the revolution has been channeled to the benefit of development and for several years has played the same role of mobilization and associationist participation as the socialist ideas born in our countries at the time of the industrial revolution.

Setting aside this privileged period of revolutionary socialist enthusiasm, the majority of associations in the countries on the path of development rest nevertheless on stimulated participation, in structures created by other agents, especially public powers, than the groups of participants themselves. On this subject we may take the example of Israel, where, besides voluntary institutions prior to 1948 (the year of national independence) was developed a vast network of stimulated participation addressing itself to recent immigrants to the country, not desirous by themselves of utilizing associationist mechanisms.

The different types of cooperative societies represent the institutions most frequently utilized by the national directors and the officers of planning institutions to get their populations to participate in development and to integrate them to the nation. The pages which follow are especially centered on the analysis of these cooperative developments. But to the extent that cooperation constitutes only one type of association among others, the cooperative example can, in the majority of cases, be extended to other forms of associations.

COUNTRIES WITH STRONG TRADITIONAL STRUCTURES

Anglophone East Africa can serve as an example of the first group of countries which have only prepared the way for their social change.[1] Far from being just a bit cooperatized, the countries of East Africa (Kenya, Uganda, Tanzania) show to the contrary the greatest degree of cooperative penetration in south sub-Saharan Africa.[2] British administration has, for several years, favored the development of cooperation in gathering agricultural crops within a system of price guarantees to producers for the majority of the products with commercial potential on the export market. The number of cooperatives and their good functioning seem to originate from the fact that these institutions are more centers for agricultural harvests than commercial organisms. Unlike the liberal European cooperative which serves them as a model, the East African cooperatives do not have a commercial function and do not compete on the market. They do not therefore have to concern themselves with problems of sales, which have been at all times and in all countries the stumbling block of cooperatives.

As agents of social change, cooperatives have however only a very limited role. Far from aiming at a capitalism for African exploitation and an organization of production, they limit themselves to a certain specialization of production in one or two commercial crops, especially cotton and coffee. To transform the conditions of production would rebound to clash with tribal customs of periodic repartition of the lands; now, these customs discourage all investment in production and therefore all modernization of agriculture.

By contrast, the traditional structures accommodate very well to cooperatives which limit themselves to channeling monetary resources to their members, but do not destroy the traditional forms of social control. The cooperatives constitute themselves in the orbit of the clan and the tribe. This also explains their number and the fact that many among them are too small to be truly effective. Tribal solidarities have victoriously opposed the rational behavior that cooperation supposes. Thus, directors are chosen from within the tribe, rather than by qualification for functions. Thefts and corruption are frequent, to the profit of the extended family, whose influence competes for the loyalty of the modern group.

Cooperation, such as these three African states know it, does not therefore really aim at a social change in modes of work and traditional lifestyles. It constitutes a sort of indirect administration of the harvest of agricultural products to the profit of the very large import-export companies, in the same way as Indirect Rule has been an instrument of political domination utilized by the colonial power. This function of cooperation is not different from that of the private merchant, who likewise does not aim at social change, does not lead the way to a modern organization of production and does not capitalize businesses. In fact, the only credits are advances against harvests; investment credits are not possible due to the nonexistence of individual titles to property.

It is, on the other hand, a domain in which cooperation plays a role, that of training of an African political elite for independence. The colonial power being long opposed to social ascent of natives by the ordinary channels of education and professional training, the Africans that are the most desirous of elevating themselves socially for a long time have not had any path of social promotion other than cooperatives. In fact, many political men have come out of the cooperative movement, where they occupied positions as secretaries and presidents of small societies.

The French colonial principle of assimilation of natives and opening other paths of social promotion has slowed the formation of cooperative movements in African Francophone territories. In other terms, the weak development and failure of cooperation in the majority of ex-French African countries can be in part attributed to the existence of alternate channels of promotion.

Currently, nevertheless, the East African countries find themselves in the situation of these Francophone countries: independence has drained the cooperative movement of its best trained men, and the possibilities of social ascent that have opened permit individuals to neglect cooperative channels of promotion. As in all the countries, cooperation has suffered from the lack of supervisory and executive personnel, much more attracted to private enterprise or to public functions (professional careers in particular) or through movements of a more lively ideological tonus (on the level of militantism).

Essentially an agricultural movement, cooperation suffers in addition from the desire to abandon the land for urban life (an aspiration common to all the countries) and the scorn for manual labor on the part of individuals having some training. In the years following independence, public function represents the greatest opportunity for the young African elite. National development, with which the public function must compete, meanwhile demands more and more well-trained specialists. Recruitment is done increasingly on the basis of competence and decreasingly on the basis of militantism; to the contrary of what exists now, in which the elite is more militant than technical. In these conditions it is foreseen that cooperation will become more a tool of national planning in the hands of the state and of a more technocratic elite.

Currently already controlled by functionaries of the national department of cooperation in all matters that concern its accounting and financial affairs, cooperation will become, in more centralized economies and to dominant politics, the unique instrument for the harvest of agricultural products by an organism of national planning. Its very inactive role in social change will doubtless not be enlarged.

This last point is sufficiently important to call for closer examination. The development of countries considered here rests in large part on two conditions: strong foreign aid and a stabilization of the flow of exports, such as coffee, cotton, and sisal. For several reasons, foreign aid, above all under the form of private investments, tends to decrease, and in spite of the investments and aid of recent years, the average national personal income has constantly decreased (between twenty and twenty-five pounds, among the lowest in Africa). In these conditions, governments will increasingly have to concentrate their meager disposable funds on some limited development; the foci can only be some cities already disposing of a certain economic infrastructure assuring a better return on investments and from which the population, already proletarianized but without sufficient work, is a constant threat to social peace. For these same reasons, rural development and the investments that it calls for in men and in equipment risks being placed in eclipse.

As to already unfavorable rates of exchange, their stabilization and international agreements (as already exist for coffee) impose a limitation and even a reduction of land under cultivation for export products. Now, these are the very products that constitute the essentials of cooperative harvesting in the three countries. An extension of cooperation is then not very desirable.

The countries in question meanwhile seek a development of cooperation in two other directions: cooperation in harvest of new products, thus differentiating an economy tied to one or two international products; and cooperation in modern economic structures, of the *moshav ovdim* type, kolkhoz, or even *sovkhoz*. These two paths of cooperative development may have little success. Both necessitate important investments that current resources do not permit, and both are going to encounter the traditional mentalities of the African peasant.

These conservative mentalities, the direct consequence of the weight of traditional structures, opposed themselves to all modernization and to all social change more profound than the simple cooperation of gathering crops (regarding which it is necessary to repeat, that it transforms nothing of the structures and modes of traditional thoughts). These mentalities moreover are also opposed to ideological penetration, the most important factor of all cooperative development, whether of the liberal or socialist type. Although miserable, the African peasant is not a proletarian from the point of view of his situation in the relations of production. His tribe and its institutions furnish him a certain material security, certainly precarious, and above all a psychological security. As long as these institutions conserve their vitality, there is little chance for the ideological enthusiasm and therefore for a cooperative and associationist development. The problems of communal development, of unionism and politics, are posed in the same way in this regard.[3]

As in developed countries, cooperation sees chances of development among the proletarian and therefore urban population.[4] African associationism of autonomous creation is now above all found in big cities. The associations that are created there remain marked by traditional solidarities (recruitment limited to a single tribe, for example), as were those of our own country during the first period of industrialization.[5] The political parties, like the unions, no longer escape these close traditional ties and only emerge from tribalism with difficulty.

All things considered, social change is far from being sufficiently started, even in the urban zones, for the victims of this change to have recourse to cooperative and associationist institutions to resolve their economic and social difficulties; that is, by the liberal path of associationist development. As to the socialist path of associationist development, it would demand at once an ideologization of the elite and a receptivity of the masses to their message. Neither one of these conditions have yet been realized: the elites are too recent, and too few (although problems of competition within the elites oblige certain of their numbers to brandish the ideological flag to assure their ascent) and still too preoccupied to consolidate their socioeconomic position; and the masses are still too much under the influence of traditional structures.

The conditions of emergence of a true associationist development of the socialist type are therefore not yet realized in depth, that is to say, beyond the phraseology of the Left that seems so popular among the African leaders. In these conditions it can be supposed that cooperative development in these countries is not for tomorrow.

COUNTRIES HAVING ALREADY BEGUN SOCIAL CHANGE

The Latin American countries can furnish us good examples of this type.[6] Setting aside certain areas distant from all progress (indigenous communities of the Andean high plateaus, for example), these countries are characterized by the presence of very old national elites, of rural origin but increasingly urbanized, oligarchic, and obstinately defending their positions. They have already realized a certain development, but their economic dependence on developed Western countries prevents them from pushing ahead to achieve takeoff. Western cultural tradition there is very old and the local universities produce an elite that is increasingly qualified technically, originating largely from the urban middle classes and opposed, for those two reasons—qualification and social origin—to the rural and military oligarchic elite.

Corresponding to the ascent of the middle classes, the associations of all types are well developed; this is especially true for the cities, which set the tone in these countries. In the country areas, the dominant regime of the great, and even the very great landed properties, and the rigid social stratification that accompanies it gives a feudal character to rural society. The associations and participation are concentrated in the limits of each social stratum. At the summit of the social pyramid, the big proprietors form closed groups whose latent function is to maintain their privileges and domination over the other social strata. Below them, the more or less permeable strata of small property owners, sharecroppers, farmers, and middle men—the rural middle class—also have their associations. As in the cities, these are the intermediate strata, which are the most conscious, thanks to their learning, of their ambiguous position in the social hierarchy and of the lack of dynamism of a society in which the paths of ascent are blocked by those at the top.

At the bottom of the social hierarchy are the innumerable agricultural workers, the peons of more pronounced indigenous origin with neither learning nor chances of social mobility, apathetic and without association participation, or momentarily explosive in popular demagogic movements or directed by charismatic leaders.

Numerous cooperatives exist on the agricultural level, and rally the landed proprietors. These are generally the societies for commercialization of agricultural products, whose product sales finally benefit the great private import-export societies, and when there are no export products involved, private networks of distribution. Such societies have constituted active agents of change on the level of agricultural modernization and of the capitalization of operations by their adherents. Thanks to the banking system, generally well organized in these countries, the cooperatives have been able at the same time to make loans for their own equipment and to incite their members to mortgage their lands.

On the social level, their action for change has especially constituted, through the bias of rationalization and capitalization of the operations of their members, the destruction of the traditional structures and the proletarianization of the masses of agricultural workers. At the same time, cooperation reinforces the political power of the landlords and that of the great proprietors whose influence is more powerful than their number in the cooperatives and in the rural associations in general.

If we add to these two factors of change—proletarianization on the one hand, accentuation of the rigidity of social structure on the other—the continued decline of standards of living due to deterioration of the terms of exchange, and the stifling of the rapid economic growth of these countries due to the increasingly strong domination by European and American capitalism, we will have a panorama of their current sociopolitical situation and can reflect on the roles of cooperative associationism in a development that will have to occur sooner or later.

The decades of stagnation—even regression in recent years—and the bankruptcy of diverse programs of Western aid do not favor a takeoff within the structure of current liberalism. One supposes rather, that following the example of Cuba the countries considered here will orient themselves toward socialist models of development, whose painful establishment will be preceded by violent social turmoil.

In these new models of development there is no doubt that cooperation will play an active role in social change, as much from the point of view of modernization as management of individuals and mobilization of the masses. Agricultural cooperation at the present moment seems by contrast too bogged down in its problems of economic management and too identified with the propertied class to play a role in the sociopolitical upheaval that is prerequisite to future economic growth.

The urban elites, currently denied power, and the associations and movements that they direct constitute the most active forces in the anticipated new stage of social change. The decline of the standard of living of the urban proletariat, up to that time privileged by relation to the rural masses, can be an important factor in organization and revolutionary participation of the rural proletariat.

The models of development originating in these social upheavals will then impose a totally different role on cooperation. This role can be analyzed by the example of a socialist country.[7]

COUNTRIES IN SOCIALIST DEVELOPMENT

Of all countries having chosen socialist models for their economic growth, Yugoslavia is indisputably the one that reserves the greatest place to structures and participation of the associationist type.[8] We will consider it as an example in this section.[9] Yugoslavia is interesting to us above all from the point of view of its participationist mechanisms in industry and the social management of collective equipment for consumption. Regarding agricultural cooperatives, after the example of other countries of the East, Yugoslavia has followed too faithfully the Soviet doctrines of rapid collectivization of the countryside and has destroyed socialist enthusiasm—existing immediately after Independence—an indispensable condition for the creation of a voluntary cooperative movement. The most widespread current type of cooperative recalls the commercial cooperatives of Western countries. Adhesion to them is not forced any more as in the production cooperatives (of the kolkhoz type) of the start of the 1950s, but participation in them is strongly promoted by animators and through mass organizations. In spite of these structures and different sociocultural contexts, the stimulated participation in Yugoslav agricultural cooperatives is the nearest neighbor of that set up in Israeli village cooperatives, to be discussed in the following section.

It is on the level of participation in different forms of industrial self-management—whose inspiration goes back, as that of Western production cooperation, to utopian socialism—that one can best comprehend the role of associationism in a model of socialist development. Self-management is a type of cooperation that has benefitted from the enthusiasm of revolution and national liberation, and which, like the liberal cooperation of the past century, intends to be the instrument of the construction of a socialist society.

Like liberal cooperation of old, the project of a new society, more fraternal and more just, motivates the sacrifices and devotion of the militants. And the stronger the hold of ideology, the more intense popular participation becomes. The central value in this ideology is that of equality, by opposition to the injustices of liberal society. Whence the very numerous rules destined to maintain equality among participants and to prevent all formation of privileges. Equality of incomes, or only a very weak differentiation according to professional responsibilities, originates from respect for this central value of socialism.

To the extent that equality among individuals (and between businesses and between regions thanks to mechanisms of national planning) can be maintained, individuals will give the best of themselves, will militate, will participate actively. They will be psychologically mobilized, and the human investment in time, in pain, in benevolent works for development will extend to the maximum. For the same reasons, national consumption will develop much less rapidly than investments and can easily be directed.

This ideological mobilization nevertheless seems to last only for a time. Relaxation is gradually introduced. Differentiation appears in salaries, or increases, individuals dream more of their individual well-being than of collective promotion, the grip of ideology and militantism diminishes, popular participation is much less intense.[10] Yugoslavia has known these diverse phenomena and those with national responsibilities attempt by all means to struggle against popular disaffection regarding self-management and against weakening of the ideological credo.

In total, the Yugoslav example shows us that the period of popular enthusiasm, and the corresponding ideologies, hold for a rather limited period of time, of some years. In other experiences of cooperation, this privileged period lasts longer, one or two generations in the case of Western or Israeli cooperatives.[11] The latent function of cooperative or socialist ideology has been, during this period, to favor the creation of fixed collective capital by restriction on consumption. In Western and Israeli experiences, the period of strong ideological tone has been sufficiently long to end in a creation of sufficient fixed capital. To the contrary, in Yugoslav self-management this period will have been too short and the militant work, accumulated in the form of investments, is still too weak: the apparatus of national production is still insufficient to satisfy the consumption needs expressed in a more imperious and demanding fashion, precisely because of ideological relaxation.

At first, beginning in the 1960s, the Yugoslav government believed it possible to struggle against these manifestations of ideological relaxation by energetic measures limiting the autonomy of businesses, by restrictions on consumption, and reaffirmation of the supremacy of central planning objectives. These measures, however, arrived too late and were unsuccessful. Individuals believed less in socialist values, and, in spite of their reaffirmation, participated less; and even if they did participate, their power of decision proved to be limited, curbed by the imperatives of a central plan that tended to become more authoritarian.[12] Thus, in spite of a different way, the forms of socialist participation merge with those of participation in the Western world—they are voluntary, but they have been promoted.

The government had to draw lessons from this setback, and, changing gears, decided to abandon all forms of control and to favor tendencies to liberalization, and notably, a greater autonomy in business. From this came the reforms introduced in 1965, characterized by the shelving of planning institutions—and therefore greater autonomy in management of enterprises—by the tacit consent given to the development of private enterprise,[13] and by total renunciation of equalitarian principles in matters of salaries and rhythms of development of different regions. Such concessions have profoundly transformed the socialist self-management model of Yugoslavia, self-management becoming one sector of the economy and national life, among others, somewhat in the same fashion as the cooperative sector represents only one part of the liberal economies.

LIBERAL COUNTRIES

This section concerns liberal countries on the path to development, in which sectors of voluntary and stimulated participation coexist. Israel can furnish us with an excellent example of this group of countries. Even more, it could be said that Israel, as a state, is an associationist creation. From the start of the century, the first cooperative agricultural colonies were conceived as instruments for creation of the Jewish state. Whether they were kibbutzim or *moshavim,* these agricultural colonies created by the first waves of Jewish immigrants presented the following characteristics: voluntary recruitment, intensely and doubly (Zionist and socialist) ideologized, of relatively high social origin and education, and in reaction against their bourgeois social mileux of origin. The agricultural colonies had to serve the double ideology of the founders: to create the Jewish state (Zionism) and to create an egalitarian and classless society (socialism), founded on productive work in the primary and secondary sectors (in reaction against the purely tertiary activities of the Jews of the Diaspora).

Thanks to ideological fanaticism,[14] the colonies constituted true microlaboratories of communist doctrines. The principles of these doctrines could be tested in them. For instance, the principle of equality was studied and applied in all domains, not only at work but in life outside of work, between men and women, and so on.

On the level of social change, the agricultural colonies carried out to the maximum the criteria issued from the top; they specialized, they capitalized, and above all they organized rural exploitation. The kibbutz is, before all else, a great enterprise that submits entirely to rational criteria and to profits, and differs in nothing from the industrial enterprise on the level of its organization. As to the social point of view (in the sense of workers'participation in management), as from the point of view of the scientific organization of work, it must figure among the most complete of modern business.

This search for application of the principles of industrial organization to the agricultural world, and simultaneously, that aiming at the application of socialist principles have only been possible thanks to the very special recruitment mentioned above. These colonies have meanwhile had to face a certain number of problems due precisely to the fact of the creation of the Jewish state that they finally brought into being.

The independence of Israel in 1948 brought new tasks to the colonies and modified their position in society. Before independence they were the only solid roots of Jewish implantation in Palestine; after independence, and especially currently, following massive immigration and great urban growth, they are no more than socialist cells in a country organized according to the principles of the liberal world. From their double historic mission—creation of the Jewish state and socialism—there remains only the second, that for several reasons they appear incapable of pursuing.[15]

In spite of the strong influence the agricultural colonies have kept in political life (parties of the Left) and in the political structures (many of the high functionaries and politicians are old kibbutzniks and *moshavniks*), the social and ideological origins of new inhabitants of Israel do not lead them to enter the old colonies, form new ones along the same lines, nor to follow leaders of old colonies in their efforts and socialist propaganda. The new immigrants are of European origin and generally from the middle classes, but unlike their predecessors have no desire to return to the land. They undertake tertiary urban activities and are in no way influenced by socialist ideologies. As to immigrants of North African or Near Eastern origin, they belong in general to the lower middle classes and to the urban proletariat. Not having sufficient resources to establish themselves in the cities as small merchants or artisans, and industrial employment being limited, these immigrants have no other possibility than to install themselves on the land as agriculturalists. Agricultural work, for which they have no experience, is for them only a makeshift.

The very large number of such immigrants, around 40 percent of the population of the country, has lead the public powers to planning cooperative agricultural villages in which they are established and placed, and to the good functioning of which their participation is strongly promoted. Hence the creation of the *moshve olim* (moshavim of recent émigrés) colonies of small individual agricultural properties in which common services such as purchase and sale of products, utilization of heavy equipment, and so on, are organized under the cooperative form.

Animators and the organizing and training personnel in these new villages often come from the old socialist colonies and attempt to stimulate the participation of new émigrés.

The number of members of colonies of the old type remains stationary and therefore greatly lower proportionately as the country grows. They now represent no more than four percent of the national population. Because socialist ideals have little grip on the majority of the new immigrants, because of national prosperity due to foreign aid, and because of the progressive integration of Israel into the occidental bloc, the cooperative socialist of the old colonies has little chance to develop at the present time. In other words, the popular echo of socialist ideals is weakened and it no longer leads to membership and voluntary participation in colonies of the old type.

Social participation is now of the stimulated type—participation stimulated by militants of the old colonies, strongly promoted in less original, less socialist forms, and more acculturated to the values of the global society than those represented by the old colonies. Like the cooperation of Western Europe that it has joined, Israeli cooperation sees itself as incapable of eliciting adhesion in its original frame and must denature itself and renounce a part of its originality to recruit new adherents and thus survive.

The cooperative structures that remain closest to the original ideals, the original Israeli colonies or European production cooperatives, are the structures that witness the most meagre new recruitment. They are victims of their own originality, and having to make an appeal to a rather intense militantism, they find fewer members in a population in which ideals that create militantism get little response. By contrast, there is more success with cooperative structures that are easily adapted to the new values of society, as is the case with consumer cooperation in Europe. Adhesion to them no longer implies militantism, and the structure specially created to absorb a population is not sensitive to socialist values, as in the case of the *moshve olim.*

ASSOCIATIONISM AND DEVELOPMENT

The application of concepts of participation and social change, set out in the first part, in the specific case of cooperative and associationist development, tends to show that cooperation assumes two different social roles in its evolution. It is first an instrument for the realization of a project of socialist society, then it becomes a simple institution of economic life.

As an instrument for the realization of a socialist society, the cooperative or self-management enterprise (industrial or rural) depends strongly on sentiments of altruism and militantism of its members. Before being a business it is a fraternal association of men united in the search for a better society. And the sacrifices that all make together to lay the foundation and to reinforce their enterprise must finally converge in the construction of socialism. The social function of the ideology that unites them is therefore, in the last analysis, to create a fixed capital, investments, to create development. In this sense, socialist ideology is a more collective manner of producing the individual plus-value of capitalist development.

This fundamental role of ideology cannot be emphasized too strongly. To the contrary, the absence of ideology, or better, the ideological impermeability of traditional societies that have not yet begun social change, explains that cooperation or other forms of socialist self-management cannot play the role in these countries that they have assumed in the liberal and developed socialist countries. In such conditions even stimulated participation, be it cooperative or more generally associationist, encounters little success and only in institutions without great disposition to social change, as is the case of harvest cooperation. And the enormous efforts at rural animation, of creation of development groups, of communitarian development, and so on, have few chances of durable success and remain generally without results once the animators depart and the experts have terminated their contracts.

In countries that have already begun a certain social change and where a real economic takeoff will soon necessitate profound disturbances in economic and social structures, cooperative associationism currently sees its greatest chances for development. History shows that the period of enthusiasm and ideological influence is rather short and that it is this privileged historic moment that must be utilized to create enterprises from sentiments of association, to take up again the terms previously employed.

The history of liberal cooperatives and socialist self-management also shows that once the period of ideological influence terminates, the enterprise can even do without the association. The cooperative or self-management cell no longer has such an imperious need for the participation of its members. Its directors are specialists, technicians whose activities and initiatives are even slowed down by the participation of members. The case is clear enough in cooperatives of the Western world, totally submitted to elected directors and to executives named by management, and in which periodic spurts of participation by members interfere with good economic functioning rather than actually favoring it.[16]

From this moment cooperatives and self-management enterprises have ceased to be instruments for the creation of a new type of society to become simple institutions of economic life of their respective countries. The direction of production and management of investments (tangible results of the militantism of former times) are reserved to the directors without member participation. As we have seen in the first part of the book, ideology survives under the form of phraseology, but signifies nothing more for those to whom it is addressed. For the directors, their posts in the enterprise are a means of applying their techniques and training and of making a career out of no matter what institution of economic life.

Western cooperation, the oldest and most engaged in the process, suffers in addition from a lack of dynamism that stems precisely from its associationist origins: due to the apathy of its members, its elected directors are in general rather aged, its appointed staff have learned on the job and are generally natives who lack the highly specialized training required by the modern economy. The lack of dynamism due to these two reasons leads staff trained in the advanced schools to disdain posts offered by cooperatives. These aspects are the survivals of the militancy of times gone by, which, dried up, are nevertheless perpetuated in negative forms, such as gerontocracy, autodidacticism, workers' control.

These facts explain the feeble role played by cooperatives in the most urgent problems to be resolved in the developed Western world: reform of distribution systems, defense of consumers, research into new modes of participation in management. The lack of dynamism is explained in part by the disaffection of members, and in its turn, reinforces the lack of interest.

Other movements born of the industrialization of the Western world, such as unions, political parties, social work associations, are afflicted with similar problems. Although the popular disaffection in their regard does not rival that which has overtaken the cooperative movement, especially the consumer coops, they thrash about in doctrinal conflicts[17] and are without response to new social problems created by mass society.

Born of the industrial revolution, all these movements can only with difficulty accomplish their reconversion in a society undergoing rapid transformation. They remain tied to issues of former times, and have nothing to say on the questions of today. Everywhere in the developed countries, both liberal and socialist, the depoliticization of modern man is the most crucial problem on the political and associationist plane. Beyond an evident satisfaction regarding new possibilities of consumption offered by modern society to progressively greater social categories, and the aspirations to new consumption created by the gigantic apparatus of production of this society, this departicipation seems to originate as much from the absence of associationist programs (political, union, and so on) that people can respond to and that propose solutions to problems born of mass society, abundance, welfare.

NOTES

1. See Albert Meister, *L'Afrique peut-elle partir?* (Paris: Editions du Seuil, 1966); idem, *Le Développement économique de l'Afrique de l'Est* (Paris: PUF, 1966).
2. The extent of penetration is weak by comparison with that of the more developed countries where it sometimes reaches 30 percent of the population. In Tanzania, where cooperatives are strongest, the proportion is 5 percent. On these issues see Henri DesRoche, *Coopération et développement* (Paris: PUF, 1964).
3. This question has been developed by me in a series of articles in *L'Homme et la société* 18 (1970) and 19, 20 (1971) under the title "Développement communautaire et animation rurale en Afrique."
4. And in certain rural regions of Kenya where European colonists have had success in detribalizing their African manual labor force.
5. On this subject see Albert Meister, *Associations coopératives et groupes de loisir en milieu rural* (Paris: Editions de Minuit, 1957).
6. I have participated in two research projects on these problems in Argentina. Albert Meister, S. Petruzzi, and E. Sonsogni, *Tradicionalismo y cambio social* (Rosario: Universidad del Litoral, 1963); H. Calello et al., *Desarrollo comunitario y cambio social* (Buenos Aires: Consejo Federal de Inversiones and Universidad de Buenos Aires, 1965); Albert Meister, *Participation, animation et développement* (Paris: Anthropos, 1969); idem, *Le Système mexicain* (Paris: Anthropos, 1971).
7. The hypothesis of a development of the liberal type has not been considered. Such a development ends up emphasizing the businesses of the developed countries. The contemporary liberalism of many underdeveloped countries is founded on political power and operates to the exclusive benefit of American and European free enterprise.
8. Excerpts from Meister's work on Yugoslavia also appear in several other chapters, drawn from the other two books that make up this volume.(Ed.)
9. See Albert Meister, *Où va l'autogestion yougoslave?* (Paris: Anthropos, 1970).
10. For detailed analysis see ibid. In addition, keeping appropriate adjustments in mind, Mexican agrarian socialism shows similiar tendencies. Cf. Albert Meister, *Le Système mexicain.*
11. One of the essential reasons for these time differences arises from the degree of hostility of the social milieu. The more hostile the environment, the stronger the participation of members in groups which contest society. In the Yugoslav case international détente and Western aid have created a climate of ease and above all, have reawakened the bourgeois and individualist values that the socialist credo claimed to have eliminated.
12. Certainly the socialist cooperatives have never known the autonomy of liberal cooperatives. The corollary of the principle of equality in socialist ideology is a planned economy. To declare, as Western cooperatives do, that socialist cooperatives are not free, is a pseudodoctrinal argument permitting the

international conclaves of cooperation to mask their political opposition to the adhesion of the cooperatives of the socialist countries. To question the lack of liberty of the socialist cooperatives is to contrast the planning system from which they originate.

13. See the chapter "The Retreat from Self-Management," in *Où va l'autogestion yougoslave?* p.341.
14. The word is employed without a value judgement. What the outside observer might call fanaticism, from the point of view of the groups themselves is only the sign of a high degree of cohesion and acceptence of group ideology.
15. I have examined these issues in detail in Albert Meister, *Principes et tendances de la planification rurale en Israël* (Paris: Mouton, 1962).
16. In addition management has become so complex in the majority of businesses that common members lack the necessary training to understand its problems. Their participation often becomes negative, their control is exercised on secondary aspects and is paralyzing for directors.
17. Doctrinal conflicts have not existed in cooperation for a long time, where the diffuse Rochedale principles are only a pale reflection of the objectives set by the English founders. On this subject see H. Desroches, "Principes rochdaliens? Lesquels?" *Archives Internationales de Sociologie de la Coopération* 10 (1961): 3-38. Thus the principles of political neutrality that sanctify the accord between values of cooperation and those of liberal society, and thus sanction the abandonment of all goals for transformation of this society, have been added since 1844. In fact, they appeared in the 1934 congress of the Alliance Coopérative Internationale.

9

ORIGINS OF COMMUNAL DEVELOPMENT AND OF RURAL ANIMATION

The intention here is not to sketch a history of communal development and rural animation, but simply to indicate very briefly some aspects that differentiate them and that are tied to the history of the societies in which they were born. In general terms, communal[1] development is the method of Anglo-Saxon countries and sees a double application in the situation of new countries: directly through Great Britain to its colonies; less directly and mediated by the United Nations, on the part of the United States. Rural animation is French and it is usually applied in the old territories of the French empire. Not only is it necessary to see these different origins, but also the different colonial situations, born of different methods of colonization, which in turn reflect different metropolitan societies.

HISTORICAL ASPECTS

Points of Application

The points of application of communal development and rural animation are not the same. That of communal development, as the name indicates, is the local community; that of animation, more vaguely, is the public. The difference must be sought, respectively, in the structure of local government in Great Britain and in Anglo-Saxon countries; and in the countries influenced by the tradition of Roman law, and later, by the ideas of the French Revolution. Anglo-Saxon local government has always been characterized by decentralization, preeminence of the legislative, cooptation of officers thanks to systems of committees, a very large range of activities, and voluntary citizen participation. The French system is the opposite. Reinforced by the revolution, it is characterized by centralization, constraining hierarchical structures, preeminence of the executive, a restrained range of initiatives, and a slight accent on local voluntary participation. Each of the two systems of local government was later exported by the mother country to its colonies, as we will see below.

In addition the French system influenced Spain, and through it, Latin America. In these countries, as in the French colonies and in the home country, the local communities have very little influence, few powers, and financial autonomy limited to raising local taxes. The legislator does not want to know local and regional differences, nor the institutions born of local tradition; he knows only The People, the public.

These differences are noted still more in the transition from the notion of local community in England to the United States and its role of development during the colonization and the frontier period. In the United States, the states and the federal state itself originated from the vitality of local communities of pioneers. And, as in the past, the same communities continue today to draw pride from their independence. As for the federal state, collector of taxes and menace to the autonomy of the federated states, its interventions are generally considered with suspicion.

It is then not astonishing, from the fact of these different origins, that rural animation and communal development do not consider the same points of application in their interventions. It is not necessary to insist here on the reproaches that have long been addressed to communal development for idealizing the small rural community with its periodic town meeting, this autonomous community that perhaps does not exist elsewhere, and certainly not in the new countries. The point of application of rural animation, its abstract notion of the public to animate is not, a priori, more appropriate to the African countries, where the traditional institutions fractionate the population into numerous categories, classes, and strata.

Voluntary Associations

The place of voluntary associations is entirely different in the Anglo-Saxon tradition. The administrative and political structures provide a large place for them and favor their action, as well as citizens' participation in and representation through such groups. In countries of Roman and Napoleonic tradition, no voluntary structure exists between the citizen and the administration and state. Although, for example, American communal groups hold a large place at all echelons of administration and government, the countries of Roman tradition view the intervention of such groups with suspicion.

Great difficulties have been caused in communal development by the transposition of the Anglo-Saxon conception of voluntary groups. Taking less account of political hierarchies and administrative structures, animators have encouraged the formation of local, and sometimes also regional committees, thinking that such groups could validly dialogue with the administration and present their points of view and their complaints to the public powers. Far from being sensitive to these pressures, the administrations and political men have viewed them with suspicion and have fought them, the animators, and the groups themselves.

Rural animators exhibit a different tendency, but which also reflects the origins of their current of thought: they are less occupied with creating pyramids of voluntary groups than with going to meet the public with the administrative structures with which they want to open a dialogue more than in the past. In addition, the centralization of French administrative and political life reduced the role of the local community, and the movements of animation have a much greater chance for effectiveness if they organize on a departmental or regional basis. The communes have few powers of decision and few financial resources to aid movements, which therefore must naturally overflow these confining structures and organize around the centers of power, the prefectures.

A second consequence of this centralization is that movements of animation are much more oriented toward political-administrative power, and dependent on it, than North American communal development groups. The persons who incarnate power are not the same: in the very autonomous local communities of North America, the real power silhouetted behind municipal institutions is that of associations of landowners, of industries, and local merchants, in a word, the business community—and it is known that very often programs of communal development are inspired and financed by this commercial community in order to alternate the consequences of its economic initiatives (changes in the location of businesses, shifting the labor force, opening highways, population displacements). Other studies on community power structure show the influence of business on local life. In France, these economic interests are certainly also powerful, but are not exercised at the level of the municipality—where their influence would have little efficacity—but at the prefectoral level, and increasingly at the regional and national levels. The interlocutor of these animation movements is then no longer the merchant or industrialist himself but the prefect, at once representing the state and mediating the influences of pressure groups.

Another aspect concerns the permeability of the public administration by voluntary groups and citizens. In the Anglo-Saxon countries, and notably in the United States, a large range of public employment is provided by election, which is not the case elsewhere. In numerous countries, those entitled to employment are recruited by the administration itself or by other procedures that do not depend on election. By virtue even of its nomination, the American public administration, and especially at the local level, finds itself nearer to the citizens and more permeable to their desires and pressure. Things go differently in other countries, where public administration is not indebted to election for the renewal of its mandate. Here, also, communal development has too often supposed a public administration sensitive to local popular pressure, although this same administration very often hopes to itself play the role of opinion leader and to follow its own criteria in matters of local amelioration or development. From this point of view, rural animation has been better prepared by French centralism and state interventionism to deal with the susceptibilities of independent administrations that have arisen from African colonization.

Influences and Currents of Ideas

The Anglo-Saxon world is not distinguished from the Latin world only by its different view of the state and of social groups, but also by a different religious situation. To the diverse and multiple sects of Protestantism are opposed centralizing Catholicism in the image of the state of the Latin countries. At the origin of animation are found certain explicit Catholic currents and a tradition of parish animation; that is, historically an animation dependent on another hierarchy, that of the public administration. In the small rural community, the curé often had an influence much stronger than that of the mayor and his communal council, and stimulated (and still does) numerous parish groups of local development. It is in this tradition of parish action and its influence on movements like those of Catholic youth that one should seek one of the sources of rural animation.

On the communal development side, religious influences are not absent either, although mediated by the ideal of charity and social Christianity. Three sorts of influences on communal development may be distinguished, beginning from English origins. First, the charity movements. Second, community centers or settlements, set off by the English Christian socialist intellectuals and proposing to bring social classes together by encounters between higher- and lower-class men. Third, the writings and militantism of Christians and socialists, such as the Muckrakers, outraged by the corruption and abuses of power by American big capital during the years that preceded World War I. These three sources define the origins of social work more than those of communal development, although the latter draws its inspiration more from social work than from the connection with agricultural extension groups, which were very active in the United States since the end of the past century.

Although sketched very schematically, these different points show us a clearly different series of positions and options between the two approaches to participation for development. As concerns communal development, the influences indicated are conjugated in programs of communal development set up in the new countries: there the accent is found on the community and on local decisions, on a mixture of agricultural extension and social work, from motivations of good will and sincere indignation, on the belief in contact between men of different cultures.

As to rural animation, at least four characteristics differentiate it from communal development. First, the habit of bringing action to bear on territorial units larger than the local community. Second, the tradition and duty of recourse to political-administrative authority. Third, the tendency bestowed as much by the political structure as by the religious hierarchy to dialogue and come to terms with a superior authority on which the animation groups have almost no leverage and which delegates animators to them (priests, for example), whose nominations and statuses escape their control and which, through that, always remain more or less foreign to them.[2] Fourth, the custom, acquired in lay movements, of taking ideological positions, of references to a moral stance and a conception of man and society, and correlatively, the habit of a certain combat for the triumph of this conception.

These historic conditions make of animation an approach to stimulated participation that is different from that of communal development. The picture must nevertheless be completed by some words on colonial conditions. Before that, however, we will examine more closely some aspects of the world view of each of these two currents, these aspects being linked to the historic conditions that we will examine later.

ASPECTS OF DOCTRINE

A characterization like the preceding one cannot fail to fall into a certain schematism, that is, a certain exaggeration of contrasts, an overly strong development of extreme polarities. There is, however, a certain virtue in that, for the systematization forces critical reflection. A good example of this polarization is our opposition between communal development, marked by its Protestant origins, and rural animation of Catholic origin: it is agreed that it is not a question of saying that the men of communal development are Protestants, although those of rural animation are Catholics. The opposition is rather one of sociological types, and is intended to express the idea that as far as rural animation is concerned, it has originated in a society in which religion has historically reflected centralization, interventionism, and social hierarchical tendencies as much as it has inspired it.

Innumerable texts have taken positions regarding communal development. In reference to the authors who best reflect the mentality of the field development agent, it can be said that communal development is conceived as "the necessary approach when one works with the people over whom one has no authority and whom it is necessary to convince that they must change." Communal development also means "a social process through which men can affront and acquire a certain control over local aspects of a frustrating world and change it." The development of personality by means of responsibility in groups is the central point.

Three complementary aspects merit emphasis: the accent put on local problems, the accord that the method seeks to obtain from individuals on the changes that they must bring about in their manner of working and living, and finally, the desire to realize these changes with the least tension possible. These three aspects are those which have been among the most criticized of communal development. First, the accent placed on local problems permits skipping over more important national realities, which it would sometimes be not very politic to criticize. Second, the profound accord of individuals with changes that they must introduce constitutes less a matter of informed and autonomous conscience than accord with the politics of change which are decided elsewhere and without them. Finally, the care to evade all conflict has often been the origin of reproach addressed to communal development for being a sort of politics of human relations similar to that established in industrial enterprises—and perhaps with the same goal, to gain acceptance of an authority whose legitimacy could be challenged and whose care is, if not to maintain the status quo, to introduce the least perturbing changes possible.

The method of rural animation is different from that of communal development. The awareness of problems of development is created through outside action and results from a translation or transposition into local language, and decisions do not arise uniquely from the local community, but from the community as interlocutor for outside animators, bearers of the technical constraints of development. In this perspective the local community is not the privileged cell of development, but the base element of an apparatus of development that goes all the way up to the national level. Just the same, as we shall see again, the felt needs that communal development tries to get expressed and on which it wants to build its program of activities, are put in opposition to the imperatives of development. Conceived as the popular organization of development plans, animation cannot bypass a certain emotive dynamic, and must formulate its slogans, create its symbols, write its proclamations. This work is often done by the political party to which it is bound and which in return utilizes it as an instrument of national integration.

Like communal development, animation claims to confide to the care of the local community the definition of its development objectives, or things of which it has need, and thus puts the accent on selection, and subsequently on the training of local leaders. The two approaches have put in focus the procedures of this selection and training: animation training generally takes place in the headquarters of districts or provinces, and assembling the animators of numerous villages can last several weeks. Following this, the animator returns to his local community and attempts to apply the methods he has learned and to bring about the participation of the other villagers. Both approaches are based on this sort of proselytism by example, and the foci on training agents of change or animators, or village workers, resemble each other in spite of certain nuances or sophistications of technique. Yet rural animation puts much less accent on the voluntary sector than does communal development. Its approach is not only more directive, but more authoritarian, though here too there are nuances. It does not underestimate the technical and economic constraints that the change brings with it. To the volunteer in a communal development association, animation could oppose the volunteer in a popular organization for mobilization.

The most profound differences between communal development and animation are to be sought in the part they give to economic action. Communal development has generally been marked by a social concern, which has been the most criticized aspect in recent years. Its origin must be sought in the influence of social work and in the training of its principal animators in this domain. In addition, the economy of the liberal countries where communal development was born has been the domain reserved by the entrepreneurs and all intervention in this sector has been practically forbidden. In countries with very dynamic economies, especially the United States, communal development has no other functions than to adapt communities to change, to occupy itself with the categories of victims of excessively rapid change and its repercussions.

In the new countries in which communal development has been applied, economic progress is extremely weak, so that all the population can in certain regards be considered as a problem population and made the object of the social solicitude of communal development. The latter is surely not possible, and before the slender resources that are to be put to work for the benefit of vast populations, communal development finds itself reduced to economic action if its goal is really individual progress. But it has little experience with this economic development, for it has been traditionally isolated from it.

What has been said of the origins of animation shows that it poses from the start the problem of economic development in the French interventionist tradition. Animation attempts an articulation of public powers with popular organizations and has for an explicit goal to associate the inhabitants with governmental economic development decisions. Animation is different in that it does not consider that material development is the result of internal transformations of man, of intangible changes, and it often presents itself as the sectorial type, destined to shoulder the burden of an agricultural development in which the structures of animation are put to the service of a cooperative development.

In spite of these differences, the two approaches converge in their belief in the possibility of harmonious development and reconciliation of men and their conflicts. Animation has been very much influenced by the humanitarian doctrines of Father Lebret and his vow of "harmonized development." Communal development of North American origin has been strongly marked by the idealization of the rural community and its creative autonomy. Not only is the addiction to the past of some thinkers responsible, but there is also a profound and very popular conception of an amiable society, one in which divergences and conflicts of particular interests are reconciled in the general interest. It is this conception that communal development conveys in the new countries, assuming that the "natural local milieu" engenders a community of interests that implies participation of all in its amelioration. In these two cases man is considered fundamentally good, and social conflict is viewed as a misunderstanding to be dissipated. The two approaches, as in a certain measure the sociologies from which they arise (this is especially true of communal development) are without explication of social conflict.

In total, and in spite of doctrinal differences, the two approaches are similar: communal development, like rural animation, aims to give confidence to the populations by showing them that the public powers remember them, that the government is not so distant from their preoccupations as it may seem. The two approaches convey this new image of power thanks to channels of communication between the local communities and public powers. Both intend to realize democracy on the local level, to the end that the desires and needs that the base communities are called on to express might be the act of all their inhabitants. In the face of these intentions, the two approaches cannot raise participation and control over the politics of development to higher levels, and they are thus reduced to becoming the politics of human relations, softening administrative intervention decided on by the public powers. This weakness does not diminish their utility, but makes both seem like slow approaches to development; even so, the problem of their utility is relatively independent of the question of their adequacy for the social structures of certain backward societies, like those of Africa.

COLONIAL SITUATIONS

Decolonization is very recent in Africa, and the colonial phenomenon still profoundly marks the young countries of the continent. We will not evoke here all the colonial situations, but only those inherited from the French and English empires. Portugese colonialism, the settlement approach, constitutes a case apart, as does the method used by Belgium in its colonies. France and Great Britain approached the problem of colonial administration in an entirely different spirit. Without entering into detail on this question, examined elsewhere,[3] we note the kinship between the English tradition and indirect administration, and that, not less evident, between French centralism and the rule of direct administration.

According to the principle of indirect rule, the colonial administration leaves the indigenous hierarchy in place. The British governed through local chiefs, and the commissioners of the district limited themselves to presiding over district councils formed by these chiefs, overseeing the legality of their decisions, and coordinating the diverse public services at the district echelon (public health, public works, agriculture).

Equally schematically, on the French side, the colonial administration was modeled after that of the metropolises and was constituted of a body of functionaries, from the summit down to the local level. Much more than the British district commissioner, the French colonial administrator of equivalent level intervened in the daily lives of populations and possessed an entire administration under his orders.

In these different administrative structures, attempts to stimulate participation are naturally different, manifest from the moment when, after the end of World War II, the colonial governments foresaw possible decolonization. On the British side, the programs of communal development were established in the setting of traditional structures. The goal was to aid local communities to adapt to change, but ensuring that the communitarian sentiment was not destroyed. Yet these very different forms of colonial administration were styled as community development, and the British administration knew the need to be as interventionist as the French. Nevertheless, with exception of the periods in which interventionism was justified by the need to maintain order, the principle of indirect adminstration molded communal development. Preceding the latter, the old base institution was that of local councils, the native authorities, whose composition was intended to reflect the population. This system was to remain in effect until after World War II, when it was increasingly questioned and gradually transformed into an institution of local government, at first destined to spread education, the essential element of White prestige, in the African population. In Nigeria, Kenya, and Tanganyika, there were attempts that became official in the 1940s. To educational activities were rapidly added health and social projects, but very few cooperatives and economic activities.

On the French side, there was less preoccupation with founding intervention on needs felt by local communities, than with associating peasants with the actions of the administration. While British communal development stressed social activities, the French colonial administration posed from the start the principle of modernization, and by means of the administrative checkerboard undertook campaigns of popularization, created cooperatives or other institutions of centralization of products, acted directly on modes of work, organized collective fields, cultural blocs, and so on.

The diverse institutions that were created, such as the Indigenous Provident Societies and the Mutual Societies for Rural Production, were not basically communal, or only very little rooted in local communities. They were centralized institutions, unifunctional, authoritarian in their creation and functioning, and generally qualified as precooperatives, for it was thought that authentic cooperatives, which would be voluntary, would emerge from apprenticeships in common action projects, stimulated through these imposed institutions.

Rural animation has sometimes benefited from these colonial structures. This was the case in Senegal, where the cooperative movement animated by it benefited from aid by the Regional Assistance Centers for Development, which are the old Mutual Societies for Rural Development transformed, and which function as centers for agricultural equipment, outposts for credit institutions, and centers of technical assistance for cooperators. Other heritages of the colonial period have been inherited by rural animation in the two other countries in which they have been very active, Niger and Madagascar.

Although British colonial administration has also sometimes been very interventionist in practice, the characteristic of these programs of communal development of the Anglophone countries remains their local anchorage and their social and educational character. French interventionism is the opposite. Behind it is the centralist tradition of the metropolis, which has marked animation projects with its nonopposition to single-party systems. The interventionism and authority of the French colonial system creates a noncompetitive system similar to that created by single parties; habituated to work in this structure, animation does not find it contradictory. Politically, as economically, animation constitutes in some way the apparatus of popular mobilization. Especially on the technical and economic level—and accessorily on the political level—the intervention of the young African Francophone governments necessitates a kind of organization of the population as a response to their intervention. The result is an organizational form, and a certain human warmth. A not very different role was taken by communal development in Ghana during the reign of Kwame Nkrumah.

Unlike communal development, rural animation started off in the old colonies in response to problems of development. The metropolitan influences were from the outset mediated by postcolonial realities and by underdevelopment. It was completely different with communal development, where doctrine has come to bear the name originating from the United Nations and has made the old British communal development administration pass into obscurity. The respective influences of American and British communal development approaches on that of the United Nations will not be traced here. At first glance, it seems that the direct British influences on the product of the United Nations are less; even so, the North American current of thought mediates the English tradition. Likewise, at first glance, the communal development of the United Nations does not seem to show great originality by relation to its American sources.

At present, particularly in matters concerning Africa, three currents of influence seem to coexist in three types of men and movements: civil servants of the old British colonial administration (always very active and present in certain countries), who have a practice of communal action and who continue to apply it in the field. The importance of this current is decreasing, as the men who represent it retire. The second current is that of North American communal development, propagated by North American or international experts and by the currents of thought originating in the United Nations. Finally, rural animation and its interventionism in the French manner, with, as a representative type of man, the old militants of associations, social movements, unions, or politics, all movements steeped in a Catholic society. There is one *type* of man peculiar to each approach: the English *civil servant*; the *social worker* become an international expert; and the *militant,* social or political, from the metropolis reconverted to overseas social action.

Always, in the field and faced with the passivity and mistrust of rural Africans, and, also and above all, in the very directive, if not authoritarian or dictatorial manner of the young African governments, communal development, like animation, assumes a very authoritarian dimension which often does not differentiate it from the public administration, itself rising from the authoritarian tradition of colonial administration. In these conditions, we continually risk being in error by misconstruing the democratic and humanitarian vocabulary in which these approaches to development express themselves, just as we may be deceived by the vocabulary of parties and political movements, to which communal development, like animation, cannot, given the context, fail to be tied. That is to say that their objective study is far from being easy, even at the level of generalization kept here.

NOTES

1. The word in French is *communautaire.* (Ed.)
2. The difference from North American communal development is considerable. In the United States pastors are elected by local communities, and, dependent on them, more often become spokesmen of local public morality than militants of other values, a role that priests named by an outside hierarchy can play. In another context, a similar difference can be claimed in the relations between the communist parties and the masses: in the Soviet Union, for example, the party finds itself above the masses and plays a directive role in national life; in Yugoslavia, to the contrary, the structures of self-management oblige members of the League of Communists to pass through the mechanisms of election in order to play their role as animators of national life. Cf. Albert Meister, *Où va l'autogestion yougoslave?* (Paris: Anthropos, 1970).
3. Cf. Albert Meister, *L'Afrique peut-elle partir?* (Paris: Editions du Seuil, 1966).

10

VOLUNTARY PARTICIPATION IN LATIN AMERICA

Whether they are unions, cooperatives, parties, or entrepreneurial associations, groups or institutions of voluntary participation work in structures that present a certain number of common characteristics that influence them, whatever their domain of activity. Without pretending to present an exhaustive list, here are some of these characteristics.

ECOLOGICAL AND SOCIAL HOMOGENEITY

Participation groups appear doubly homogeneous: in regard to ecological recruitment of their members and as to recruitment in social stratification. The two criteria overlap. Ecological homogeneity implies reduced size and the predominance of interests and localized objectives.

The poverty of Latin American economies coincides with a rigid social stratification, whose goal is precisely to prevent thrusts toward more equalitarian redivision of a low plus-value of social work.[1] These conditions, which were those in Europe before and at the beginning of industrialization, lead to barriers to participation: associations, groups, and institutions of participation are constituted not only within each social class, but within strata formed by differences of incomes or resources. This double homogeneity permits distinction of categories of population within which groups with voluntary participation are formed.

Rural Marginals

The marginal label can be extended to the whole of the illiterate rural population, dispersed, poor, almost isolated from the monetary system, living at a subsistence level, without permanent remunerated occupation. The voluntary participation is not characteristic of these rural marginals. Cooperatives, unions, political parties are unknown to them, and participation in other respects is perhaps more intense than in other population categories; to them there remains participation in the family, the ethnic or locality group, institution or religious sect.

The activities that have been set up for them intend their integration into national life, or an amelioration of the conditions of life (certain programs of communal development, for example), but do not really pretend to lead this population into an effort at national construction.

Rural Proletariat

Participation is generally low because of the miserable conditions of life and the very low level of education. Participation is essentially confined to unions, although it is limited by the difficulty of implanting unionism in areas still under the grip of feudalism, with its protective relationships that interweave both peon and employer.

Urban Marginals

This category is comprised of innumerable inhabitants of the shantytowns, sometimes almost half of the population of certain capitals, that girdle all Latin American cities. Without permanent employment, more or less recent immigrants from rural zones or the transition shantytowns of secondary cities of the interior, often of distinct physical appearance (*métis, cabecitas negras*), illiterate and without urban callings, the urban marginals tend to reproduce in the city the forms of participation they have known in the country. The groups they constitute are first dispensers of psychological security against the hostile and new urban environment and attempt to prolong the solidarities and loyalties of the countryside. These groups are generally made up of individuals of a single geographic origin. The groups are secondarily means of urban integration and adaptation to a more modern environment. Union participation is of little importance because employment is unstable, there are no cooperatives for there are not sufficient resources or regularity of resources, and there is little political participation because there is little experience with political process. By contrast, religious phenomena are important, particularly participation in sects. And, because of the fact of syncretism and imperious religious needs, even established religions sometimes become sects again. The sect is solely a means of conferring a certain psychological security while satisfying religiosity, but it is equally, and in this regard interesting for our thesis, first an instrument of adaptation to the urban world. Comparable to religious and socialist sects of nineteenth-century Europe, and addressing itself to the same populations of rural émigrés, the sect seems to be a phenomenon linked to the rural-urban transition and to psychological modernization. For these reasons, it is found in the urban proletariat and in the lower middle class. More than all other participation groups, the sect is turned in on itself, primary, expressive of aspirations and of psychological needs of its members, more than it is oriented to material change and participation at the secondary level.

Urban Workers

This category is distinguished from the marginals by its qualifications, by permanent employment, and sometimes even by a certain security. The characteristic participation group is the union, much more than the cooperative, which seems above all the province of nonmanuals.

Employees

This is the social category that has seen the greatest growth in recent decades, thanks in particular to the expansion of public services and to the tertiary character of Latin American economic growth. The world of employees, from which cadres will always be excluded, sees a greater diversity in participation groups than in the preceding categories: unions, cooperatives (consumer, savings, residential), cultural and professional associations, political parties. Even outside of public employment, employment security is much stronger than in the workers' world, and it is perhaps not foreign to higher participation.

Cadres[2]

The most modern techniques of the highly developed countries of the Western world have received less extensive application in Latin America, though they are found to some degree in advanced industries, in modern public administration, in institutions of higher learning and technology, in some private service industries, and so on. However, because of the low level of training in the traditional employee world, the gap between cadres and employees is much more marked than in the developed countries. Having high incomes, often keyed to North American salaries, almost always with a university education, generally from the urban bourgeoisie, the high level technical and administrative cadres (to which we could add university professors) show rather different participation from other categories distinguished here. Their social origin and the status that their societies confer on them because of their competence renders them strangers to participation groups like unions or cooperatives, which constitute means of social promotion for the preceding categories. In addition, the demands of the unions generally do not concern levels of living like theirs. Their training has rendered them very critical of traditional political action, in which they pertinently analyze the power struggle game as detrimental to the realization of a program. Having often been influenced by Marxism (especially those trained in the human sciences), they consider that the participation that existing groups offers them lead nowhere if not to a slow development of existing social and political structures or to an action of social assistance for the disinherited.

The cadres are attracted by their business rather than by associations. The modern enterprise constitutes a participation center for them: the new methods of administration and particularly the decentralized methods of management, the increasingly collective process of decision making at the management level, the absorbing and complex technical elements of decision—all these result in making businesses into participation groups at the managerial level. The new management techniques create conditions of a sort of self-management recruiting its participants at the summit of the business hierarchy. Certainly only modern businesses show these tendencies, but such businesses exist in Latin America in certain advanced sectors and under the influence of North American management techniques. The same tendencies are found in research institutions, increasingly centered on interdisciplinary projects or collective studies, in technical units (such as computer or planning operations), and even in the army.

These tendencies are more apparent in certain countries: it is not by chance that they are disclosed more often in the more advanced countries like Brazil or Mexico. They are less apparent in others, although enclaves of high technical development are found, more or less isolated from their environment, but whose decisions affect this milieu.

Small Rural Landholders

We may include in this category the farmers and sharecroppers of all sorts, beneficiaries of agrarian reform or Mexican *ejidatarios*; in brief, all the Latin American small peasantry, whose principal national characteristic is the small holding, often the minifundium, a familiar unit of work, the investments of a low order, and low level of technique and economic organization. Like the urban artisanate, the small agricultural proprietorship is characterized by its lack of participation groups; cooperatives for purchase and sale of products are not widespread, even when taking account of the efforts made to organize the producers. Everything goes on as if a very low level of economic independence (small proprietorship or petty artisanate) were incompatible with participation in groups; family production and consumption enclose the family group and prevent it from opening itself to outside participation. In these conditions it is not astonishing that traditional values, and particularly those of the family and religion are the most vital in this category of the population.

With the exception of some areas where big efforts at cooperative organization have been undertaken, and in spite of the political power of certain peasant unions (in Mexico, for example), the small rural proprietorship possesses no economic weight in questions of product commercialization and in organization of markets. These matters are regulated without it and outside of it.

Larger Landholders

Whatever the degree of advancement of diverse agrarian reforms, the big and medium-size holdings maintain economic and political power in the rural world.[3] On the economic plane, the cooperative for sales and purchases is more characteristic of the medium than the large holding. Thanks to a very developed banking network in all the countries, the cooperative has aided much in capitalization of exploitation of a moderate size and to rationalization of its production. On the political level, by contrast, the medium holding is submitted to the leadership of the big landowners and often organized in the same associations for the defense of rural interests. Such associations play a powerful role in pressure groups. Elsewhere, the big landed families have always fed the parties with political men, and continue to do so once converted to urban ways; successors of the old armies of *caudillos,* even modern national armies still often witness on the highest levels links of kinship to the big landed estates. Perhaps the most important manifestation of participation of the medium and large landowners is political leadership. It gives direct access to the government and its power.

The Business Bourgeoisie

This category is situated above the small merchants and artisans, whose situation resembles that of the small rural proprietors. We exclude the free professionals from the business bourgeoisie, for the nature of their participation seems to have been profoundly transformed in recent decades. Previously at the service of rural aristocrats, the Latin American urban bourgeoisie has gradually found in industrialization and development of the tertiary sector, an autonomous economic and political power. The movement has taken shape during these last years thanks to foreign investments, of which the business bourgeoisie has become the manager. Professional associations of all sorts are characteristic of the participation of the business bourgeoisie: professional associations, chambers of commerce, entrepreneurial groups, assume an increasingly important role as pressure groups.

The Free Professions

Those characteristic figures of Latin America, the doctor and the lawyer, have lost their political importance. Sons of landed aristocrats or urban bourgeois, the lawyers—and in a certain measure the doctors, whose title was a symbol of social status—were formerly political delegates of the classes from which they emanated. They were the participants and the moving spirits in all social groups. Today the traditional lawyer is relegated to the associations, parties, unions, and parliament, although the executive posts, and especially the cabinets and planning offices that surround them, are increasingly in the hands of technicians.

To sum up, it is necessary to underscore anew the homogeneous character of recruitment of each of these participation groups that is constituted in each of these categories. Social mixture of these participants does not exist, apart from commissions of specified powers. The result of it is not only a fractioning of groups, but also a lack of communication and coordination among them.

ABSENCE OF SECONDARY PARTICIPATION

With the exception of political parties that can convey their demands in parliament, it is only exceptionally that Latin American countries provide a channel or institutional mechanism permitting secondary participation to groups, institutions, and organs of participation. It does not follow that groups cannot make their voices heard, but they must do it by means other than in the organisms for consultation or decision: the consultation is informal and groups that are heard are so by consequence of their weight as pressure groups, or thanks to the relations, joint presentations, good offices of extortion of their directors (and this weight can be considerable, as the Chilean labor unions showed in 1973).

The problem of secondary or institutional participation is the problem of institutionalization of pressure groups that confer a right to be consulted, or to decide, to groups whose experience shows that the law of the stronger at work in lobbying otherwise reduces them to silence. This institutionalization supposes a theoretical view of the society and of the game of social pressures, a view which goes counter to liberalism; and it is not by chance that one of the rare attempts at institutionalization of pressure groups in the occidental world has seen the light of day in France (in the Economic Council), at the moment of the ascendancy of socialist and planning ideas in the postwar years.

Although reflecting the general situation, these tendencies admit of some exceptions and one can indeed indicate some examples of institutional participation: in Venezuela, the Federación Campesina has an office at the National Agrarian Institute and a representation in other local, regional, and national official institutions; in Colombia, a representative of the National Agrarian Institute, which brings together rural unions, sits in the Colombian Institute of Agrarian Reform (INCORA); in Mexico, the Confederación Nacional Campesina does not participate directly in government but has representation in the Partido Revolucionario Institucional. If these are not the only cases they nevertheless give the impression of exceptions, and the general panorama that has been presented here is not modified by them.

Some important consequences can be identified in relation to the absence of secondary participation. First, groups of less political impact, emanating from social categories lagging behind a development that all the countries want to be industrial (associations of small proprietors, rural unions), are never heard or consulted by political organisms or by those charged with elaboration of the politics of national development. Second, given the influence of the liberal model, the participation groups have extremely few chances to see built up mechanisms of consultation; to the contrary, it can be supposed, from the example of the United States, where pressure groups are well established and operate without restrictions, that only the more powerful will continue to be able to support the expense of representation in the corridors.

Finally, ignoring participation groups without political weight, the public powers underestimate or misestimate their activities at the moment when they put development programs in operation: whence the creation of new institutions originating from the executive in place of implantation of programs through existing participation groups. By relation to the public services that have created them, these new organisms do not generally benefit from a listening post or a channel of communication, but are dependent for their relations with the powers, on their animators' good personal relations with political men who make decisions concerning the financing and continuation of their programs. As in the participation groups, the man who stands behind the institution is much more important for its survival than its accomplishments, and often the institution grows or weakens due to variations in the position of its animator.

The characteristics enumerated, and especially the absence of channels of institutional participation in the majority of countries, necessarily result in a purely defensive concept of activity by participation groups. Each one of them, according to the extent of the networks of personal relations of its directors, tries to gain some advantage: some fiscal exoneration for cooperatives, some salary increases for unions, some schools or some gerrymandering for parties. The activities, and the pressures they lead to, necessarily assume a segmentary character and never pose the problems of the whole milieu in which the groups operate.

One consequence of protest activities and of the climate of tension in which it unfolds is the exclusive character of the protection that the groups offer their members thanks to the services of all kinds that they can produce following their demands. This tendency is particularly clear in the unions, although it is found in cooperatives, professional associations, and even in social clubs. From the time when one of the groups obtains some success in its demands, it translates them into services and equipment to the benefit of its members alone, such as social services, hospitals, and cultural activities. It becomes a protector, like the hacienda. It is exclusive, and closed, like the old European society for mutual aid, which also tried, in a hostile world, to gain some advantages for its adherents. And the hypothesis can be made that the more powerful and organized these groups are in such extensions or services, the fewer the chances for collaboration with others, the more they will appear as privileged "citadels," and the less likely they will become institutions open to a national development perspective.

PARTICIPATION GROUPS AS CHANNELS OF INDIVIDUAL ASCENT

All participation groups constitute a mechanism of elite selection: thanks to election activities, individuals emerge to animate, direct, or represent the group to the outside. The individuals who thus emerge are those who best represent the values of the group, and when this later is compatible with the wider society, the values of the global society. In Western societies at the time of the industrial revolution, the leaders that emerged from this process of selection represented not only militant values but possessed the personality traits of the entrepreneur of atomic liberal capitalism. The union, cooperative, or political leader was not only an animator of his troops but also a sort of business head putting a product (an ideology) on the market, jealous of imitators, keen for gain (in terms of new adherents and advantages of all sorts for his group). So therefore, and in spite of opposition by these participation groups to the society of the time and its values, the militants who emerged from it assume some traits of the liberal entrepreneur, who was nevertheless their enemy. In the same way, it can be shown that the leaders of participation groups in socialist countries reproduce the personality traits of the leaders of socialized businesses, more functionary than entrepreneur, more anxious to conform and execute orders, than to put their own plans to work or oppose received directives.

If we transpose these regularities on the societies that occupy us here, we can sketch the portrait of the director of the participation group and explain certain aspects of the functioning of these groups. For that it is necessary to make reference to the still profoundly feudal character of Latin American societies and especially in the rural milieu. In the country, the relation between employer and worker is still generally that of protection-fidelity, through which the employer not only assumes material charge of the life of his people, but represents them to the outside world. For his part the vassal owes fidelity and obeisance not only in his work life but in all aspects of existence. This scheme is no longer current, and the peons attached to the glebe in certain parts of the Andes are now the exception.

But if capitalist relations have replaced feudal protection-fidelity, expectations and styles of relations still remain those of the past. There is always the persistent feeling that the employer represents those who depend on him, that he is the only one able to speak in their name, that he incarnates the finalities of the group that he constitutes with them; there is the persistence of the authoritarian relation between superior and inferior, between those who command and those who obey. These two traits, internalized for generations, are always present and the equalitarian relation has not yet taken precedence over relations of authority. The right that the superior has to represent his subordinates has not disappeared; he who speaks, he who responds, is the master and the inferior waits until the master may have spoken or defers to the master who expresses what it is necessary to say in the name of all. These traits seem to subsist very strongly among officers, animators, directors of groups and participation organisms. They carry with them in their groups the same attitudes and norms of authority and representation as those that continue to be in force in the ambiant milieu. And these styles of relations are expected by group members who know no others and are habituated to them.

Although these traits are more apparent in the country, they subsist no less in the urban participation associations and groups. This partly explains the personalism and sometimes even the *caudillismo* of the leaders of certain unions and political parties; and above all it will help to understand why participation is sometimes stifled by leaders, why certain turnabout tactics and policies are accepted by the base, why questions of personality are so important in social, cultural, and political life.

In cooperatives, unions, or political parties, leaders everywhere are more important than the programs of groups they direct and represent; the collaboration or coalitions between groups are generally the result of their personal dealings and the sharing of power among them, much more than the result of concordance of programs, doctrines, or ideologies. In the same way we can understand the mechanism of participation of groups in official organisms, states, regions, municipalities, or planning organisms: although there are only rare cases in which the channels of institutional participation have been arranged, participation occurs all the same through contacts, networks of relations, friendship links, and camaraderie of the leaders of participation groups.

Mexico furnishes us with a very interesting but not unique case of this informal secondary participation. The intense Mexican "participationism," supported by an unchallenged official ideology, has resulted in a veritable elite of leaders, directors, and officers of cooperatives, unions, cultural and political groups. The revolution having eliminated the old oligarchy of power posts, the door was found open to the ascent of this new elite. In spite of the antagonisms that can separate them (for example, union heads and directors of entrepreneurial associations), the leaders meet and informally negotiate agreements, exercise together or separately pressure on the public powers, multiply alliances with politicians, and so on. Each of them is tied to his group by the protection-fidelity relationship and exerts himself to achieve the success of his programs. Although Mexico represents this tendency in a clearer fashion, it also appears in all the countries; in each of them there exists a stratum of parapoliticians, intermediaries of participation. Limited in number, the people that compose the group know each other and are often linked by pacts of friendship; if the success of the programs of their group ensures them personal success, they can equally sometimes obtain more success by betraying the interests of their group, and without the rules of the game condemning such perfidy.

SURVEY OF ACTIVITIES AND FUNCTIONS OF VOLUNTARY PARTICIPATION GROUPS

The conditions in which Latin American participation groups work are not generally favorable to the emergence of a dynamic and innovative leadership. The rigidity of stratification too often limits the action of groups to one particular social stratum, and the existing weak economic expansion cannot break down these barriers. This can be usefully demonstrated by a brief review of the activities and functioning of some of the groups already surveyed. To these will be added some institutions like the church and the universities, sometimes intense centers of participation, and which, from near or far, influence national development.[4]

Cooperatives

Even though cooperatives of all kinds are found in Latin America, their distribution seems nearer to that of the United States (especially agricultural cooperation) than to Europe (a predominance of consumer cooperation). In spite of the diversity of situations, a list can be presented that includes the great majority of these groups.

Dispersion. With some exceptions, the Latin American cooperative is small, isolated, and without strong relations with its sister societies. It works independently, without horizontal or vertical integration with the rest of the cooperative world. In spite of the tendency toward economic development of big units under the impulsion of giant U.S. firms, Latin American cooperative development is atomic, following the example of liberal capitalism from which this form issued.

Federalization. Although cooperative federations exist, they are more nearly friendly societies of managers or supports for pressure activities than centers for the elaboration of development plans for the cooperative movement. If there are cooperative development plans in certain countries, their initiative and elaboration generally do not come from cooperative federations but from the official services (organized for agrarian reform, for example). The federations are not then considered as possible partners for cooperative planning. The latter occurs without their initiative, a sign of the disaffection of technicians responsible for national planning of popular institutions.

Ideological and Doctrinal Default. Entangled in the difficulties of everyday life, cooperation no longer constitutes a movement of thought or reflection in matters pertaining to development. Indeed, cooperative publications are characterized by their doctrinal dependence on European or U.S. movements.

Absence of Favorable Laws. Latin American legislation is not distinguished by laws very favorable to the growth of cooperation, even if the sum of laws concerning them is voluminous. Moreover, the official institutions supporting or aiding cooperation are weak or nonexistent. Such is the case with long-term credit institutions for provision of fixed capital for the societies.

Unionism

Although the development of unionism is very unequal from one country to the next, and though it has sometimes come to play a primary role in national life—more or less ephemeral as in Bolivia or almost institutionalized as in Mexico or in Peronist Argentina, certain generalizations seem possible.

Inequality of Internal Development. The powerful union is more often based on a single sector of production or on a single category of workers: here, the miners are the base of the union power; there, the petroleum workers; in another place it is uniquely the urban workers, and so on. This domination of national recruitment is accompanied by a great insufficiency of development in the other sectors, and because of the political game within each movement is even opposed to a powerful unionization of other sectors. In addition, even if certain kinds of unionism can constitute forces in national political life, the unity is often only formal and is limited to pacts of friendship among leaders and to sometimes fragile coalitions.

Ideological Insufficiencies. Union ideologies (socialist or socialist tendencies, Christian, Marxist or Marxist tendencies, and so on) establish the vocabularies more than the motive force of action; they are justifications rather than frameworks that inspire and restrain. This weak ideologization brings about a certain laxity in activities, recruiting, and alliances. Consequently, the unions seem to be politicized because of the very deficiency of their ideological thought, that is, by the absence of guides to conduct in the political field, by the very insolvency of their political thought. Note that the liberal criticism which says that unions should refrain from playing politics is not being repeated here; to the contrary, my criticism rests on the fact that the unions are not playing their own politics and are only actors in a political theater production, toward the writing of which they have contributed neither plot nor stage directions.

Isolation from Economic Dynamism. The channels of institutional participation being the exception, the unions find themselves relegated to defensive action vis-à-vis private and official initiatives. Whatever the strength of the movement and its will to influence national evolution and to influence the course of development, however dense its network of alliances with public powers and parties, and its compromise with private enterprise, unionism is not associated as a partner to important decisions that affect economic life; it only becomes a partner at the moment of putting decisions into practice, at a moment when it can only defend positions.

Antiunion Hostility. This isolation often also increases hostility against the unions, which is not moreover that of single businesses but equally from public powers and other national forces (army, university, church) and foreign enterprises. To unionism are imputed the personalization of power of leaders, corruption, alliances with politicians—all characteristics that arise much more from the social structure in its totality, as has been seen. In other words, unionism is not considered a counterpower to the dynamism of private enterprise, but as a corrosive force on the social peace desired by liberalism.

Employers' Associations

Employers' associations of all types—professional chambers, chambers of commerce, chambers of agriculture, boards, coalitions—bring together entrepreneurs from different economic sectors just as the professions do. Several characteristics may be assigned to them.

Participation in the Power Elite. Although the cooperatives and unions remain groups of contestation and social promotion, the employers' associations recruit their members, and especially those who take responsibilities in them, in the higher social strata. Because of this recruitment and through the levels of education and lifestyle of their members, these associations thereby participate intimately in the power elite. And this characteristic is true even in the less advanced countries, there where the old landed oligarchy is still powerful: by tradition the commercial bourgeoisie was at its service and its aspirations were to imitate its modes of life. In other terms, whatever the country, and in spite of the contradictions and tensions within the power elites, a strong cohesion—augmented by the force of aspirations to popular participation—seems to be characteristic.

Awareness of National Development. The mental habit of conceiving of national development within the structures of liberalism must be underlined, even if it is not a conscious ideology. More than a century of European neocolonialism has, at one and the same time, created this reflex and the social class that incarnates it. It is, moreover, interesting to underscore the double hostility to socialist planning, foreshadowed by unionism and U.S. managerial rationalism.

The two forms of hostility are characteristic of business employers still very often familial, habituated to high profits depending on commercial capitalism much more than on industrial capitalism, and for which national development is not envisaged, other than as an indefinite prolongation of the past. The leaders of employers' associations have always found the doors open to their pressure. They are nevertheless decreasingly alone operating in this way. In addition to the popular movements that it is less easy to reduce to silence, they increasingly encounter a state will, affirming its own priorities in matters of development, possessing too a knowledge of economic life and a managerial ambition.

Political Parties

The majority of the characteristics set down in relation to union movements apply to political parties as well. The list can be completed, as follows.

The Decrease of Political Caudillismo. The long-term tendency goes against personalization of participation movements. The progressive acceptance of mass consumption is contrary to the personalized relations evoked above. It is not always certain that it leads rapidly to a greater instrumentality in the choice of political leaders nor especially to greater political participation.

Passivity. The majority of the aspirations created by the consumption society are not perceived as capable of satisfaction through traditional political action. Certainly there will be no lack of objections that the combats which occur periodically in the universities testify, to the contrary, of an intense political participation. This apparent contradiction will be explained further on. With the exception of these agitated sectors, Latin American political life seems characterized by weak participation—and especially where it is still possible, by weak contestive participation, immediate thermometer of political participation—and by the absence of mobilizing issues.

Intervention in Political Issues. There is no need to point out the terrible repression that has crashed down on the most advanced countries of the continent and whose evident goal is a gigantic clean sweep of all who think otherwise, a surgical operation considered as an indispensable condition for the ultimate resumption of "normal" political life, in which each group will retake its place in the social order without more dispute. No country is sheltered from such repression and in fact, intervention in the political process multiplies everywhere. Besides outlawing communist parties, it is necessary to recall the multiple traps that prevent progress of political life: disbanding militants, imprisonment of leaders, rigged procedures, withdrawal of funds, prohibition of publications. Added to the inquisitiveness of national and foreign political police, these interventions create a climate of conformism and double the growing apathy toward political participation.

Public Institutions

What are the possible forms of participation of individuals and of their groups at various echelons of the hierarchy of public institutions, from the commune to the central state? Beyond the diversity of the countries and the situations in each of them, some characteristics can be enumerated.

Excessive Centralization. In spite of the federal constitutions that imitate that of the United States, it is necessary to underline the excess of decentralization of deliberations by relation to the centralization of means necessary to give force to these deliberations in order to make relevant decisions. This contradiction is particularly clear at the level of the municipalities of which it is claimed that they are deprived of all financial means to put into operation a development politics. Scarcely less marked, this situation is found again at the departmental or provincial levels.

Degradation of the Political Process. The contradiction between decentralization of organisms for deliberation and centralization of financial means ends in a degradation of the political process: on the level of participation, the dominant sentiment in the majority of the countries is that participation serves no purpose, leads to nothing. Whence the weak direct participation of individuals in the organisms of power, especially the municipalities, and the neglect of the lower levels of power by participation groups, and their constitution into pressure groups with the goal of reaching and influencing the higher levels, where decisions are really made.

Public Structuring Unpropitious for Development. If the federal structure permitted the United States the maximum of liberation from obstacles to the initiatives of private business, it does not follow that this same structure is also favorable when the development is of another type. In fashioning their constitutions after that of the United States, the Latin American countries have made the hypothesis that development would follow the same lines. We see daily that development does not precisely follow the liberal line and even, as we will see, that it increasingly risks becoming the deed of public powers, the national technical bureaucracies. In this more centralized structuring of decisions, decentralized public institutions become the brakes on initiatives, each decision being discussed and debated by intermediary organisms located between the top and the populace. From this arises great slowness, and since the central organisms also control the means, the degradation of decision-making structures provided by the constitutions.

Development of Parallel Structures. From the time that development became a national affair there was witnessed in the majority of the countries the creation of technical planning organisms and implementation of development programs. These organisms, created on the side and without liaison with parliamentary institutions,[5] raise several questions: if they want to be efficient and to escape political pressure for division of resources, and therefore to escape from the danger of dissipation of budgets, the central governments have no other possibilities than to create institutions directly dependent on them; when such institutions also have as a goal setting up programs resting on popular participation, the local programs that they create with this goal will be constitutionally independent from regions and municipalities. The result of this is the dissociation of development programs (and therefore of instigated participation by some of them) from the financing of traditional activities by the administration, the latter arising from the constitutional political structure, although the development activities originate from parallel hierarchies. In other terms, the political is dissociated from the economic, and the economic is decreasingly submitted to political control: increasingly, to the extent of the complexity of options and techniques of development, decisions are the deeds of the planning offices that report directly to the central powers, and because of this they escape control of parliaments, regions, and municipalities. The technicians who make decisions decreasingly come under the control of political institutions and themselves determine, and therefore arbitrarily, the zones or activity domains in which they will ask for or instigate the participation of the population.

The Enterprise

When speaking of participation in the business enterprise reference is not made to structures that provide for it, such as workers' councils, organs of joint consultation, or even of business committees. Some such juridical forms that permit participation do exist in Latin America, but their rarity authorizes us to ignore them. What is at issue here is more the participation of individuals offered by their work itself, the possibility to have a complete view of it and because of this to freely decide certain aspects, ways of doing or proceeding, or of participating in discussions and decisions concerning these aspects. In this order of ideas, three situations can be distinguished.

Participation in the Traditional Enterprise. Corresponding to a still rudimentary technical level and without much division of labor, this form of enterprise permits a great participation of the individual. In the artisanal enterprise or in agricultural exploitation, the worker or peon still has a whole view of the production process: in the structure of received orders—whose necessity he understands for they only achieve coordination of ways of doing things that he knows well and that present no novelty by relation to tradition—the worker or peon participates in the tasks that he must fulfill; on occasion, he can discuss the best way of doing them with the patron for the patron scarcely knows how to do them any better than he. The way of undertaking work is therefore participant. If we recall in addition the nature of the social links that unite employer and worker, and in particular the feudal relation of protection-fidelity spoken of above, we will understand that the unity of traditional life is not broken by work and economic activity or the business that organizes it; whence, also, the resistance offered by this unity of life to the novel forms of participation that might destroy it. The difficulties of innovating in matters of participation must be in part explained by the persistence of this type of enterprise.

Rupture of the Traditional Participationist Schema in the Liberal Enterprise. The increased division of tasks, a stronger technology, the imperatives of yield due to a more developed capitalism, the hierarchization of command, lead to a rupture in the traditional participationist schema. The old participation in work or trade is inhibited in life outside of work. The majority of Latin American businesses belong to this type.

Emergence of a New Schema of Participation in Modern Enterprise. The modern business, of great size, highly capitalized, under managerial rather than individual or family direction, of high technological development, supposes and demands new forms of participation. This new form is situated among the executives, established at the time of determination of the politics and objectives of the business and continued in daily activities. Participation is the consequence of a certain level of technique and capitalization. Although slow by relation to industrial enterprises, modern agricultural businesses know the same evolution.

Modern business is gradually expanding in Latin America and offers to an increasingly significant number of young executives the possibility of participation. Although still in limited number, they already tend to give the tone to certain economies such as Brazil, Mexico, Venezuela, and Argentina. The participation they offer is creative, concrete, a source of reward in status as much as in material advantage, security-bestowing because it is expressed in technical terms, apparently free of ideology, and nonpoliticized. We have already glimpsed at the possible effects of this variety of apoliticism, encouraged by the ideological stagnation and skepticism concerning the utility of political action, and conveying the acceptance of novel views that are outlined for Latin American development.

The University

The university constitutes the sole institution of education that gives rise to participation on the part of its members, professors as well as students. Some tendencies can be enumerated.

Inverse Relation between Participation and the Status of Occupation. Participation of all forms—political, cultural, associationist—is stronger, both among professors and students, than in the professions exercised by students after graduation which are new and therefore little organized, uncertain as to opportunities and still not socially recognized; it is the case, notably, of occupations based on the social sciences, psychology and especially sociology. At the other extreme, the older disciplines (exact sciences, medicine) and the technical branches (agronomy, for example) lead to professions that are socially honored and recognized as trades.

Intense Participation. University participation in disciplines originating from the human sciences, whether close to them or afar, is at once intense, violent, tending to global contestation of the society, finding its vocabulary now in Marxism, now in texts of the church reformers. Apart from some exceptions, this participation is nevertheless very weakly organized, or only in groups that are ephemeral and of reduced size.

Participation of Limited Duration. However intense it may be, this participation is limited in time and scarcely persists after some years of university. Even among the professors, it tends to decrease rapidly after some years of exercise of the function. After leaving university, young people find themselves outside of the generative milieu of participation and must face the problems of their professional careers in isolation. In spite of the extraordinary development of the tertiary sector, especially the public part, the offers of employment are rare, notably the more prestigious jobs, that is to say, those calling neither for work on the land nor residence outside the capitals. The job hunt, and later the attention given to the professional career and the preoccupations with security, which intervene with marriage and the creation of a family, diminish very strongly the tonus of participation, and rather rapidly eliminate all participation tied to the established university groups. It corresponds therefore to the period that extends between the moment when the adolescent escapes from the family circle and that when he finds himself integrated into occupational structures. It does not always follow that this participation has been useless for him. If nothing that he wanted actually happened, such as structural transformations or revolution, this participation will nevertheless have been responsible for a greater openness to social problems, and for a tendency that is extremely important, a certain will to insert into development activities some of the notions of the juvenile commitment, in particular the tendency to planning of instigated participation activities.

The Church

We will not evoke here the participation tied to the traditional church, participation rising from feudal relations in the same measure as the church has been incorporated into the landed feudal structure. It is appropriate rather to clear up some characteristics of actions instigated by the renewal of the church in Latin America.

Very Limited Experiences. From the first, and in spite of their extreme interest, it is necessary to underscore the limited character of participationist experiences of the church. The spirit of renovation only breathes on very limited fractions of the clergy, and Chile in the 1960s included, is still, most of the time, very timid. It has been excessively exaggerated.

Contestive Character. In spite of their limitation and their timidity, certain experiences of animation, of social work, or cooperative development, of union and political organization, and so on, are perceived as a profound contestation of the bases of society and of the liberal economy.

Nonmissionary Character. The developed activities attack social problems before seeking to save souls. Certainly, it is a question here of a new way of tackling proselytism and it must be remarked that the struggle against under-development offers to the Church an unexpected chance to maintain itself as a social force in Latin America.

Technicity of Interventions. The animators of participation activity have very quickly become aware that sincerity and devotion cannot palliate the lack of technical training. Whence a great effort at technicity in intervention and in animator training—this last activity being perhaps the principal element of action of "the new church."

The Army

The army is traditionally a powerful group in Latin America. Its role in anticipation and repression of social agitation is extended.

Increased Technicity. We return to this characteristic regarding the army as well. It is notably due to the utilization of more complex armaments, to the more theoretical training of the officer corps—including training in ideological struggle—and its training in counterrevolutionary struggle and in the strategies of modern war. The superior officer thus becomes more and more a technical expert whose particular domain is, certainly, different from those of the executives and administrative technicians and from production, but whose technical nature can permit him dialogue with these latter elements.

Modification of Ties with the Landed Oligarchy. The still rather habitual representation of the power structure of Latin American countries as landed oligarchies ceased to be accurate a long time ago. The oligarchy has divided its power with the urban bourgeoisie, especially those sectors of the latter that manage foreign investments. In the course of this intervention, and in spite of recruitment that is still of oligarchic origin in certain cases, the army has moved away from the ancient masters of the countries and recruits predominantly in the middle classes. In the majority of countries it has today quit its role of power arbiter in order to exercise it without opposition.

Police Role. Gradually assuming the industrial or developmental role of the urban elites, the army comes to play its role of a police body against social agitation, no more with a view to maintain the agrarian status quo but within the structure of modernization. An increased participation of the army in the concrete tasks of development is also witnessed.

The Revolutionary Way Out

The *salida revolucionaria* constitutes another—perhaps the most intense—of the paths offered for participation. It leads to the maquis, and as the events of recent years have shown, to physical elimination. At the present hour it seems that the revolutionary path is less than ever capable of leading to the general revolt, national or continental, that its adepts among the followers of Che Guevara wanted.

Faithful supporters of U.S. policy, intolerant of a second Cuba on the continent, the national bourgeoisies can only reject all ideas of a mass participation in power and in decisions that concern development. In this determination they are supported by the rising class of executives and technicians, whose interests in obtaining a greater portion of power have driven out the generous and populist intentions of their university years.

The bitter discovery of the current impossibility of all revolutionary resolutions counts for much in the discouragement of numerous executives, intellectuals, and animators. Their bitter duty to devote themselves to employment at purely bystander tasks, band-aid work (paños calientes), where only radical surgery could bring change—Will it lead them to hostile indifference or to interested collaboration or yet to contemplative cynicism? I have proposed three attitudes, and it is very possible that the participation instigated in the technocratic development cadre, that has been hypothesized for the future, will be precisely a combination of the three attitudes.

NOTES

1. Social *work,* as in Marxist theory, not *social* work, as in the U.S. helping professions. (Ed.)
2. The word *cadre* is always troublesome for English translations of French, and Professor Meister and I agreed to try to adjust to the context. Here it is something like junior executives or bureaucrats. (Ed.)
3. Whether the great estates become cooperative or social (Peru) does not alter matters at all.
4. This section is the start of chapter 5 in *La Participation pour le développement.* Some irrevelevant transitional material is omitted. (Ed.)
5. For example, CORDIPLAN in Venezuela or INDAP in Chile before 1973.

11

NEW FORMS OF ASSOCIATION AND PARTICIPATION IN POSTINDUSTRIAL SOCIETY

The postindustrial society that is taking form under our eyes, and above all in the most advanced country, the United States, scarcely seems to fulfill the hopes of the democrats nor of those—but are they still numerous today?—who identify the progress of techniques with development of a more just society. From their side, hardly in the process of emerging from their respective Stalinisms, the most developed socialist countries make haste to faithfully imitate both Western technologies and lifestyles. As for the bourgeosie or ruling classes of some underdeveloped countries, islands of modernity and high consumption in the midst of seas of misery, their styles of life and even the models that they follow for development are directly inspired by the rich countries, liberal or other. A sort of world unity seems therefore to be growing up around technological advance, from the riches and fashions of the consumer, and thanks to the dynamism and to the relations of domination of the country, or the small group of the country that is found to be the center or centers of this irradiation.

But the society that thus takes form is far from being uniform, and it is no longer possible to make fun of the uniformity and conformism of rich societies, as was generally done 15 years ago in relation to the United States. To the contrary, the postindustrial society appears profoundly divided, as has been illustrated in preceding chapters. And it is in the structure of these divisions—I hestitate to speak of classes, although it might be asked if we are not witnessing the formation of new class oppression—that it is necessary to view the questions of association and participation.

It is necessary to distinguish successively participation at the level of the technostructure, at the level of those who currently contribute to the orientations of the society, to decision making (contributory participation); participation at the level that Daniel Chauvey[1] calls the zerostructure, at the level of those who have nothing to decide, who are integrated to the objectives and to the systems of aspirations that the technostructure manipulates at its own intention, whose participation is dependent and cannot be more than an identification-participation with these objectives and aspirations; participation at the level of the leftovers of progress, the marginals, that is, primary participation, oriented toward the turning of small groups into themselves without impact on the larger society and having no other goal than helping individuals to survive (survival participation); finally, contestation-participation, revolt against the system, and sometimes construction of cells of life and/or of new work (communes, for example). This participation moreover fluctuates (notably the last three), in the images of the social categories in which they develop.

CONTRIBUTORY PARTICIPATION

According to Galbraith, the technostructure is the totality of those who participate in decision making and the organization that they constitute. It is those who know, who hold back information and release what they believe it is necessary for others to know, who innovate, who control, who negotiate. At the level of the big business, as at the national level, the technostructure is however not monolithic without exception; it is, to the contrary, marked by tensions, although as has been seen, the conflict itself is institutionalized, proceeds according to the accepted rules of the game and among partners who recognize each other as valuable interlocutors. Whether they be big businesses, administrations, state powers, unions or political parties, big associations or social movements, these partners compose parts of the technostructure and "this society of apparatuses, dominated by the big businesses, at one and the same time political and economic, is more oriented than ever toward power, toward truly political control and its internal functioning and its environment. This is why imperialism's consciousness of its apparatuses is so keen."[2] But the fundamental aspect of the ascendancy of the technostructure is its control of the access of knowledge. Decouflé has described this process.

The mark of the passage to postindustrial society is not the constitution of a *society of knowledge* in which each would have equal access to information; it is the fact that the social differentiation in it is founded on cultural factors. It is because knowledge is not distinguished from power that its effective distribution has a tendency to be, in spite of the generalization of teaching, more and more discriminatory. The trans-industrial society is profoundly inegalitarian in its very foundation. It only distributes elementary knowledge at the price of a generalized manipulation, from which only those escape who, starting from a quantum of particularly extensive knowledge, can move on to a new culture, defined from this point of view as a place of exclusion from manipulation. To the others, knowledge continues to be distributed at a rudimentary level and under the form of immediately consumable products, even though the veritable culture consists precisely in mediated knowledge. The saturation of the average man of the transindustrial society by an organized and controlled cultural flux has, it would appear, the function of creation of an aristocracy of knowledge: a new class of leaders fully adapted to the structures of postindustrial civilization.[3]

Far from leading to sharing, the knowledge and information lead to separation. Elected or named to a function because of knowledge that opens doors for them, the leaders perpetuate and even reinforce the separation.

Who are these leaders? Analyses of postindustrial society have placed more attention on the authoritarianism and rationality of the system than on the men who compose it, in particular by lack of research data on the latter. And yet it would be necessary to know better the categories of men who control it: directors of big businesses, high-level functionaries, union and political interlocutors, intellectuals and university professors tied to the system and who ensure its reproduction, high international functionaries, faithful clients of the international lines, of university or equivalent training, whose incomes situate them at the top level, and so on; all these categories tending to support one another. The common denominator of these men is that they contribute to decisions in the groups, committees, the councils which, although able to disagree on means and tactics, all have as a final goal quantitative development (the greater the gross national product, the greater the employment, the more the schools, the greater the comfort) in the present framework—even if certain groups employ or continue to employ a revolutionary vocabulary.

Beneath them are some categories or fringes of intermediate technostructure—executives, technicians, marketing specialists, information specialists—who represent, within industries and services "the essentials of the work force itself calculated less in number of workers than in stock of intellectual capacities and aptitudes for internal professional mobility in the branch of activities considered. This professionalism elaborates its own rules of conduct regarding the directing technostructure . . . practicing not an ideology of competition but of participation."[4]

But the essential character of all the system, and which constitutes its binding force, is rationality. It derives directly from the acceptance (once more, it is not a matter of philosophical acceptance but the acceptance implicated in daily practice) of development goals of postindustrial society. The lack of controversy about these ends among the groups and constituents of the technostructure permit programming by the most rational means in order to attain the ends and to confer a high degree of logical coherence in proposed measures.

This rationality is only a rationalization, and every effort of the system will be made to forget it.[5] And it is in this that it succeeds magnificently, to such a point that "we leave an exploitative society to enter into an alienative society."[6] Although in the industrial society or in the society on the path to industrialization, groups and systems of values in opposition with those of the directing class permit awareness of exploitation, the species of ideological unification that is produced in the postindustrial society around acceptance of themes of growth[7] creates or generalizes alienation, that is to say, acceptance of exploitation—which objectively has not diminished or has only partially changed form.

We add again that the growing authoritarianism of our postindustrial society does not consist so much in a political regime as in a degree of alienation, in the ascendancy of dominant values and in the degree of rationality attained by the system. Although it is this very rationality that indicates the rational measures that authority must take in order to be respected, it is the extent of alienation which permits and authorizes different forms of repression. We will see, moreover, that precisely because of its authoritarianism, the system has need of dispute so that it might draw dynamism from it. But before that we will consider the identification-participation and the integration to which it leads.

IDENTIFICATION-PARTICIPATION OR DEPENDENT PARTICIPATION

Those who are unable to contribute to decisions, those whose occupations submit them to instructions and routines,[8] those who compose the zerostructure, must be integrated. To the end that they keep in their place, the system occupies itself with their state of mind, with their work satisfaction, tries to integrate them to their work, and since they are separated from participation in decisions, attempts to identify them with the politics and the measures taken for them. "Alienation is therefore the reduction of social conflict by means of a dependent participation."[9]

Increasingly numerous groups thus have no other role than to adapt the individual to his social frame; they are generally centered on consumption activities: the club for collection of key rings not only adapts its members to the consumer society but makes adepts of them, seeking new products whose premiums will augment their collections; the tourist association attempts to create a friendly and fraternal world for the limited period of vacations, a world that will render less painful the return to work and urban anonymity, and that the association promises to make still more enchanting the following year.

In the manner of the businesses, these integration groups make a great effort to diffuse a favorable image to the public. Thanks to the techniques of public relations, thanks to stylish hostesses and the personalized contacts that these techniques permit, the individual senses himself immediately at ease with no matter who, feels well, and happy. And as these groups are themselves in accord with the values of the consumer society—their success often depending directly or indirectly on the sale of a product—they are the intermediate body aiming at the integration of individuals.

Certain such integration groups have existed in the past, and they too were centered on consumption of a product or of free time: for example, the club for bowling or cards, or the cycling society. Nevertheless, these groups remain marginal by relation to the great movements of civic, political, and social participation. In addition, the products to be consumed were less numerous and free time was reduced. It is very much different today, when the products to be consumed are daily more numerous and in which free time has increased. It can even be said that the function of leisure is to favor consumption.

The role of these integration groups is enlarged by the disaffection of individuals for old conflict groups or by the placing of the fundamentals of society in question and even if they continue to participate, by the progressive inclusion and institutionalization of these groups into the system. In addition, in their entirety, the mass communication media assist integration groups: diffusing information more than opinion, conveying commercial publicity, mixing texts and ads, and often not even making distinctions between editorial rubrics and publicity; whether they be visual or auditory, these media of diffusion promote consumer participation and, in developing its needs, integrates its individuals with their society.

I have presented this integration only in reference to participation groups, a reference which is perhaps too strict, to the extent that the individual can very well integrate himself to society by individual consumption. Beside these leisure groups, our time is also characterized by the withdrawal of the individual into small informal groups having little structure, and into his family, to the increasingly comfortable home, center of ever more imperious consumer needs and therefore of integration into society.

Beyond this tendency, we must note the progressive dilution of the notion of participation. By opposition to the rites of initiation that mark groups of the traditional society, by opposition to participation rising from an engagement or from dues habitually paid, the new participation groups of the consumer society reduce the notion of participation to that of the commercial clientele. At the extreme, a simple purchase and we become members of a club. In competition with one another, but inspired by the same values, different groups and participation movements become strong as far as memberships are concerned. At the extreme—and this is what we have established in our inquiries—the individual never knows very well what groups he actually belongs to. The participant becomes a simple client or a simple user; and it is perhaps no exaggeration to advance that this identification participation is as far from participation contributing to the life of the groups as kitsch is from art.[10]

The rapprochement between participation groups and enterprises—especially distribution enterprises—must still be completed by another aspect of the problem: like these businesses, participation groups call for remunerated personnel and one which tends to resemble those of the businesses; no longer proposing exaltant finalities, the participation groups must replace benevolent militants by remunerated animators whose goal is to animate, to make people stir, to make them adhere to or use the group. The techniques of animation resemble those of the salesmen of the commercial enterprise; businesses now speak of sales animators, thus showing the transformation of sales techniques that consists in the seller no longer remaining behind his counter awaiting the client, but drawing the client to him, acting so that he would not go elsewhere, to animate sufficiently that he buys. Although he sells other products—and immaterial products like participation—the animator often uses techniques similar to those of the salesman. The examples are numerous, since the animator who attempts to arouse civic participation at the moment of elections, or who attempts to lead the elector to pronounce himself for this or that candidate, up to the social worker who endeavors to integrate the members of bands of young delinquents into legitimate activities, and thus to society. In all these cases, the animator has replaced the militant, this militant whose work we have already witnessed.

The notion of association is transformed, parallel to the transformation in participation. Increasingly institutionalized, associations are less and less concerned with members. These members are increasingly the general public, since the member is scarcely differentiated from the nonmember. And it also leads to an increasing uniformity in the context of their public communications. Submitted to the totalitarianism of the mass media (in the sense that their message is uniform and omnipresent), caught in the trap of "the economy of futility" and of the incessant quest for useless goods, manipulated at the time like the worker, like the resident, and like the consumer, man in transindustrial societies is neither the man of new crusades nor even, all proves it, of "new frontiers." He is interested neither in the adventure of the conquest of space nor in that of the solitary development of a humanity that is in large part frustrated in its enjoyment of the most necessary goods and services. And finally he appears incapable of grasping the tragedy of his own situation. There only seems to remain to him, in all its forms, the most barbarous and unstinted violence.[11]

The violence seems to be manifest more and more often not in the service of a cause but for itself alone. It is sudden violence in which the destruction is like a brief festival, quickly consumated, and which appears to have no other consequence than reinforcement of the apparatus of repression. But there are other forms of conflict that it will be necessary to examine, for they imply other forms of participation. Formerly, always, it was necessary to speak of participation of the entire mass of the leftovers of progress; what is more, the integration that has been in question here is still far from affecting all sectors of our postindustrial societies in construction, or transindustrial societies as Decouflé calls them.

SURVIVAL PARTICIPATION

In addition to the leftovers of expansion and modernization already considered (aged workers, the handicapped, the poor), it is necessary to take account of the differences in rhythm of modernization and therefore of the persistence of traditional activities, still little touched by technical innovations and management: the mines, building trades, small farmers, small commerce.

Although one might think that these activities will progressively modernize, the slowness of their evolution situates them in mid-path between the integrated working class and the true leftovers, the unwanted, the misfits. And it is not by chance, as has been seen, that it is precisely in these retarded categories that participation groups can still be born, originating in the organizational forms and slogans of the era of industrialization.

The majority of leftovers are found in the production sections: migrant laborers or seasonal workers, racial minorities, manual and nonqualified workers, and the poor. Inaccessible to help, to welfare programs and the struggle against poverty, sometimes even beyond reach of the benefits of social security, without sufficient income to acceed to the consumer civilization, often even situated in an economy of underconsumption, if not mere subsistence, shoved aside (increasing segregation being perhaps the most apparent factor if not the most dramatic), not easily integrated into unions and political organizations, these different categories of the forgotten ones can only develop limited participation, aiming more at the survival of small primary groups, notably in the form of mutual aid and exchange of services, and yet occupied in the established structure of traditional solidarities such as the family or place of origin. At the same time as they aid these small groups to survive, these kinds of participation isolate them still more from the rest of society. These same kinds of participation have, in addition, the function of reducing aggression against the outside world, of the kind that characteristically exists not so much among the forgotten themselves, whom the society risks to see produce these brusque passages from apathy to revolt; revolt that seems much more characteristic of the less poor, those less resigned to their fate.

To the extent that they enclose the forgotten ones in their "culture of poverty," this primary participation contributes to reinforce the neglect in which they are held by the rest of society. And one is correct to ask oneself whether postindustrial society will not increasingly consider them defects of its integration projects, rebels from its benevolent integration programs.

The progressive segregation contributes at one and the same time to this neglect (as in the Black quarter?) and to the good conscience of the integrated ones ("see what they have done to their houses"). The ideology of the rationality of our postindustrial societies is propitious for the reappearance of the notion of pauperism mentioned above in regard to the American Protestant rationality of the beginning of the century. And it is not farfetched to think that our societies will consider these forgotten ones as inevitable, in the same fashion that they risk viewing as inevitable some aspects of violence.

CONTESTATION-PARTICIPATION

All this violence is not due to contestation, nor are all contestations products of the postindustrial society. It is necessary therefore to begin by a kind of classification in which the categories are not exclusive, and more or less interpenetrate, since it is of the very nature of these manifestations to be fluctuating, fluid, and thus by the same token elusive.

A first form of contestation, or better, of refusal of contestation, is *apathy.* In the liberal society the voluntary sector (participation and associationism) constitutes a defensive reaction against a society that has made little provision for the needs of man, against the excess of liberty, against the indifference of the powers in face of this or that need; in programmed societies, to the contrary, apathy appears a means by which the individual resists collective pressure, and the solicitude, certainly benevolent, but in the long run oppressive, of programs and institutions that occupy themselves with him, with his case, with his needs. To take refuge in apathy and indifference permits him a certain liberation. An elementary flight response, nontheoretical—different from the refusal to consume—even indolent, it is no less a sort of refusal and permits, although it is characteristic of the lowest levels of education, the conservation of a certain personal autonomy. It is also a sort of fatigue in the face of the tedious repetition of incessant mass media messages, and also witnesses the erosion of its messages, as elsewhere with political messages, and information itself.[12] The apathetic perhaps constitute a good proportion of "the silent majority," taken up in the anxieties of daily life and for which change, of whatever type it may be, has finally no more significance than nonchange. The fatigue of urban life and the diffuse awareness of the absurdity of the human condition and life in society risk to increase apathy in the years to come, reinforcing by this very fact the power of the technostructure.

A second form is *violence for violence's sake,* a sometimes sudden liberation from an apathy that no longer suffices—and in which destruction becomes a festivity. It can be assimilated to a sort of physical exercise, all the more necessary as urban life offers few occasions, even taking account of sport, for muscular relaxation and concomitant liberation from aggressivity. It is not surprising that this form of violence is found above all during the ages of physical growth. Even insofar as it is social contestation, it has a very limited effect. The pulsation is ephemeral and quickly lapses, even when the material damage is important.

This violence for the sake of violence that is not often found in the pure state must not be confused with violence as a means to support a demand or to draw the attention of the public and its powers to a problem. The gulf between the masses and the powers, the deepening chasm between lifestyles and aspirations of the technostructure and those—and in spite of the programs and activities launched by its intentions—of the zerostructure, the absence of all systems (in spite of surveys and other inquiries) for listening to the needs and registration of popular sensibilities, the authoritarianism of the directing classes and the rigidity of organization that they control make violence the only means by which many social categories can make themselves heard, and not only those deprived of representation or of access to media of information.[13] Violence appears therefore as a means of establishing a dialogue, and increasingly risks becoming part of the normal language of communication. It is not excluded, at least for a time, that it may become a normal element of political and social discussion, in public life as well as within the great participationist institutions such as unions. For a time, that is: until the moment when escalation of violence-repression constitutes a threat to the system, and, above all, until the moment when shortcomings of programming technology and manipulation catch up and permit integration of groups that still resist.

We come now to partial contestation which does not oppose the postindustrial system itself but contests certain abuses in it. A good example of it is furnished us by consumers' societies whose objective is to arrive at a more intelligent consumption of products. Some of such groups are struck almost spontaneously, as, for example, in the United States, when mothers united in a struggle against high prices at supermarkets and in opposition to use of premiums. Other examples are offered by renters' associations whose buildings are threatened with demolition, by certain associations of parents of schoolchildren, and increasingly by action groups seeking protection of the environment, improvement in transportaion, and reduction of pollution. In all these cases, it is a question of consuming better and more intelligently, and of products and equipment. The flourishing of groups and associations in these domains is due in great part to the incapacity of associations born during the era of industrialization and centered around themes of production, facing new problems of consumption. This field of consumption of products, of equipment and environment, is new, less clear, less organized than that of work; and "the most 'sensitive' social problems are those in which the technocracy, consumers, and professionals find themselves more directly opposed, that is to say, those who deal with teaching, public health, and the organization of social space."[14]

From the associationist point of view, it is very likely in these domains that one will witness to the most numerous creation of groups in the coming years. Due to the shortcomings, already indicated, of programming and manipulation, especially sensitive in these domains, it can also be supposed that violence will have to be one of the most frequent means of intervention of these groups. It is not excluded, either, that certain among them may open into less partial forms of contestation of the postindustrial order.

Another form of refusal, which might be called *stoic refusal,* consists in a limitation of individual or collective consumption, in some communes[15] or marginal communities. Considering either groups or individuals, this attitude originates in the sentiment well expressed by Marcuse, but already present in a number of socialist experiences,[16] that "it is principally the *quantity* of merchandise, of services, of work, of diversions, that in the over-developed countries permit damming-up of liberation. By consequence, the qualitative change seems to presuppose a *quantitative* change in the evolved standard of life, that is to say, a reduction of *over-development*."[17]

On the practical level, such an attitude is represented as well in the rejection of television and Muzak, in a hostility against all forms of organized leisure and integrative culture, as in the new types of consumption (biological products, for examples), and in general, in a refusal of all forms of organization. As it is individual, this type of refusal is of an aristocratic nature; it supposes a cultural autonomy and is encountered frequently among intellectuals. It is not incompatible—to the contrary, for it supposes higher resources than the average due to the higher cost of individualized consumption by relation to the reflected habitual consumption—with an "objective" integration in the postindustrial system. In a country like France, where a tradition of aristocratic humanism still lives, a number of intellectuals and even decision makers of the system adopt such a form of refusal, which also corresponds in part to a more or less pronounced desire for social distance. As to the contestation of industrial society, this refusal does not go very far, for it constitutes only an adaptation of a certain lifestyle to new conditions, adaptation that moreover often engenders a sort of cynicism manifesting the difficulty of living by a system while holding oneself at a distance. On the contestation plane, the communities constituted by those who have had the courage to extract themselves from the system are much more interesting.

It is not useless to mention anew the popularity of the new cults and the initiatory sects, for they constitute a sort of refusal, or better, flight into myth or fantasy. At the rudimentary level, for the most part that of fantasy, it has been noted that there is a vast reflux movement of the "average man" toward purely magical modes of knowledge like astrology, whose "consumation" does not cease to break records.[18] Consider too the fortune of initiatory metascientism—whose journal *Planète* has the biggest circulation in Western Europe. This level proceeds by questioning our materialist civilization and is a quest for a greater being. It is found in a more exacting form in the new cults which often give way to spiritual communities where, as Edgar Morin notes "one seeks religion more than God, that which is going to unite humans to each other and with the world."[19]

With *sectorial contestation* we come back to the more violent forms of refusal. I include in this category the struggle for the Third World (struggle against the war in Vietnam, for example), the struggle for sexual liberation, the contestation of the women's movement, that of the Blacks, and so on, all forms of struggle that are much more virulent in the United States, but which, as for so many other things, announce future forms of contestation in other countries. Starting out from limited sectors, these contestations often end up in global contestation of the postindustrial system, supporting one another and finishing by mixing together in a unique and total contestation.

The latter is then *contestation of the quality of life.* To start from David Riesman's question—"Abundance for what?"—the questioning extends to all aspects of life, from the omnipresent meddling of the mass media and publicity to the models of social success and modes of utilization of science completely the inverse of the growth in quantities of goods proposed by society, the demands are qualitative: it is necessary to change life. Passing through all other forms of refusal and contestation examined up to the present, and of which certain ones are truly ameliorative, it is mutation that is in question here. All the contestations, partial and sectoral, are rejoined: it is thus, for example, that the struggle against pollution becomes only an exterior manifestation of a claim for authenticity: in cleaning the outside, it is the inside that is cleansed, it is the old man who is swept clean. In the same way as it absorbs all contestation, this total contestation borrows from all theories and doctrines. Speaking of the American, Morin writes:

> The theoretical aspect is much more rich, in my eyes, in its blundering syncretism when it mixes and juxtaposes its elements diversely drawn from psychedelic experience, from grand interior voyages, from Far Eastern vulgates, from the Marxist vulgate, and from different prophets: McCluhan, Marcuse, Buckminster Fuller, William Burrough, Timothy Leary, and so on, who are not theoreticians in the sociopolitical sense of the term, nor thinkers in the university professor sense of the term, but truly prophets of an eschatalogical quest. There is among them something in movement, in search, candid, intuitive, confounding materialism and mysticism, hedonism and asceticism, that touches me and interests me very much.[20]

The commune is the local par excellence of this total contestation, since it permits, besides the critique, experimentation with new forms of life.

Initiation-contestation must be mentioned prior to the experiences of the communes, for however total it may be, it remains temporary (many communes are ephemeral too), linked to the passage from adolescence to integrated adult life. With its risks of blows, of torture, of prison, this revolt is a veritable voluntary self-initiation. But everything goes on in our societies, where the attachments and familial socialization are weakened, where institutions like military service, student societies, and apprenticeship fraternities no longer play a role, long assumed, as institutions of passage to adult life; all goes on as if our societies had rediscovered some very old institutions from societies of the past, that were believed to be forever buried in history.

The characteristics they share with archaic initiation rites are extraordinary: just as the youth once quit the village to isolate themselves in the dreaded forest, modern youth go into the underground, into the new ghettoes or savage nature; just as archaic youth had to confront spirits, genies, ancestors, modern adolescents come to face the "pigs," and the barbarian gods of the polis; the same as the archaic initiation supposed torture and the bloody test, the modern initiation supposes the risk of death, be it in the game, be it in delinquency, be it among the new urban guerrillas. The sole and capital difference is that the archaic institution is entirely controlled by the social hierarchy and the adult class, even though the new institution under construction is self-directed by the adolescent class that wants to conquer the adult state.[21]

The modern initiatory revolt perhaps lasts longer than the archaic, one or two years after high school and/or one or two of the first years of college. Sometimes much less, for the less turbulent elements participation at one or two barricades suffices. For the others, to the contrary, it is developed or is prolonged in the communes in political action or is extinguished bit by bit in drugs.

Finally, *communitarian* or *communal* contestation, at once retreat, flight, experimentation in new forms of life and creation of economic activities permitting these groups to survive. To brush a panorama of all these groups would exceed the bounds of this essay;[22] we limit ourselves to indicating the two phases that dominate their existence. First, that of experimentation or putting into practice the common idea that unites the participants: to smoke together, to tolerate one another, simply to pass some hours or days together (the experience of commune can be very ephemeral), to give and to give oneself, to share and to share oneself, to listen and relate, to try to live together in spite of differences of tastes, of temperament, of situations (bachelors and couples with or without children), to attempt to manage one's own affairs, to work or to make something together, and so on, all these terms found in an infinite variety of combinations. But the commune very quickly finds itself confronted with the problem of material resources: although the phase of experimentation finds its material support in the resources or pocket money of this one or that, if it wants to last, the commune must find a material base. In addition to a place to live, an urban house or an old farm to patch up, or a caravan in the case of itinerant groups such as musicians, a minimum of return from the sale of artisanal products, biological agricultural products, services (public art, photos, production and sale of a paper, concerts). These economic activities characteristically demand little capital in the beginning, but for the majority, a certain artistic talent.

But from the moment when the group centers on production, material or intellectual, it enters into a second phase and reveals a division between those of its members more preoccupied with establishing the material base of the group and those who remain centered on experimentation, or better, on the expression of their sentiments. It is at this moment that the first crisis is produced, and the departure of a certain number of members, and even the disappearance of the group, takes place. For, since it wants to produce, it encounters the constraints of enterprise: it is necessary to work regularly to tolerate delays, to pay clerks, to name officers for contacts with the outside (and who will gradually become the heads). And it goes even further, in the sense that the recruitment of new members will be done with an eye to production. Drugs can no longer be accepted, or temperaments that menace group cohesion, or visitors who come simply to size things up and eat at the communal table. The community will have to become respectable, beginning with good contacts with neighbors and evading police raids. At that moment, the commune repeats the history of the production cooperatives and communities of work that also began in experimentation but very quickly were constrained to transform themselves into businesses. The worker elements that composed them in the majority did not have the resources or backgrounds of the young people of the middle classes who make up modern communes. The analogies between the communes and communities of work are not only formal, for the latter—as other socialist cells, notably kibbutzim—equally propose another mode of life, another structure of family relations, different modes of administration of productive activities, total equality among members, and often a nonurban life or a combination between industrial and rural work, and so on.[23] Little by little, meanwhile, these groups have had to re-enter the "world order," have become businesses like others, even if they continue to practice a certain self-management. They have gradually been assimilated rather than put down as other forms of social and political contestation were in the past. Will it be the same for the current contestation and modern communes?

ASSIMILATION, REPRESSION. . .

Assimilation,[24] repression, or surpassing—I will return to this question further on. In Europe, and particularly in France, the contestation has only just begun, so attention must be directed toward the United States if the future is to be considered. The first contestation to present itself at the door during the extreme rapidity of evolution was the hippie phenomenon: in a few years, beginning from its golden age, 1966-67, it passed quickly to repression and decadence in 1969-70. Such rapidity of change shows how well the programmed society had learned to react to social agitation, somewhat in the same fashion as it has learned better to head off economic recession. Whether rapid programming capacity to face new phenomena or self-defense reflex against the perils of its overgrowth,[25] the reaction witnesses at once to the sensitivity of the society, and also, in the face of the amplitude of the repression, its rigidity. Writing of the American cultural revolution, Edgar Morin sees it divided into three branches: the first, part of the hippie revolution of love and peace, risks finishing in begging and drugs; the second "is going to mature into political revolt, dissociating or mixing the new urban guerrilla movement (attacks and assaults) with the magical aspirations that the other drug, "Marxism-Leninism," procures; finally, the third branch is perhaps going to constitute an original social fabric in the neoartisanal sector and in communitarian experiences."[26]

The last current appears more assimilable by society, in the same measure that it has succeeded in creating a demand for its products, because of which it must submit to the constraints that weigh on the life of all businesses. Marketing specialists have quickly understood the commercial possibilities this current offers:

> The techniques of market study, and in particular sectoral analysis, must be utilized to determine who the clients are who, without kinship to the counterculture, are likely to gain by certain tendencies that it has launched. One could also try to find out if there are needs that are common to this sector of the clientele and other clienteles. The adepts of the counterculture, opposed to the consumer society and representing only a small fraction of the population, are therefore in the end of interest especially for two reasons: they can be considered as authorities influencing their contemporaries, and who crystallize and give form and force—because they talk a great deal about them—to existing tendencies or aspirations that the larger public already feels more or less deeply.[27]

It can therefore be supposed, at least in an early period, that a sort of symbiosis is produced between the world of production and industrial distribution and the neoartisanal sector, its opposite. But one can also think that, subsequently, even artisanal production, and especially its distribution, may gradually be integrated. After all, biological wheat originating from a great industrial domain *could* have the same quality as that from a small agricultural community.

From the point of view of social control, flight into drugs can also be considered as a kind of assimilation, in the same way as begging. Drug users and beggars put themselves apart and no longer represent a danger to social equilibrium. From the point of view of contemporary rationality that admits as normal that the social fabric, like all others, produces a certain number of defectives, the existence of young beggars and semibeggardly drug users is perfectly tolerable. It is even to be predicted that certain drugs that are not very dangerous for the organism but reducers of aggressivity will be put on sale with the goal of diminishing the menace of social adaptation. After all, our societies have always used alcohol like that.

There remains political contestation, more difficult to assimilate but that can be channeled, and in the extreme, capable of becoming the object of brutal repression. Channelization is nothing new and our great political and union associations have long known how to deflect the combativity of their member bases through their petitions, or in the repetition, a veritable catharsis, of demonstration slogans. This same channelization can lead to the attraction to certain areas in the public domain for brawls and settling accounts between opposed groups, areas of tolerance where the right to fight will be respected. In fact certain university campuses, where tradition opposes the entry of the police, have already played the battlefield role. To the extent that violence is recognized as inevitable, it is in the logic of our rational societies to circumscribe the field to the end of confining damage to it, and to the end of keeping the social peace elsewhere.

As to violence as a means to achieve demands otherwise impossible of realization, or violence of the initiative type, it is channeled with difficulty and therefore encounters habitual, classical repression. But on this point also, a change in attitude may be supposed; it is not excluded that it might gradually come to be considered inevitable: knowing their conditions of life—Is it not inevitable that the poor and the other forgotten ones revolt sometimes? Knowing the role of violence in the education of the integrated adult citizen—Is it not inevitable that his initiatives take violent form? Is violence then not a necessary evil to maintain social equilibrium?

Our programmed societies are not yet so exhausted that they cannot formulate these hypotheses in terms of contestation and politics instead. Their self-knowledge and their instruments of self-control are not yet sufficiently developed to institutionalize contestation thus—even if they already seem entered on this path. For the incorporation of the neoartisanal sector, the free sale of certain drugs, the creation of areas of tolerance and the recognition of the "right to fight" do indeed constitute a sort of institutionalization of contestation, an institutionalization that is complex and pluralist, but which reflects well the complexity and plurality of our societies. The current escalation of repression is perhaps only transitory and manifests only the disarray of the directing class, taken unaware by the rapidity of the phenomenon and still incapable of drawing logical instruction from the change. In other terms, the police repression is to be considered as a sign of insufficient development of the means of manipulation and of a reticence to avail themselves of existing ones.

One could go even further and imagine that our societies will come to recognize the creative character of contestation and destruction, the two aspects—creation/destruction—being indissociable. It is not farfetched to think that what is witnessed at this time is a sort of assimilation of the socially creative, somewhat in the same manner as the recordings of brainstorming sessions on magnetic tape, serving to retain the impulsive and fleeting ideas of their participants. A programmed society, knowing the thresholds of collective aggressivity that are not to be passed, sufficiently self-controlled that it permits the existence of zones or kernels of contestation within itself, kinds of laboratories of collective social creativity, knowing that the revolt is functional and brings a new dynamism into the entire system—such a society would come to program its change within itself. A harmonized change for those who, optimists, dream of such surpassing.

. . .OR SURPASSING

The analyses of the preceding pages are not full of optimism and the societies toward which we seem to be moving recall Huxley's *Brave New World* or *1984,* the political fiction of George Orwell. These societies seem to be so structured and organized that their citizens will no longer have any initiative to take and participation groups, manipulated and quickly assimilated, will no longer offer any resistance to arbitrary, benevolent, distant, and noncontrolled powers. The sole participation—but is it still a matter of participation?—requires the individual's conformity, completely alienated, submissive without surrendering to the eulogies that power renders itself—he is plainly happy and does not imagine another world than his own. Besides, if he does not want to conform to what society expects of him, it knows how to go about putting him back on the right path. The hidden microphones and camouflaged cameras no longer belong just to *1984,* and the intrusions in private life can only increase. In brief, such a society has no more need of citizens, that is to say, of conscientious men who participate in its destiny and in its control, who try to influence it by participating in its groups and its civic and political life. There remain only collections of individuals, crowds, or individuals isolated but knowing neither how nor being able to turn back to themselves, constantly under the dominance of the dissemination, and listening, of the mass media. This society killed participation and therefore, at the same time, civic life and democracy.

One cannot hide the fact that this vision is currently very prevalent, corresponding to the reflux of optimism of the late 1950s and early 1960s, at the end of a period of great economic expansion, in the disappointed hopes concerning the development of new countries, in the disputes and contestations of recent years—themselves in part the consequence of preceding factors. But is there no alternative? Can it not be imagined, if only in play, or to end on a less somber note, that there is another way? The gigantic progress of science, notably of electronics—must it not serve as the basis of what could be another hypothesis? The rationality of our postindustrial societies—Does it not prepare the way to a utilization of information at the level of daily life and participation? Beside the *1984* hypothesis, cannot one dream of "a computer hypothesis"?

LET US DREAM FOR A MOMENT. . .

First, it is necessary to think again about participation in traditional society. In this society the place and roles of individuals are determined by a kind of logic that is outside of them. All the society, like ours in the Middle Ages or the traditional societies of Africa now, is explained in reference to an entity external to it, God or tradition. Religion or tradition explains the relations between men, assigning to them their place in the world, surrounding them in a vision of the past and the future, in a cosmogony. Each one, in his place, participated in the good functioning of society, of a society that does not have as goal to transform itself, to change.

With modernization, and especially industrialization and urbanization, these explanations of the world are transformed and it is the men themselves who claim to explain the world, its past, its future, and its change. The denial of an external logic, of all transcendence, whether it be in religion or tradition, leads to diversity of explanations, to multiplicity of paths of search and to means and techniques necessary for it. Man believes he holds his destiny in his hands and thinks that he can help himself to create more adequate social structures to help realize his conception of himself and the world. Whence the diverse conceptions that are opposed to each other, whose participationist aspects we have studied. For his leap ahead, as for this research, the man increasingly has recourse to machines of two sorts: material tools and logical or intellectual tools.

Regarding the first, material tools, we have long known how much they impose their constraints on those who use them. The studies of sociologists and psychologists of work have abundantly shown us the consequences of work subdivided into small units, and of repetitive work, where the user sometimes becomes the slave of his machine, which dictates his rhythm. It is not of these machines that it is necessary to speak, but of those which aid man to surpass himself in his intellectual work. To comprehend well this point with its very clear implications for participation, it is useful to make an incursion into the life of the economic enterprises and to attempt to follow the consequences of the introduction of thinking machines in the management of businesses.

Three moments can be distinguished: the first is that of individual management, a prolongation of the typical running of a liberal enterprise by a captain of industry, by an entrepreneur. It is implusive management, by jerks and jolts, that transposes the dynamism of the entrepreneur on the economic plane, his flair, that sixth sense that permits him to detect the moment or domains where there is business to be done. Thanks to the importance of the flair, of business sense, this management is not purely rational: in his calculations the entrepreneur takes account of very numerous factors, but its analysis is not explicit and often contrary to logic; if he brings it off it is often because he has guessed well.

At a second moment, often corresponding to the growth in size of the business, the entrepreneur surrounds himself by an apparatus—office personnel and machines—that assist him in the administrative aspects of his management: with personnel and machines to calculate salaries, do clerical work, extract sales data. In many cases, these machines can be very elaborate, comprising systems of perforated cards and even electronic computers. But the system of management itself is not yet transformed: the machines constitute an administrative appendix of the personality of the entrepreneur.

It is in the third moment that things change, when the machines cease to be simple administrative instruments, in order to become auxiliaries of management. For example, when the computer ceases to manufacture only salary information, and solves management problems, aids in the choice between several hypotheses, between alternate business policies. Thanks to its speed in calculations, the machine permits the most logical choice between alternative hypotheses in record time. In this case it is no longer a simple administrative tool but a collaborator in management, a collaborator that does not have the flair for business, but a collaborator that does not deceive itself, that does not commit logical errors, that tempers dynamism and the business spirit by purely rational considerations. At this moment, the machine is a brain tool with which it is necessary to communicate—it is the goal of very numerous training institutes for business heads and executives, and even a tool of education, in the sense that it teaches its logic to those who manipulate it.

This digression on the evolution of management in business has only apparently led us away from problems of participation, for as thinking machines have become more widespread we have perhaps entered into a completely new conception of participation. It is also for this reason that we have spoken of self-management groups, part association, part business groups. By relation to the participation and to the traditional society subject to an exterior logic, to a system of explanation and transcendent authority—God or tradition—and by relation to the society on the industrialization path, and even the contemporary society that refuses all transcendent authority but which has not yet replaced all ancient beliefs by new ones, nor has been able to prevail in certain other modern beliefs in order to restore a unity to society and to the world, by relation to these societies, the society toward which it seems that our more modern societies orient themselves will be marked—and is already in part marked, for the new society is already profiled in the present—by the restoration of a unity: no longer a transcendent unity, but the immanent unity of rationality.

In such a society, according priority to logical choice, participation assumes a new significance and proceeds by new methods. The machine, or the logic that imitates that of the machine, does not accept or retain ideologies, slogans, or beliefs, and the choices that it proposes will be neutral. Whether in a business or in a participation group, rational thought indicates that if one wants to go, for example, to goal B, the most efficient route will be to pass by FGK and not by FMK, GMK, or still other paths. In other terms, the most efficient means are chosen so as to reach the goal as rationally as possible. Still, it is required that the goal be decided, and it is on this point that the thinking machine has exercised a decisive and formative influence on individuals: in order that the machine understand them, it is necessary that the goals be clearly defined and rendered operational for it, which is not generally the case with group participation goals. There is nothing new in this, it will be said; goals have always had to be previously defined to obtain the greatest chance of reaching them. But if the principle is true, and there is nothing new at this level, it is the generalization of application of this principle that is new. Until now, it was only taught but not lived—it is only necessary to look around us to perceive the lack of clarity of goals of the majority of the groups that solicit our participation. To the contrary, thanks to the logic of the machines, the principle is currently leaving the manuals of logic and lesson to pass into daily life. It is becoming a sociological phenomenon. The principle is partially achieved in business, and we know that participation groups tend to model themselves after businesses.

Two great consequences of the penetration of this logic into daily life must be considered. First, the necessary reformulation of participation group goals in terms comprehensible by the machine, or if it is preferred, by rational thought. Such global goals as liberty, socialism, fraternity, the care of fellow man, and like terms that have become vague and charged with emotional elements will have to be redefined and specified into precise objectives comprehensible by the machine whose neutral brain will indicate the most rational means to attain them.

Second, the brain machine, being quicker and taking count of many more variables than man, gives us the most rational means to follow to attain the goal, the participation of men will no longer be called for in order to determine the means, but only in order to define the goals. And that is immense progress: Who of us has not been exasperated by the loss of time in assemblies of certain participation groups occupied with interminable discussion on the choice of means to attain goals? How many of us have seen the lassitudes and discouragement that are the consequence of such discussions and such dissipation of energy?

Thus, according to the computer hypothesis, participation will be rid of all rhetoric. It will no longer focus on means but solely on expressed rational choices. It does not follow that these choices will in turn be more rational, for in them are expressed the finalities of the participation groups, their ideologies. It does not follow from this that the society and its men will be better; they will simply be more efficient, participating and deciding with better reasons.

By contrast, having seen that the choices posed to men must be put in rational terms, the most extremist choices, the most revolutionary finalities, that propose a total overthrow of society—these contestive and global ends risk being much more frequent. Precisely because of a constraining logic, the choices men make risk being those of the possible, of the concrete, by opposition to the ends of numerous modern participation groups, unreal and unrealizable. These choices will remain ideological, but decreasingly marked by utopian elements. In addition, to the extent that the logic is universal, a reduction of the infinity of finalities of modern participation groups to some fundamental choices may be supposed, with a progressive unification of groups around these less numerous choices. In sum, this hypothesis tends to take account of the growing rationality of participation and of what I have called "ideological unification." In the process, the thinking machines are called to play a more and more important role.

Although the *1984* hypothesis is pessimistic and presupposes that our societies are moving toward totalitarian dictatorship, the second hypothesis does not prejudge the political form of that society. It is limited to showing the possibility of a greater rationality in the decisions of men and in the choices they cannot long avoid making regarding this intelligent participation in a mass consumption society. An example can show us how necessary such choices are, but also how nearly impossible it is to make them under current conditions. We take this example from the many-sided industry of gadgets that invade the market and with which only collectors could be happy. At this writing we do not have any information on the number of persons occupied in this industry, we do not understand its weight in the national product, and still more we do not have any idea of the economic repercussions, social and regional, that the eventual closing of related workshops or industries will bring. Our attitude before the gadget phenomenon originates uniquely from moral considerations, from feelings: the phenomenon is saddening to some, while according to others, it represents only the legitimate luxury that every affluent society is always offered in history.

Right now, in the absence of valid information, we can neither render account of the scope of the phenomenon nor act validly in relation to it. Only machines are capable of rapidly digesting the innumerable items of information touching the phenomenon and specifying for us the consequences of the choices that we might be called on to make. And to participate is precisely to make a choice, to decide.

The immense resources and energies developed by the genius of man militate in favor of new forms of decision on some phenomena of which it cannot, by itself, measure the breadth and all the interdependencies with other phenomena. Only these decisions will permit him to take his destiny into his own hands and no more simply submit to it. Never mind his apprenticeship in communication with the machines that teach him more logic; the essential thing is that he might soon formulate rational choices and thus restore some meaning to participation and participation groups, from which disaffection also originates, in great part because they have nothing to decide, they have neither information nor logical structures. In this conquest of rationality, economic enterprises are already advanced, as are certain large public administrations. It is likely and desirable that this tendency will gradually make itself felt equally in participation groups—in civic and political life.

The dream ends here, at the moment when, waking, the dreamer brutally perceives that neither the direction of the enterprises nor the ruling classes desire to share their power, to diffuse the information they jealously control, to share in place of integrating. It is true that enterprises and large administrations base their decisions more on the rationality of computers and that there is in this proof of a certain enlargement of the restrained circles in which decisions are made. But this enlargement does not signify democratization, for it is confined to the highest levels of the technostructure. Participative management by objectives is limited to higher executives and reinforces powers and privileges that would be diminished, if not menaced, if they were less concentrated. In these conditions, even if the dream could be realized and rational choices proposed to the members, to the users, to the people, it would no less remain that the computer programmers, those who feed the machine with information and establish programs in it, would continue to command an extremely extended power and be more powerful than our modern technocrats. Marcuse is surely correct when he writes that "the right of power to freely elect some masters does away with neither masters nor slaves."[28]

The dream of a society controlled by means of information constitutes a sort of answer to the technocratic myth of a national plan with its vision of economic development harmonized with social development. This dream is also that of self-management, warmly advanced by Daniel Chauvey,[29] paraphrasing the celebrated aphorism of Lenin: "democratic socialism = information + self-management." No doubt this theme constitutes a kind of second wind for many associationist groups, all the more necessary as the old myths that stimulate participation are gradually emptied of their content. What remains is nothing less than the fundamental problem of self-management, or more generally, that participation in power occurs by taking power. For it is necessary to understand that there is no programmed society, but only ruling classes, programmed and programming their domination. The new character of our postindustrial societies resides in new forms, still more alienating than domination, so subtle that participation in them is already occurring and risks finding itself more and more ensnared there.

NOTES

1. Daniel Chauvey, *Autogestion* (Paris: Seuil, 1970).
2. Alain Touraine, *La Société post-industrielle* (Paris: Denoel, 1969), p. 13.
3. André-Clément Decouflé, *Problèmes sociaux et objectifs de politique sociale des pays industriels avancés membres de l'O. C. D. E.* (Paris: OCDE, 1969), pp. 80-81.
4. Ibid., pp. 44-45.
5. The surprise attacks or the outrages commited by those who propose to destroy the system are also rational.
6. Touraine, p. 141.
7. I am not saying that there is an "end of ideology"; at the very most there is a dissappearance of the ideals of the past.
8. Chauvey, p. 141.
9. Touraine, p. 15.
10. Such an insight merits further development, the purchase of the kitsch object becoming progressively all of participation. See the study of Abraham Moles , *Le Kitsch: l'art du bonheur* (Paris: Mame, 1971).

11. Decouflé, p. 64.
12. This apathy seems to be general in planned societies, even more than in our Western ones. See Albert Meister, *Où va l'autogestion yougoslave?* (Paris: Anthropos, 1970), p. 149ff.
13. In their recent work *L'Ecole capitaliste en France* (Paris: Maspéro, 1971), p. 179ff. Christian Baudelot and Roger Establet show that the violence of children in elementary school is a way of manifesting their hostility to the scholarly apparatus and to a training submitted to the dominant ideology, and whose function is to prepare for their docile integration into the lower ranks of the zerostructure.
14. Touraine, p. 101.
15. The word *commune* is used here in the American sense that became popular in the 1970s, i.e. a radical community, and not the French civic unit.
16. Meister, p. 228ff.
17. Herbert Marcuse, *L'Homme unidimensionnel* (Paris: Seuil, 1970), p. 295.
18. Decouflé, p. 81.
19. Edgar Morin, *Journal de Californie* (Paris: Seuil, 1970), p. 74. Also J.-F. Revel, *Ni Marx ni Jésus* (Paris: Laffont, 1970), p. 236ff.
20. Ibid., p. 22.
21. Ibid., pp. 239-40.
22. See the recent book by Henri Gougaud, *Nous voulons vivre en communauté* (Paris: Bélibaste, 1971). For French communes, see also the bulletin *Communauté*, published by Michel Faligand.
23. See also Meister, p. 225ff.
24. The French word is *récupération*, for which neither the author nor I can find an adequate English expression. The intended nuance has its roots in a recent idea referring to the recycling of junk, with political or social innuendo. (Ed.)
25. Decouflé, p. 61.
26. Morin, p. 139.
27. Hélène Bulla, "La Contre-culture: mal du siècle ou promesse d'avenir?" *Revue d'Economie d'Entreprise* (May 1971): 23-25.
28. Herbert Marcuse, *L'Homme unidimensionnel* (Paris: Seuil, 1970), p. 35.
29. Chauvey, p. 191ff.

BIBLIOGRAPHY

Baudelot, Christian, and Roger Establet. *L'Ecole capitaliste en France.* Paris: Maspero, 1971.

Bernoux, Philippe, Dominique Motte, and Jean Saglio. *Trois Ateliers d'O.S.* The Hague: Mouton, 1962.

Bishop, Claire H. *All Things Common.* New York: Harper & Row, 1950.

Bouglé, Celestin. *Socialismes français.* Paris: Colin, 1933.

Bourgin, Georges, and P. Rimber. *Le Socialisme.* Paris: PUF, 1957.

Bulla, Hélène, "La Contre-culture: mal du siècle ou promesse d'avenir?" *Revue d'Economie d'Entreprise* (May 1971).

Calello, Hugo, et al. *Desarrollo comunitario y cambio social.* Buenos Aires: Consejo Federal de Inversiones and Universidad de Buenos Aires, 1965.

Chapin, F. Stuart. *The Social Participation Scale.* Minneapolis: University of Minnesota Press, 1937.

Chauvey, Daniel. *Autogestion.* Paris: Seuil, 1970.

Cherubini, Arnaldo. *Dottrine e metodi assistenziali dal 1789 al 1848.* Milan: Guiffre, 1958.

Considérant, Victor. *Le Socialisme devant le vieux monde ou les vivants devant les morts.* (Reference incomplete in original text, ed.)

Cooperator, The. (Reference incomplete in original text, ed.)

Coulon, Marc. (No title) *Pour* 18-19, 20 (1971).

Decouflé, André-Clément, *Problèmes sociaux et objectifs de politique sociale des pays industriels avancés membres de l'O.C.D.E.* Paris: OCDE, 1969.

Desroche, Henri, "Coopératives, communautés et mouvement ouvrier," *Communauté* 2, 3, 6-7, 8 (1953).

Desroche, H. "Principes rochedaliens? Lesquels?" *Archives Internationales de Sociologie de la Coopération* 10 (1961):3-38.

Desroche, Henri, *Coopération et développement.* Paris: PUF, 1964.

Devine, Edward T. *Pittsburgh the Year of the Survey.* New York: Survey Associates, 1914.

Di Franco, Joseph. *The United States Cooperative Extension Service.* New York: State College of Agriculture at Cornell University, 1958.

Dillick, Sidney. *Community Organization for Neighborhood Development Past and Present.* New York: Woman's Press, 1953.

Dolléans, Edouard, and Gérard Dehove. *Histoire du travail en France.* Paris: Domat Montchrestian, 1953, 1955.

Drioux, Joseph. *Etude économique et juridique sur les associations.* Paris: Librairie Nouvelle de Droit et de Jurisprudence, 1884.

Duveau, Georges. *La Vie ouvrière sous le Second Empire.* Paris: Gallimard, 1946.

Galbraith, John K., "La Crise des sociétés industrielles," *Nouvel Observateur,* nonseries (1971).

Germani, Gino, "Comparación típico-ideal entre le sociedad preindustrial rural y la sociedad industrial urbana," in Gino Germani and Jorge Graciarena, *De la sociedad tradicional a la sociedad de masas.* Buenos Aires: Universidad de Buenos Aires, Departamento de Sociología, 1961.

Godard, J. *Travailleurs et métiers lyonnais: les origines de le coopération lyonnaise.* Lyon: No publisher, 1909.

Gossez, Rémi. "Circonstances du mouvement ouvrier, Paris, 1848." Paris: ms., 1951.

Gossez, Rémi. *Les Ouvriers de Paris.* Paris: Société d'Histoire de la Revolution de Paris de 1848, vol. 24, 1967.

Gougaud, Henri, *Nous voulons vivre en communauté.* Paris: Bélibaste, 1971.

Gurvitch, Georges. *La Vocation actuelle de la sociologie.* Paris: PUF, 1950.

Handlin, Oscar. *The Uprooted.* Boston: Little, Brown, 1953.

Journal Officiel. Paris (19 November 1875):9466.

Kennedy, Albert J. *The Settlement Heritage.* New York: National Federation of Settlements, 1953.

Laidler, Harry W., *Socialism in the United States.* New York: League for Industrial Democracy, 1952.

Lane, Robert E. *Political Life—Why and How People Get Involved in Politics.* New York: Free Press, 1965.

Lavergne, Bernard, *La Révolution coopérative.* Paris: PUF, 1949.

Lewin, Kurt. *Resolving Social Conflicts: Selected Papers on Group Dynamics.* New York: Harper, 1948.

Lipset, Seymour M., Martin Trow, and James S. Coleman. *Union Democracy.* Glencoe, Ill.: Free Press, 1956.

Marcuse, Herbert, *L'Homme unidimensionnel.* Paris: Seuil, 1970.

Martin, Gaston. *La Révolution de 1848.* Paris: PUF, 1948.

Martin Saint-Léon, Etienne. *Histoire des corporations des métiers.* Paris: Alcan, 1922, 3rd. ed.

Meister, Albert. *Coopération d'habitation et sociologie du voisinage.* Paris: Minuit, 1957.

Meister, Albert. *Associations coopératives et groupes de loisirs en milieu rural.* Paris: Minuit, 1958.

Meister, Albert, *Les Communautés de travail.* Paris: Entente Communautaire, 1959.

Meister, Albert, *Sociologie du Travail* 3 (1961): 236-52.

Meister, Albert. "Participation organisée et participation spontanée: quelques études sur les 'petits groupes' aux Etats-Unis," *L'Année Sociologique* (1961): 113-61.

Meister, Albert. *Principes et tendances de la planification rurale en Israël.* Paris: Mouton, 1962.

Meister, Albert. *L'Afrique peut-elle partir? Changement social et développement en Afrique orientale.* Paris: Seuil, 1966.

Meister, Albert. *Le Développement économique de l'Afrique de l'Est.* Paris: PUF, 1966.

Meister, Albert. *Participation, animation, et développement.* Paris: Anthropos, 1969.

Meister, Albert. "Développement communautaire et animation rurale en Afrique." *L'Homme et la Société* 18 (1970), 19-20 (1971).

Meister, Albert. *Où va l'autogestion yougoslave?* Paris: Anthropos, 1970.

Meister, Albert. *Le Système mexicain: les avatars d'une participation populair au développement.* Paris: Anthropos, 1971.

Meister, Albert, *Vers une sociologie des associations.* Paris: Editions Ouvrières, 1972.

Meister, Albert. *La Participation dans les associations.* Paris: Editions Ouvrières, 1974.

Meister, Albert, L. Petruzzi, and E. Sonsogni. *Traditionalismo y cambio social.* Rosario: Universidad del Litoral, 1963.

Melman, Seymour. "Pentagon Bourgeoisie," *Transaction* 8 (March-April 1971): 4-12.

Merton, Robert K. *Social Theory and Social Structure.* Glencoe, Ill.: Free Press, 1951, 2nd ed.

Michels, Robert. *Political Parties: A Sociological Study of the Oligarchic Tendencies of Modern Democracy.* New York: Dover, 1959 (1911). Trans. Eden and Cedar Paul.

Milbrath, Lester W. *Political Participation.* Chicago: Rand McNally, 1965.

Mills, C. Wright. *The Power Elite.* New York: Oxford University Press, 1959.

Moles, Abraham, *Le Kitsch: l'art du bonheur.* Paris: Mame, 1971.

Morin, Edgar, *Journal de Californie.* Paris: Seuil, 1970.

Murcier, A. "Business en France." *Le Monde* (16 June 1965).

Nadaud, Martin. *Les Sociétés ouvrières en France.* Publishing information not available.

Picht, Werner. *Toynbee Hall and the English Settlement Movement.* London: Bell, 1914.

Revel, J.-F., *Ni Marx ni Jésus.* Paris: Laffont, 1970.

Riesman, David, "Flight and Search in the New Suburbs," *International Review of Community Development* 4 (1959): 123-36.

Riesman, David, Nathan Glazer, and Reuel Denney. *The Lonely Crowd,* abr. ed. New York: Doubleday Anchor, 1953.

Rose, Arnold M. *Theory and Method in the Social Sciences.* Minneapolis: University of Minnesota Press, 1954.

Sanders, Irwin T. *Balkan Village.* Lexington: University of Kentucky Press, 1949.

Scelle, Georges. *Le Droit ouvrier.* Paris: Colin, 1929.

Sinclair, Upton. *The Jungle.* New York: Airmont, 1965 (1906).

Smith, Constance, and Anne Freedman. *Voluntary Associations.* Cambridge, Mass.: Harvard University Press, 1972.

Tchernoff, Iouda. *Associations et sociétés secrètes sous la Deuxième République.* Paris: Alcan, 1905.

Thrupp, Sylvia. "Gilds," in David L. Sills, ed., *International Encyclopedia of the Social Sciences,* 17 vols. New York: Macmillan & Free Press, vol. 6, 1968.

Touraine, Alain, *La Société post-industrielle.* Paris: Denoel, 1969.

Weber, Max, "Geschäftsbericht," *Verhandlungen des Ersten Deutschen Soziologentages vom 19-22 Oktober 1910 in Frankfurt a.M.* Tübingen: 1911. Trans. Everett C. Hughes in *Journal of Voluntary Action Research* 1 (Winter 1972):20-23.

Weber, Max. *The Protestant Ethic and the Spirit of Capitalism,* trans. Talcott Parsons. New York: Scribner's, 1958.

INDEX